62

The nonprofit sector in Hungary

This volume provides an unusually perceptive analysis of the emergence – or rather re-emergence – of citizen organizations in Central and Eastern Europe following the break-up of the Soviet bloc in 1989, an event of profound importance in the history of the nonprofit sector.

Éva Kuti explores the rich historical roots of nonprofit activity in Hungary, particularly in the early Middle Ages and in the late nineteenth and early twentieth centuries. She shows how some forms of voluntary organization persisted throughout the forty years of communist dominance, thanks to the perseverance of the Hungarian people and the *modus vivendi* they reached with the local Communist regime. She argues that the burst of activity after 1989 drew on these strong traditions of voluntarism.

By placing the current Hungarian nonprofit scene in context, both in relation to its Hungarian origins and in relation to developments elsewhere, Éva Kuti makes a major contribution to our understanding of the role nonprofit organizations are playing in the post-Communist transition process now underway throughout Central and Eastern Europe.

Éva Kuti is an economist, founding member of the research association called Research Project on Hungarian Nonprofit Organizations, Budapest, Hungary

Johns Hopkins Nonprofit Sector Series
edited by Lester M. Salamon and Helmut K. Anheier
Institute for Policy Studies, The Johns Hopkins University

Manchester University Press is proud to be published this important new series, the product of the most comprehensive comparative analysis of the global nonprofit sector ever undertaken. The growth of the sector between the public and the private, known variously as the nonprofit, voluntary or third sector, is one of the most significant contemporary developments in societies through the world. The books in this series will cover the development and role of this sector in a broad cross-section of nations, and also provide comparative, cross-country analyses.

Johns Hopkins Nonprofit Sector Series 2

THE NONPROFIT SECTOR
IN HUNGARY

Éva Kuti

Manchester University Press

Manchester and New York

distributed exclusively in the USA and Canada by St. Martin's Press

Published by Manchester University Press
Oxford Road, Manchester M13 9NR, UK
and Room 400, 175 Fifth Avenue, New York, NY 10010, USA

Distributed exclusively in the USA and Canada
by St. Martin's Press, Inc., 175 Fifth Avenue, New York
NY 10010, USA

British Library Cataloguing-in-Publication Data
A catalogue record for this book is available from the British Library

Library of Congress Cataloging-in-Publication Data applied for

ISBN 0 7190 4905 9 *hardback*
     0 7190 4906 7 *paperback*

First published 1996

00 99 98 97 96   10 9 8 7 6 5 4 3 2 1

Typeset in Great Britain
by Northern Phototypesetting Co Ltd, Bolton
Printed in Great Britain
by Bell & Bain Ltd, Glasgow

For Dávid and Máté
who peacefully tolerated
that I worked instead of playing with them

CONTENTS

Contents

TABLES

ix

List of tables

FOREWORD

This book is one in a series of monographs on the voluntary or nonprofit sector throughout the world that have resulted from the Johns Hopkins Comparative Nonprofit Sector Project, a major inquiry into the scope, structure, history, legal position, and role of the nonprofit sector in a broad cross-section of nations.

Launched in May 1990, this project has sought to close the glaring gaps in knowledge that have long existed about the thousands of schools, hospitals, clinics, community organizations, advocacy groups, day care centres, relief organizations, nursing homes, homeless shelters, family counselling agencies, environmental groups and others that comprise this important sector. Though known by different names in different places, these organizations are present almost everywhere, albeit to widely differing extents. More than that, there is significant evidence that they are growing massively in both scope and scale as faith in the capability of government to cope on its own with the interrelated challenges of persistent poverty, environmental degradation, and social change has declined. Indeed, we seem to be in the midst of a global "associational revolution" that is opening new opportunities for organized private action and placing new demands and responsibilities on private not-for-profit groups. As a result, it has becoming increasingly important to understand what the scope and contours of this nonprofit sector really are, and what its potentials are for shouldering the new demands being placed upon it.

The Johns Hopkins Comparative Nonprofit Sector Project was conceived as a way to meet this need, to document the scope, structure, revenue base, and background of the nonprofit sector, and to do so in a way that not only yielded solid and objective information about individual countries, but made it possible to undertake cross-national comparisons in a systematic way. For this purpose, we identified twelve (later thirteen) countries representing different religious and historical traditions. Included were seven advanced industrial societies (the US, UK, France, Germany, Italy, Sweden, and Japan), five "developing" societies (Brazil, Ghana, Egypt, Thailand, and India), and one former Soviet bloc country (Hungary). In each of these countries we recruited a Local Associate and undertook a similar set of information-gathering activities guided by a common definition, a common classification scheme, and a common set of data-gathering forms and instructions. The result, we believe, is the first systematic attempt to put the nonprofit sector on the social and economic map of the world in a solid and empirical way.

The present volume, *The nonprofit sector in Hungary*, is one of a series of books and monographs reporting on the results of this work (other titles are listed opposite the title page). Prepared by Dr Éva Kuti, our Local Associate in Hungary, this volume provides an unusually perceptive analysis of what is perhaps one of the historically most important developments in the recent history of the nonprofit sector, the emergence — or rather re-emergence — of citizen organizations in Central and Eastern Europe following the break-up of the Soviet bloc in 1989. Contrary to widespread misperceptions, Dr Kuti shows the rich historical roots of nonprofit activity in Hungary, particularly in the early Middle Ages and in the latter nineteenth and early twentieth century. Even during the forty years of Communist dominance, some forms of voluntary organizations persisted, thanks to the perseverance of the Hungarian people and the *modus vivendi* they reached with the local Communist regime. As Dr Kuti puts it: "The 1956 revolution revealed that communist governments could nationalize industry, 'collectivize' agriculture, develop a nationalized system of social services, and dissolve most of the voluntary organizations, but they could not completely eradicate citizens' autonomy, solidarity and private initiatives, even though they tried their hardest." As a result, however, the nonprofit sector that emerged after 1989 bore marked resemblance to what existed immediately before rather than the idealized new creation often pictured by popular accounts. By placing the current Hungarian nonprofit scene in context both in relation to its Hungarian origins and in relation to developments elsewhere in the world, Dr Kuti's book makes a major contribution to our understanding of the important role nonprofit organizations are playing in the transition process now under way throughout Central and Eastern Europe. As such, it is a model of clear thinking and solid analysis, and of the special advantages that can be derived from careful and systematic comparison in any complex field.

From its outset, the Johns Hopkins Comparative Nonprofit Sector Project has been a collaborative effort among an extraordinary group of scholars with support from a wide array of funders and advisors. The team of Local Associates — Martin Knapp and Jeremy Kendall in the UK, Edith Archambault in France, Paolo Barbetta and Pippo Ranci in Italy, Helmut Anheier, Eckhard Priller and Wolfgang Seibel in Germany, Éva Kuti in Hungary, Tadashi Yamamoto and Takayoshi Amenomori in Japan, Leilah Landim in Brazil, Lawrence Atingdui and Emmanuel Lareya in Ghana, Amani Kandil in Egypt, Amara Pongsapich in Thailand, Sven-Erik Sjöstrand, Filip Wijkström, and Thomas Lundstrom in Sweden — has worked together at every stage to perfect the information-gathering forms, develop the basic definitions and classification scheme, and interpret the results. To all of them, I owe a deep debt of gratitude.

Thanks are also due to the numerous individuals who served on the International Advisory Committee to this project, to the members of the national advisory committees we formed to oversee the work, to Richard Purslow of Manchester University Press for the crucial encouragement he has provided in bringing this work to publication, and to the foundations, corporations, and government agencies throughout the world that provided support to make this work possible.

Finally, I want to acknowledge a special dept to Dr Helmut Anheier, the co-editor of this series and the Associate Director of this project, who helped guide the work with great energy and dedication throughout.

It was more than 150 years ago that the Frenchman Alexis de Toqueville identified the "art of associating together" as the mother of all science. Today we appear to be in the middle of an extraordinary explosion of associational activity as new forms of organized citizen action are taking shape and expanding their role in widely disparate parts of the world. Our hope is that the series of monographs of which this volume is an important part will help make this process of change more visible and more understandable and thereby contribute to its success. We are convinced that important values hinge critically on this result.

L.M.S.
Baltimore, Maryland
April, 1995

PREFACE

It is now four years since Lester Salamon invited me to join the international comparative project designed to shed the first systematic empirical light on the nonprofit sector. In that time, there has been an astonishing growth in the Hungarian voluntary sector. As a member of the international team, I was privileged to discuss these developments with a group of exceptionally experienced, intelligent and thoughtful researchers and philanthropic leaders – Takayoshi Amenomori, Edith Archambault, Lawrence Atingdui, Gian Paolo Barbetta, Elizabeth Boris, Michael Brophy, Robert d'Archy Shaw, Raymond Georis, Virginia Hodgkinson, Akira Iriyama, Dirk Jarré, Amani Kandil, Jeremy Kendall, Martin Knapp, Leilah Landim, Emmanuel Laryea, Reynold Levy, Amara Pongsapich, Pippo Ranci, John Richardson, Gabriel Rudney, Susan Saxon-Harrold, Caleb Schutz, Wolfgang Seibel, Siddhartha Sen, Ben Shute, Russy Summariwalla, Marylin Taylor, Sylvie Tsyboula, Tadashi Yamamoto, Perri 6 – who helped me to see what happened in my country in an international perspective. In carrying out my work, I was guided and counselled by two of the most prominent scholars of the nonprofit field, Lester Salamon and Helmut Anheier. This book would not have been born without their generous help and perceptive assistance.

Similarly, I was aided by an extraordinary network of researchers and nonprofit leaders in Hungary, as well. The moving spirit of the whole Hungarian research project was László Harsányi. He played a fundamental role in creating the organizational background and raising the necessary funds for the study of the emerging nonprofit sector in Hungary. He and Ágnes Czakó worked with me at every stage of the empirical survey – to design the survey, to develop its questionnaire and to analyse the information we managed to gather. Edit Balogh helped us with sample selection, data processing and other computer work. A series of background papers and case studies were prepared by József Bagó, Magdolna Balázs, Anna Mária Bartal, Anikó Gayer, István György, Gábor Hegyesi, Béla Jagasics, Annamária Kovács, Éva Mérő, György Pataki, György Várhegyi and Krisztina Voit. Ildikó Gyergyói and Péter Kirschner helped me to interview politicians who play a crucial role in developing the policy toward the nonprofit sector. In addition to these direct participants, the Hungarian project also benefited from the advice and comments of some other researchers and key nonprofit leaders – Gabriella Ágoston, György Bódi, János Bocz, Gábor Csizmár, Ferenc Farkas, Antal Gyulavári, Miklós Marschall, László Reisz, István Sebestény, László Sík, Zsolt Somogyvári, János Szabon, Ágnes Vajda and Julie Walton.

A number of people at the Johns Hopkins University also assisted me with this project. Kusuma Cunningham and Wojciech Sokolowski edited the tables, catching many of the errors and inconsistencies which escaped my notice. Jacquelyn Perry, Donna Schaub and maybe other colleagues, as well, provided important administrative support. Editors of Manchester University Press also helped me a lot with the preparation of the final printed version of this book.

Finally, our participation in the comparative project would not have been possible either without the financial assistance of the "big" supporters of the international project, or without the help of some Hungarian institutions – Lukács Foundation, Ministry of Culture, Ministry of Welfare, OTKA (National Scientific Research Fund) – which provided the financial basis for carrying out the survey of the Hungarian nonprofit sector.

I owe a debt of gratitude to all these individuals and organizations and wish to express my deepest thanks to them. Naturally, they cannot be blamed for any errors of fact or judgement: I take full responsibility for the text.

Éva Kuti
Budapest, Hungary
November, 1994

Chapter 1

INTRODUCTION

Rationale of the third sector research in Hungary

A striking upsurge has taken place in voluntary activity in post-communist Hungary. The nonprofit organizations have mush-roomed, their social importance and economic strength have soared, the number of donors and the amount of charitable donations have multiplied for the last couple of years. This sudden growth is puzzling even in the context of the "global associational revolution" (Salamon, 1993). The scope and scale of the phenomenon suggest that something really exceptional is happening in the Hungarian economy and society. A country is looking for its future social, economic and political system. As Konrád and Szelényi (1991, p. 60) stated: "we know better what we are leaving behind, rather than what lies ahead of us. The emergent new social formation may be socialistic, but it may also represent convergence with Western capitalism, and it also may be of a different quality, it may be located on some kind of 'third – or Central European way' which is as different from Western capitalism as it is different from any form of socialism presently known to us". The proliferation of voluntary organizations is a clear sign of the citizens' intention to actively and directly influence the formation of their future. The emergence of non-profit organizations in many fields of the economy, their beha-viour and actual activities are obviously an expression of the society's attitudes and aspirations, and at the same time they are, of course, greater or lesser important factors and also indicators of the development process.

The research challenge is manifold, then. We have to find the answers to three different, though interrelated, questions: *What* is

happening, *why*, and what are its *impacts* on the social and economic development in Hungary?

First, what is actually happening in the third sector in Hungary?
How large is the nonprofit sector, how large is its share of the
national economy? How many voluntary organizations do exist in
different fields? What are their activities? How much and what
kind of services do they deliver? How extensive are their advocacy activities? How much money do they spend? Who has established and who is financing the thousands of new voluntary
organizations? What are the sources of third sector revenues?

Second, what are the interests, motivations, aims and efforts
behind the establishment of voluntary organizations? How large
is the role of traditions, democratic aspirations, political and professional ambitions, economic and financial interests? How are
these motivations manifested in the actual behaviour of the main
actors influencing the development of the nonprofit sector?

Third, the outcome of both collective and individual actions is
always somewhat different from the results expected by the
actors. Thus it is reasonable to investigate the actual impacts of
voluntary movements and nonprofit activities, to inquire what
roles are played by the third sector institutions and initiatives in
the changing Hungarian economy and society.

Research methodology, definition and data sources

The aim of the research project we have carried out was to make
the first steps in the direction of answering these questions.
Although the voluntary associations had not been completely
neglected either by researchers (e.g. Harangi, 1986; Katus and
Tóth, 1986) or by statisticians (*Egyesületek Magyarországon*, 1970,
1982, 1989) in Hungary, we still did not have a solid base from
which to start analyzing the above listed problems. Voluntary
organizations had only a limited existence in Hungary in the state
socialist period. Most of them were fully state controlled and state
financed, nobody had the idea that they should have regarded
them as institutions of an independent sector. If Western democracies considered the market and the state as the "islands of meaning" in their conceptual maps of social and economic life,
organized their economic reporting systems and their public poli-

cies in accordance with this "two sector conceptualization" (Salamon and Anheier, 1994, pp. 1–2), then Hungary was a "one sector economy" (Marschall, 1990) where the omnipotent state was directly responsible for both public welfare and the daily operation of the business sphere. Accordingly, the differentiation between economic sectors was missing from the (otherwise quite developed) Hungarian statistical system. Voluntary associations were accounted, their activities were analysed as an interesting social phenomenon, but nobody tried to conceptualize them as a sector, nobody investigated their relationships with business firms and public institutions.

Accidentally, the collapse of the state socialist regime, the renaissance of the three sector economy in Hungary, occurred in the same period, when the dissatisfaction with the welfare state challenged the "two sector conceptualization" of the social reality in the Western countries. This coincidence offered an exceptional opportunity to the Hungarian researchers. We were not alone in the midst of conceptual confusion, we could cooperate with our colleagues in developing the definition and classifications of the nonprofit sector, the general approach of the research, and the basic scheme of the statistical information to be gathered about the sector. The comparative project provided us with a frame of reference, it helped us to look at our findings in their proper perspective.

In order to establish the boundaries of the nonprofit sector for the purpose of the comparative project, it was necessary to develop a common definition. This "structural/operational definition" (Salamon and Anheier, 1992b) applied to the Hungarian situation in 1990 (the base year of the comparative project) surprisingly well, especially if we have in mind that this was the very first year of democracy after four decades of state socialism.

The core definition developed for the purposes of the comparative project consists of seven components.

1 *Formal*, i.e. the organizations are institutionalized to some extent, they have some formal character. This criterion does not cause any difficulty in Hungary. Although there are some researchers who argue that theoretically there is no significant difference between informal groups and formal voluntary organizations, the formal character of the nonprofit organizations is generally accepted. (Hungary is a traditionally bureaucratic

country – not only in terms of organization, but also in terms of mentality.) Groups without legal charter are not regarded as organizations.

2 *Private*, i.e. the organizations are formally part of the private sector and are institutionally separate from government. Nonprofit organizations are neither part of the governmental apparatus nor governed by boards dominated by government officials. In principle, this requirement was also met by the Hungarian nonprofit organizations in the base year of the comparative project. They were all registered under private law as private organizations. In practice, the situation was much more complicated. There were formerly state-controlled organizations which played an oppositional role in the new regime; foundations created by the former government with boards in which the supporters of the new government were not represented at all; organizations which had been established by members of the former opposition who became supporters or even members of the new government; foundations set up by state enterprises which then became privatized, etc. Originally I thought that Hungarian nonprofit organizations were generally more closely connected to the government even in 1990 than is usual in the United States or in Western Europe. In light of the result of the comparative project I am less sure about it now. Anyway, the private character of the Hungarian nonprofit sector has weakened since 1990 because a recent change of the Civil Code made it possible that foundations and associations be established under public law.

3 *Non profit-distributing*, i.e. the organizations do not distribute profits to their owners and members. The non-distribution constraint is imposed on all Hungarian nonprofit organizations by the laws regulating their activities. Nevertheless, there are some fake foundations which explicitly serve their founders' interests. Their filtering out is almost impossible because they obviously won't give information on their illegal acts. It is to be feared that this abuse is more frequent in the newly emerging and quickly changing Hungarian nonprofit sector than in the developed countries.

4 *Self-governing*, i.e. the organizations have their own internal decision making structures and internal procedures for governance, they are not controlled by outside entities. This criterion

must be met (at least formally) by every Hungarian nonprofit institution.

5 *Voluntary*, i.e. the organizations have some meaningful degree of voluntary citizen involvement, either in the actual conduct of their activities or in the management of their affairs. There is no problem with this requirement. Quite a few nonprofit organizations use voluntary work; many nonprofits have voluntary members, get voluntary donations; and almost all of them have non-compensated voluntary boards.

6 *Nonreligious*, i.e. the organizations are not involved in the promotion of religious worship, they are not congregations, synagogues, mosques or other primarily religious institutions. This criterion can be easily met in Hungary because churches constitute a special group of organizations. Their regulation is slightly different from the general regulation of the voluntary organizations. (They have more privileges.) Service agencies supported by churches are normally registered as foundations or associations, so they are automatically included in any empirical survey of the nonprofit organizations.

7 *Nonpolitical*, i.e. the organizations are not primarily engaged in supporting candidates for political office. With some exceptions the Hungarian nonprofit organizations met this criterion in 1990. The public financial support of the political parties was so generous during the period of the first democratic elections that it was in the political organizations' best interest to become political parties if they wanted to put their members into public office. On the other hand, there is nothing in law that would prevent nonprofit organizations from lobbying or cooperating with political parties, the present legal regulation of the non-profit sector does not guarantee the non-partisan character of voluntary organizations. Accordingly, several politically engaged nonprofit organizations have appeared since the base year of the international comparison, the Hungarian nonprofit sector is more politicized now than it was in 1990.

In short, the structural/operational definition is – by and large – applicable to the Hungarian nonprofit sector. Operationally, its use is quite easy because the Hungarian legal system is very clear about institutional forms. In 1990 there were only two legal forms available for the nonprofit organizations: those of the foundations and voluntary associations. The actual activities of these two kinds of nonprofits are not necessarily different, but they significantly differ in their organizational structure, nature, legal and tax regulations.

Foundations are organizations governed by a voluntary board (mostly named by the founders). They must have an endowment and cannot have members. They enjoy both tax exemption and tax deductibility. They can be grant-making bodies (like most of the private foundations in the United States), grant-seeking, fund-raising organizations, and also service providing, operating foundations.

Voluntary associations are membership organizations with officers elected by their members. They enjoy tax exemption, but the donations they receive are normally not tax deductible. They can be both member-serving and public-serving organizations; lobbying and advocacy are also among their usual activities.

Both foundations and voluntary associations are registered by the court. This register is an important source of information on the size of the sector and also a starting point (either as a list of addressees of questionnaires or as a base for sample selection) in any empirical survey. In our case it played the second role. For lack of systematic statistical information on the nonprofit sector, we had to carry out a sample survey in order to estimate the size and structure of the Hungarian nonprofit sector. The results of this survey are the main source of our description of the Hungarian nonprofit sector in 1990 and its comparison to the third sectors of the other project countries (France, Germany, Italy, Japan, United Kingdom, United States). The changes which have taken place since the base year of the comparative project were mostly evaluated on the basis of the official data from budget reports and tax records, and from a survey carried out by the Statistical Office of Hungary in 1993. The empirical research was completed by an overview of the literature, a study of historical documents, an inquiry into the changes of legal and economic regulation, and a series of interviews with top nonprofit leaders and decision makers who may influence the policy towards the sector.

Key findings of the Hungarian research project

As it was to be expected, the Hungarian nonprofit sector proved to be the smallest among the project countries in 1990. Its operating expenditures (excluding expenditures for capital items such as buildings or machinery) represented only 1.2 per cent of the gross domestic product, while the seven-country average was 3.5 per cent (Salamon and Anheier, 1994, p. 35). As a result of a very impressive growth, this share reached 3.2 per cent by 1992, which is still lower than the seven-country average was in 1990, but higher than the same figure in Italy and equal with that of Japan.

By contrast, the growth of the nonprofit share of total employment was much slower than that of the expenditures. It reached only 1.5 per cent by 1992. Consequently, the gap between Hungary and the developed countries is narrowing at a much lower rate in terms of nonprofit employment than in terms of expenditures.

Nevertheless, our data suggest that the economic importance of the Hungarian nonprofit sector is definitely larger than it is generally presumed to be. Its dynamism, which is in sharp contrast with the general decline in other parts of the economy, deserves far more attention than it attracted in the first years of the transition period. While the size and structure of the third sector was deeply influenced by the "heritage" of the state socialist regime (old voluntary associations still dominated the sector) in 1990, the newly emerging nonprofit organizations are already the institutions of the new area. They represent the society's response to the new challenges. Their large scale emergence in the fields of education and health care express the government's and citizens' willingness to increase the supply and quality of services which were previously monopolized by the state. The mushrooming of advocacy organizations suggests on the one hand that citizens are determined to take matters into their own hands and to develop institutional guarantees of their participation in decision making at all levels. On the other hand, the proliferation of these nonprofits may partly be an organizational expression and consequence of the degree of upheaval, upward and downward social mobility, and instability of Hungarian society under the conditions of the transition from state socialism to a market economy.

Our data on the revenue side also seem to prove the importance of private initiatives in the striking development of the nonprofit sector. The largest share (57 per cent) of the total nonprofit income originated from private earnings, i.e. fees, sales, investment and business activities of the nonprofit organizations themselves. This suggests that the Hungarian nonprofit sector is more entrepreneurial than those of the other project countries. (There was just one country, Japan, where the share of the earned income proved to be higher than in Hungary; the seven-country average was only 47 per cent.) Similarly, the income from private charitable giving (including gifts from individuals, corporations, churches, unions, foundations and other voluntary organizations) accounted for about 20 per cent of the total nonprofit income, which was the highest among the project countries and double the seven-country average. These surprising results probably have to do with the very generous tax treatment of the nonprofit organizations' business income and with the unlimited tax deductibility of donations to registered foundations.

In contrast with the generous indirect state support, the direct government support to nonprofit organizations was rather parsimonious in Hungary in 1990. Its share (23 per cent of the total nonprofit income) was the lowest among the project countries, barely surpassing half of the seven-country average.

Without wishing to deny the importance of facilitation and encouragement on the part of government and from some Western foundations and official aid agencies, we can state that the renaissance of the Hungarian voluntary sector started in 1990 mostly as a result of private initiatives. People, who wanted to act at last as citizens instead of being subordinates, established nonprofit organizations in order to exercise some control over social processes, decision making and the provision of welfare services. Solemnly speaking, many of these voluntary organizations were born as the institutions of civil society. In a more pragmatic interpretation, they appeared as alternative policy makers directly expressing the interests and aims of social actors.

Anyway, their extremely impressive development would have hardly been possible without a very old, rich and strong tradition of the voluntary sector in Hungary. It is very clear that all elements of this complex tradition have had some influence. The genuine democratic aspirations, the distrust between government and citizens, the "second society mentality" and the pre-modern character of the society and economy all played some role in the remarkable growth of the nonprofit sector, when the basic conditions for this development were dramatically improved by the political changes of 1989.

After a flying start, the further development of the sector has been possible because the patterns of problem solving offered by nonprofits have been also acceptable, in some fields even attractive for the government. The nonprofit institutional form is generally considered to be an appropriate means of facing the social and economic challenges of the transition period.

After decades or even centuries of mutual distrust and either latent or manifest conflicts, cooperation has become the leading principle in the government–nonprofit relationship. To put this principle into practice, to stabilize, institutionalize the mechanisms of cooperation and still preserve the independence of the voluntary sector – this is one of the key issues facing the nonprofit sector in Hungary in the years immediately ahead.

Political independence is all the more a great concern for voluntary organizations, because they are aware that government assistance is inevitably needed in raising the necessary funds for their programmes. The more the Hungarian nonprofit organizations are striving to enlarge their service-providing activities, the more they are dependent on direct and indirect state support. Although the private giving is growing and one can find numerous moving examples of citizens' generosity, the fact remains that individual donors' contribution to third sector development is negligible, at least in financial terms. The low income level, which is treated as a psychological barrier to charitable behaviour by some analysts, does not completely prevent people from donating to third sector organizations, but does hinder any significant growth in the relative importance of individual donations.

This greatly increases the government's responsibility. The harm done by the nationalization of nonprofit organizations after 1945 cannot be fully repaired, but the government should make amends for it. It has to continue supporting the voluntary sector and at the same time it must stop foundation abuse, increase the accountability of nonprofit organizations, and develop a comprehensive system of economic regulation without seriously decreasing the autonomy and independence of the nonprofit sector.

The responsibility of the nonprofit organizations themselves is also enormous. After the rather chaotic period of extensive growth, they should really organize themselves, develop their own rules of ethical behaviour, establish their umbrella organizations, improve cooperation and information exchange within the sector, and significantly increase the professional quality of their activities.

The structure of the book

This book is the result of an effort to bring together all the relevant information on the Hungarian nonprofit sector which is available at this stage from research dealing with it. Accordingly, our data are sometimes fragmentary, the quality of the figures used in different chapters is uneven, both the data sources and the applied approaches vary from chapter to chapter.

Chapter 2 explores the history of nonprofit organizations in Hungary. It identifies the major trends and main historical periods as they relate to the development of the voluntary sector, pointing out important events that shaped the history of the sector and its component organizations. It analyses some long-term historical factors that seem to account for the size and nature of the voluntary sector.

A detailed description of the major periods of Hungarian nonprofit history provides the reader with information on developments and changes in the voluntary sector as they relate to the social, political and economic situations over time. An analysis of the changing roles played by nonprofits over their history sheds some light on the division of labour between different sectors. An overview of the changing legal and economic regulation, financial conditions, aims and activities of nonprofit organizations help the reader to understand the tradition which has its deep and manifold impact on the recent development of the nonprofit sector in Hungary.

The chapter identifies some key features of the nonprofit history, namely the repeated necessity of existing on the edge of illegality; the limited role played by organized religion in the development of the voluntary sector; the ambivalent state–nonprofit relationship; and the lack of a comprehensive regulation of the nonprofit sector.

Chapter 3 presents a discussion of the legal position of the nonprofit sector. It gives an overview of the basic legal principles shaping the nonprofit regulation in Hungary. It describes the legal context and examines the characteristics of the major laws dealing with the voluntary sector. It discusses in detail the regulation of the main legal forms of nonprofit organizations and gives a detailed description of the tax treatment of nonprofits.

In addition, the chapter identifies the main legal issues, namely the problems of efficiency, independence and public control in the tax treatment of nonprofits; the emergence of public law organizations among the nonprofit legal forms; and the legal problems of contracting out services. Finally, it gives a short summary of the missing items of the legal agenda: the ethical issues and the problems of political commitment and campaigning activities of nonprofit organizations.

Chapter 4 presents a discussion of the economic and social importance and the role of the nonprofit sector in Hungarian society in the period of transition, and, using the full spectrum of available empirical data, tries to test the validity of both theoretical hypotheses and conventional beliefs about the sector. It compares the figures for the size, structure, activities, expenditures and revenues of the Hungarian nonprofit sector with those of the nonprofit sectors of the other, more developed project countries.

Besides presenting the results of the empirical survey, the chapter also tries to give an interpretation of the statistical data. With the help of a lot of background information it identifies the main causes and motivations behind the renaissance of the voluntary sector in Hungary right after the collapse of the state socialist regime.

Chapter 5 describes and analyses the development of the Hungarian nonprofit sector since 1990, the base year of the comparative project. It presents statistical data on the growth of the number of organizations, the expenditures and the employment in the third sector. It examines the changes in government support and individual donations.

With the help of some detailed figures for structural changes, the chapter looks in more detail at some of the subsectors, and tries to identify and explain the variations that exist among major components of the sector.

Chapter 6 describes the overall position of government towards the nonprofit sector. It identifies the divisions within the government and discusses the impacts of the sometimes contradictory government measures. An analysis of the changes in government attitude helps the reader to understand the problems nonprofit organizations have to face in post-communist Hungary.

The chapter also examines the roles played by nonprofit organizations as vehicles of policy. It differentiates three possible nonprofit strategies (the problem-solving approach, the responsive, ensuing approach and the dynamic creative approach) and analyses their usefulness in introducing, shaping and implementing social policies.

Using the results of interviews with politicians, government officials and top leaders of the nonprofit sector, the chapter identifies the current issues of the Hungarian nonprofit sector, namely the reduction of the tax privileges, the limited amount of individual and government support, the staff payment and staff training problems, the lack of a comprehensive nonprofit regulation, the politicization of nonprofit organizations, the accountability and ethical issues, the internationalization of the nonprofit sector, and the lack of information sharing within the sector.

Chapter 7 tries to bring together the various theoretical implications of the research findings discussed in the previous chapters. It discusses how the existing economic and political theories of the nonprofit sector relate to the Hungarian case, and to what extent the evidence presented for Hungary enrich our understanding of the nonprofit sector.

This concluding chapter also gives a short summary of the major policy implications of the comparative project for the Hungarian nonprofit sector.

Chapter 2

THE HISTORY OF THE NONPROFIT SECTOR IN HUNGARY

Origins and early history

The history of voluntary organizations (if it is appropriate to use this very recent term in a historical context) is almost as long as that of the Christian state in Hungary. Nomadic Hungarian tribes arrived in the present territory of Hungary about 896. The failure of their wars of conquest in the west of Europe (the battle of Augsburg in 955), and the limited size of the country, forced them to change their way of life. Agriculture, and with it the feudal system, started to develop. Prince Géza (970–997) and his son King István I (997–1038) decided to join Christian Europe and transform Hungary into a feudal state – at that time the most modern kind of state. They obliged their people to become Christian, confiscated the property of rebellious pagan leaders and donated a large part of it to the Catholic Church and the religious orders they invited to Hungary. According to some analysts (Kecskés, 1988, pp. 110–11), these endowments (followed by many others from both kings and feudal lords) were the very first charitable foundations in Hungary. They met all the criteria twentieth-century foundations have to meet. The donor could not withdraw the endowment, the endowment had to serve a permanent public purpose, and the donor had the right to set conditions for letting the donee use the income from the endowment.

The Church was supposed not only to proselytize, but also to help people in need. In his first Code of Law, King István I obliged the Church to care for widows and orphans. In his second Code of Law he even ordered one-quarter of the income from tithes to be devoted to helping the poor (Pataki, 1993, p. 1). The Church must have obeyed, because the very first monasteries (e.g. Pécsvárad, established in 999) already ran hospitals which were actually a kind of cross between almshouses and infirmaries. Some documents (Somogyi, 1941, pp. 18–19) show that the relief of poverty was also a common condition stipulated in private endowments. Besides large donations, the Church also received small gifts in kind, mostly corn, wine, honey and oil (called "oblations") from the members of its congregations. Food given in this way was distributed to the poor by the bishop after Sunday mass. Clients of monastery hospitals were also regularly sent out to the neighbouring villages in order to solicit gifts (Hahn, 1960, p. 9).

In short, the secular authority (the king), the Church organizations and the lay people all played some part at a time when the Hungarian society was first trying to face at least some of its social problems. The lay element in social care significantly increased in the next centuries. Besides the monasteries, numerous lay fraternities (*fratres conversi*) and brotherhoods were created. Originally most of them simply took over the economic and charitable activities of the monasteries, cultivated their lands, ran their institutions (including their hospitals and almshouses) and distributed alms to the poor, but some of them became independent and were known as "hospitaller orders" (*ordo fratrum hospitalariorum*) throughout the Middle Ages (Somogyi, 1941, pp. 20–1 and 28).

Some orders of chivalry also engaged in charitable work. For instance, the second hospital in Buda was established by Master Artolfus, who was Master of the Order of the Holy Ghost. (The founder of the first hospital was the king himself.) Master Artolfus sold some properties in order to build this hospital in 1330 (Zolnay, 1975, p. 124). Some decades later, at the beginning of the fifteenth century, the hospital was already owned by the Buda municipality. Its board consisted of the most respectable citizens.

In the deeply pious atmosphere of the Middle Ages all the orders of chivalry, fraternities and brotherhoods were constituted as religious orders, but in practice many of them were lay organizations which today we would call voluntary associations. A good example of such lay orders of chivalry is the Saint George Society (Societas Beati Georgii) which was established in 1326 by fifty knights. Its main purpose was the protection of the king, but its members also promised to mutually support each other. Eighty years later the king and queen themselves initiated the creation of the Dragon Order, which had a membership of no more than twenty-four persons of the highest rank. The society's aim was to form a solid alliance, to provide a framework for collective decision making, to serve the public good, to protect the country against enemies, and to promote its development (Erdélyi, 1925, pp. 253–8).

Just as nobles had their orders of chivalry, the common people had their fraternities and their trade or city brotherhoods. These groups were associations for charitable and social service as well as for leisure time and religious activities. For instance, the "Corpus Christi" Society, which was established in Nagyszeben in 1372, donated an altar to the local church, paid a chaplain who celebrated masses for the salvation of the souls of its members, and saw to the burial of poor people whose families could not afford to finance a decent funeral (Szádeczky, 1913, p. I/29). Wills in Eperjes in the fourteenth century regularly used phrases like this: "I bequeath my property to the Society of Cobblers, to wit, to the Altar of the Virgin" (Szűcs, 1955, p. 116).

Despite their constitution as religious societies, these brotherhoods of craftsmen were in fact predecessors of the guilds. Nevertheless, the tradition which was born from the religious character of the fraternities of craftsmen proved to be very long lasting. Most newly created guilds continued to worship at the altar of their predecessor's patron saint, and some of them would take the name of the saint or refer to the saint in their coat of arms. Besides their economic role, the craftsmen's fraternities and the guilds that followed them also functioned as mutual benefit, member-serving organizations providing services for the mutual benefit of their members. There were strict rules and regulations which guided the behaviour of the members towards other members and towards their families. Nursing sick members, organizing and financing their funerals if they died, and helping their widows, were all considered to be proper tasks for the guilds. Several guilds also had rules regulating their charitable activities. Fines paid by their members were often used to help the poor or other charitable organizations in the city. In some cases the guilds obliged members whose products fell below the standard size or quality to give these non-standard products to charitable organizations (Szádeczky, 1913, pp. I/34, I/215, I/230–231 and II/9).

Journeymen also formed their own societies which were more or less (but rather less) independent of the guilds. (The first examples of this kind of voluntary organization come from the fifteenth century: a society of journeyman weavers was established in Kassa in 1429; a society of journeyman bakers was formed in Pozsony in 1433.) The main functions of these organizations were to guide the journeymen's behaviour, to protect their interests, to help them to find jobs, to assist them in case of sickness or other trouble, and to help and find accommodation for journeymen who arrived in the city as guests of the guild. (Szűcs, 1955, pp. 158–62)

The development of the guilds kept pace with the development of the cities themselves. Some centres of international trade received privileges from the king as early as the beginning of the thirteenth century. Charters giving liberties and privileges to the inhabitants of fortified cities and fortresses became much more frequent after the Tatar invasion of the country in 1241, which forced the king to realize the military importance of the cities. The regular conflicts between the kings, the Church and the feudal barons also obliged the kings to turn to the cities for support. Under these favourable conditions about 25–30 Hungarian settlements became real cities by the fifteenth century in both the legal and the economic sense of the word (Szűcs, 1955, p. 19). In addition, there were about 800–900 small agricultural towns (Bibó, 1986, p. II/495) which also had charters granting liberties.

As soon as they felt strong enough, the cities and their citizens set about taking control of the welfare services. As Zolnay (1975, p. 198) notes, the first schools in Buda were run by the Church, but the city government "patronized" them. Several documents show that citizens preferred naming the magistrates or other leaders of the city as trustees when they established foundations. János Omechin, a councillor in Nagybánya, explicitly stated in 1408 that his foundation was exclusively to serve the poor and its trustee must be the magistracy of the city and not the master of the church hospital. The wording of the founding statute of a hospital established in Debrecen in 1529 was even more blunt. In order to prevent the misuse and squandering of the endowment, it strictly prohibited any clergyman from gaining full control of the hospital. Another article of the same founding statute (requiring the employment of a priest) shows that the founder's intention was not to weaken the religious character of the hospital (Somogyi, 1941, p. 93).

People as private persons were deeply religious in the Middle Ages in Hungary, but as citizens they seemed to prefer to exercise control over the use of both public funds and lay gifts through the city authorities. A series of documents (e.g. from Pozsony, 1391; Körmöcbánya, 1393; Szakolcza 1431) prove that individuals, when they established hospitals and almshouses, often decided to do so in cooperation with the city government (Somogyi, 1941, pp. 54–6). The institutions they created were neither classic nonprofit nor classic public institutions, but something in between. Thanks to their founders they had endowments, and were the beneficiaries of private gifts, foundations and bequests, but at the same time they were supported by the city governments, as well (Csizmadia, 1977, p. 17). The city's support consisted both of direct financial support and of privileges. The masters of the institutions were named and the employees paid by the city authorities, but a large part of the actual services were often provided by volunteers (Hahn, 1960, p. 11). The guilds were generally among the supporters of the city hospitals, but this was not pure philanthropy on their part. The condition of their contribution was often a well defined set of services their members had to receive from the institutions they supported (Hahn, 1960, p. 15).

As suggested by both the authors cited, and many other historians and political analysts (e.g. Bibó, 1986; Pach, 1966; Wallerstein, 1983), the early development of the Hungarian economy, society, and consequently of the voluntary sector in Hungary was not significantly different from the development in other European countries up to the end of the fifteenth century. The central secular authority often came into conflict with the Church on the one hand and the feudal barons on the other. Simultaneously, the bourgeoisie of the cities were establishing their own status, developing their own administrative sphere and methods and selling their support to the king in return for charters of liberties. As an example we may mention the city of Buda. It helped King László IV to dismiss the synod which was likely to excommunicate him in 1279 for not being zealous enough in proselytizing the nomadic Kun tribes recently settled in Hungary (Karácsonyi, 1985, pp. 34–5). King Róbert Károly also needed the help of Buda in 1311 when a rebellious feudal lord, Csák Máté, attacked him, and the city was ready again to protect the king against the besieging army (Salamon, 1885, pp. II/313–14).

Under such relatively favourable conditions, thanks to royal support and the liberties and economic privileges the cities had been granted, the rise of the urban "third estate" started, but the political balance among the competing groups was unstable. The king, not having a permanent armed force at his command, had to rely on the feudal obligation of his vassals to perform military service. Rule was still personal, and relationships between lord and vassals and not between state and citizens were the dominant elements of the political structure.

As Wallerstein (1983) points out, the whole European development reached a critical juncture in the sixteenth century. The evolution of a new pattern of division of labour and the development of the "European world economy" pushed Eastern Europe into a backward position on the European periphery. This was also the point where the development of the Hungarian voluntary sector was diverted for centuries along a different route from that followed by Western Europe.

The first two centuries of this period, which are called the "cul de sac of Hungarian history" by Bibó (1986), were really fatal to the development of the voluntary sector in Hungary. The second serfdom and the alliance formed by the lower and upper classes of nobility after the failure of a peasant revolt in 1514 were stabilized by the Turkish invasion of the country in 1526. The central part of Hungary was occupied and literally destroyed by the Turks. It belonged to the Turkish empire for 150 years. The rest of the country was divided into two parts. Its western counties became a province of the Habsburg empire. Transylvania remained more or less independent. It was the repository of the sense of Hungarian nationhood and a foothold for the repeated (1551, 1591–1606, 1683–1686, 1697, 1703–1711) and repeatedly unsuccessful wars of independence against the Turks and Habsburgs.

These centuries are black pages in the history of the voluntary sector in Hungary. Economic development, the growth of the cities, the process of embourgeoisement, the evolution of a modern society, the development of "small circles of freedom" (Bibó, 1986) all came to a halt. When the Turkish army left and the country was unified again, the Habsburg emperors still remained in power. Their policy towards Hungary was clearly colonialist. While in their own country they supported the bourgeoisie, protected the peasants, limited the influence of the feudal lords and thus helped social development, in Hungary, which was only important for them as a protective military zone and a source of cheap agricultural products, they allied themselves with the nobles and helped them to conserve the privileges guaranteed to them by the feudal system. Being the leading force of the Counter-Reformation, the Habsburg dynasty made Catholicism a state religion again. Thus the Catholic Church and its institutions could hardly play any role as non-governmental, voluntary organizations. From our point of view this means that the Hungarian society, deeply divided as it was, remained frozen in this state, the development of the "third estate" stopped, the cities went into decline, and therefore the social basis for the development of the voluntary sector was lacking. Although the guilds, some foundations and voluntary associations survived, one can say that the Hungarian nonprofit sector had only a very limited existence in the sixteenth, seventeenth and even in the first half of the eighteenth century. Its modern history started in the second half of the eighteenth century and can be divided into four very different periods.

Pre-industrial period

After the Turkish occupiers had left and the Rákóczi War of Independence (1703–1711) had failed, the Habsburg emperors established themselves in Hungary on a permanent basis. Although they considered Hungary a colony, they still promoted some very limited modernization of the country, especially in the period of the enlightened absolutism of Maria Theresa (1740–1780) and Joseph II (1780–1790). Besides the introduction of a new system of taxation, the regulation of serfs' rights and obligations, and reforms in education, social care and health care, they also payed some attention to the voluntary and semi-voluntary organizations. As Szádeczky (1913, pp. 140–75) points out, this was the period when the central regulation and control of the guilds intensified – formerly their activities had been regulated mainly at municipal level.

Several efforts were also made to gain control over private foundations. (This seems to prove that there were private foundations to be controlled in Hungary in the eighteenth century. They must have been quite important if it was worth dealing with them at the highest political level.) A first law regulating foundations was enacted in 1723. This law gave the Emperor, as King of Hungary, the right to control the activities and the financial accounts of the foundations (Kecskés, 1988, p. 111). As the passage quoted below shows, the monarchs took this right seriously. A directive issued by Maria Theresa in 1768 says:

> in order to make the necessary arrangements to feed the poor, the County Administrators must carefully find out how many and what kind of foundations for poverty relief exist in their counties. Where are these foundations? How are they managed? By whom? Does their management meet the requirements set by the founders? Is their permanency guaranteed? If their endowment or a part of it has been lost, who is to blame for it? Is there any hope of getting back foundation properties? (Pataki, 1993, p. 5)

On the other hand, the monarchs not only tried to control, they also created foundations. In many cases they did it as private individuals (e.g. the establishment of the Foundation for Helping the Orphans by Maria Theresa in Debrecen in 1775 (Szűcs, 1872, p. 885) or her foundations supporting the higher education of talented young people), but it happened quite frequently that they simply exercised their authority. For instance, when the Jesuit order was dissolved in 1773, Maria Theresa did not nationalize its properties. Instead, she established an Education Fund, which worked as an independent foundation under public law (Kará-csonyi, 1985, pp. 319–22). After the dissolution of other monastic orders Joseph II also ordered, in a decree issued on 10 September 1782, that their properties (165,000 Hungarian acres, i.e. 234,300 English acres of farmland) had to be put into a Catholic Religious Fund called Cassa Parochiorum (Voit, 1991, p. 2). Similarly, when the largest Catholic University was secularized, it did not become a public institution; rather, it became a self-governing foundation under public law.

Despite all its internal contradictions and inconsistencies, enlightened absolutism brought about some development and modernization in Hungary. This relatively peaceful development also resulted in a recovery of society. Paradoxically enough, the sense of Hungarian nationhood was actually strengthened by forced "germanization". (The most alarming measure in this germanization was a decree of Joseph II in 1784. He ordered that both schools and government offices of all levels had to use German, and only German, in their everyday activities.) The reaction of Hungarian society was a movement of language reform and the creation of a series of voluntary associations promoting culture, progressive ideas and the national language.

Voluntary associations called "reading circles" were established in the 1790s, mostly by intellectuals and particularly enlightened nobles. These groups were actually political societies. "Reading and culture served as vehicles for social reforms and weapons against Austrian colonization in their programmes" (Fülöp, 1978, p. 33). It is not accidental that secret agents payed a lot of attention to "reading circle" activities in their reports (Benda, 1957, pp. 155–7) and two of the founding members of the Buda Reading Circle, József Hajnóczy and Ferenc Szentmarjay were executed for conspiracy in 1799 (Benda, 1957, p. VIII). Not only were the "reading circles" banned, but even the public libraries were forced to close down by the Austrian emperor after the failure of this "conspiracy", which was actually a secret society of the "Hungarian Jacobins" who wanted to modernize the country and transform it into an independent republic (Kósa, 1939, p. 463; Kulcsár, 1943, p. 29). When libraries could open again in 1811, their number was limited, the nature of their collection (only rigorously censored, mostly German books) and their activities were strictly controlled. The decree of the emperor stated that "public libraries were not allowed to have public reading rooms and to cooperate with scientific societies" (Gárdonyi, 1930, p. 85).

Some continuity was preserved by the literary societies of students (Bodolay, 1963), which were less involved in politics than the "reading circles" but not less saturated with ideas of enlightenment and independence. Although the existing societies were banned in 1799, students formed new literary societies of the same inspiration in the years that followed. These voluntary associations served as training grounds for the activists of the forthcoming reform movement.

The main goals of this reform movement (1825–1848) were the industrialization of the country, the reform of the still feudal legal system, and national independence. Voluntary associations, "reading circles", "casinos" and literary societies played an active role in spreading reform ideas. Many of the associations' articles spelled out that "development of agriculture, industry and trade; support for fine arts, literature and theatre; promotion of the national language, urbanization and civilization; maintenance of high ethical standards; relief to people in need, etc. were among the aims of these basically cultural associations" (Fülöp, 1978, p. 100). A good example of this large scale activity is offered by the history of the Social Club of Szeged Inner City (Czimer, 1929). During the first ten years (1829–1838) of its existence it established a voluntary theatre company, a nonprofit orchestra, a kindergarten, and a charitable association of women, and it initiated the establishment of a Turkish bath. Similarly, the Social Club of Debrecen efficiently supported the Society for the Protection of Domestic Products, initiated the establishment of the first local savings bank and steam–mill, helped the construction of a local hospital and organized a fund raising campaign in order to develop street lighting in Debrecen (Boldisár, 1933).

The literary societies of students became much more radical and sharply political during the 1830s and 1840s. Although they were banned in 1836 and, when re-established, all claimed not to be involved in politics, they continued to support the most radical groups of reformists. The Austrian emperor ordered them to be banned again in 1845, but both the Protestant Church and the regional authorities resisted. They declared that "banning the students' societies would not have conformed with either the spirit of the law, or the ideals of education, nor with the general interests of the Hungarian nation" (Bodolay, 1963, pp. 60–3).

Scientific societies and charitable associations had fewer conflicts with the authorities, but – albeit in an indirect way – they also played a very important role in the reform movement. While they fulfilled their primary functions (carrying out research, and establishing orphanages, kindergartens, almshouses, shelters, workhouses, hospitals, etc.), they also offered an opportunity for people to meet, to form alliances, to face the country's problems, and to develop short-term solutions and long-term strategies. In a backward, feudal system these voluntary associations were the organizations in which people learned how to think and behave as citizens instead of being simply privileged or subordinate subjects of the Habsburg empire. Although the leading force of the reform movement was the nobility and the newly emerging intelligentsia, the lower classes also became involved. In addition to the most influential voluntary associations formed by the aristocracy and the lower nobility, the bourgeoisie and the workers also began to create their own voluntary organizations in the 1830s and 1840s. There appeared even some "sheepskin coated clubs", peasants' voluntary associations (Kovalcsik, 1986, p. II/51).

The short history of the Association for the Protection of the Domestic Industry (APDI) clearly shows how large the influence of some voluntary organizations was. The APDI's members committed themselves to buy Hungarian products even if their foreign counterparts were significantly cheaper. The aim of the movement was to protect domestic industrial products against foreign competition. The APDI was established on 6 October 1844. When its next meeting was held on 17 November 1845 it already had 138 regional organizations with a membership consisting of nobles, bourgeois, workers and peasants (Pajkossy, 1993, p. 7). The attitude of its members was definitely that of citizens rather than that of ideal subjects of a feudal state, or that shown in the typical benefit-maximizing behaviour of individuals in market economies.

This does not mean, of course, that all voluntary associations of the 1830s and 1840s were civic associations with a high social and political awareness. A great many of them wanted only to solve particular concrete problems or to develop various new kinds of service. Nevertheless, even these pragmatic voluntary organizations played an extremely important role in drawing together the problems of national independence, industrialization, embourgeoisement and the social economic and cultural development of the country, and in developing citizens' awareness of the importance of these matters and their responsibility for the future of the society. This was one of the rare moments in Hungarian history when all progressive groups and social classes joined forces in order to promote the development of the country, and all of them seemed to understand the importance of citizens' initiatives and cooperation.

The role played by voluntary organizations in Hungary before 1848–1849 has nowhere been more finely expressed than by a contemporary author:

> The state authorities, both the legislative bodies and the government can, at best, understand the general interests and promote the public good as a whole ... In Hungary, as much as anywhere in the world, the freedom of association is a right of crucial importance, and its protection is one of the most important tasks of the Hungarian opposition. If

23

we scrutinize recent developments, we cannot identify any progress in any social field which has not been initiated by voluntary associations. These voluntary organizations have directly or indirectly contributed to the mitigation of prejudices and hostility between social classes, to the evolution of sciences, arts and education, to the introduction of modern agricultural methods, to the development of trade and industry. In Hungary, voluntary associations must serve not only the relatively narrow local and minority interests, their assistance is also necessary for the development of the whole country and nation. This development would be paralysed without the support of voluntary organizations. (Lukács, 1847, p. 96)

In short, the flourishing of voluntary associations was not just a concomitant, but an organic element of the reform movement. It is not surprising, then, that most voluntary associations were persecuted when the allied Habsburg and Russian armies quelled the 1848–1849 Revolution and War of Independence, obliterated the first Hungarian republic and restored Habsburg rule in Hungary.

Industrialization and inter-war period

The voluntary associations were not literally banned after the failed Revolution and War for Independence of 1848–1849, but most of them were practically abolished, petrified or at least persecuted. By way of illustration, I give here a short overview of what happened to one of the most prominent, completely loyal, politically neutral voluntary associations, the Hungarian Royal Society of Natural Sciences, in the period which is called "the age of despotism and absolutism" by Hungarian historians.

June 1849–June 1850: The only note in the annals of the Society in this period is a quotation from a well-known Hungarian poem:

"The sun has gone down, but the stars
have not appeared. The sky is dark.
Nowhere near can one find a light."

June 20, 1850: The Society gets a special permission to recommence its activities, but its meetings can only be held under the supervision of a superintendent named by the authorities.
March 1852: The seal of the Society is confiscated by the Police, because the picture on it is similar to the Hungarian coat of arms, but does not contain the crown. (The sensitivity of the Court is explained

by the fact that Hungarians actually decided to change the national coat of arms when they dethroned the Habsburg emperor and declared Hungary a republic in 1849. The irony of it is, that the seal had been carved in 1843.) However, the Society was obliged to change the seal.

March 1853: The articles of the Society must be submitted to the authorities for their approval.

June 1854: The Society is prohibited from holding an assembly.

June 1855: The authorities do not approve the Society's articles, and a new version must be submitted.

July 1859: The minutes of the Society's meetings must be sent to the governor's office.

January 1860: The articles of the Society are revised for the fifth time because the authorities did not approve the fourth version.

May 1862: The Society is obliged to pay taxes.

October 1865: On a fresh request from the governor's office, the Society has once again to revise the articles, which still have not been approved.

August 24, 1866: The articles of the Society are approved.

(Kátai, 1868, pp. 117, 127, 131, 135, 139, 163, 164, 183, 194, 201)

These excerpts from the history of the Hungarian Royal Society of Natural Sciences show how difficult it was to run a voluntary association in Hungary between 1849 and 1867. It is very impressive that about half of the voluntary associations created before the revolution of 1848–1849 still survived, or rather were revived after some years of stagnation, and that despite all obstacles, new organizations were also established. Attempts to create the "Transylvanian Museum Society", one of the first associations to be established in the post-revolution period, were described in a contemporary report as "a triumphant struggle with the three-headed dragon of centralization, germanization and bureaucracy" (Kovalcsik, 1986, p. II/68).

In 1862, when the first official list of the voluntary associations was prepared by the Academy of Sciences, the number of organizations was not significantly smaller than it had been in 1848. Pajkossy (1993, p. 8), who tried to make a list of each individual voluntary association, based on all the available information in order to find out how many there were in all, states that there were at least 600 voluntary associations in Hungary in 1848. The Academy of Sciences found slightly fewer, only 579 organizations in 1862 (Magyarország különböző egyletei, 1862, p. 269). These were obviously not the same voluntary associations, but the overlap between the two populations can be estimated only in an indirect way, because the year of establishment was not recorded in the list prepared in 1862. Fortunately, this was done in the first statistical survey of voluntary associations carried out by the Hungarian Statistical Office in 1878 (Vargha, 1880).

Table 2.1 clearly shows that the Hungarian society was eager to keep its voluntary organizations alive and to create new ones as soon as the political environment made it possible. The growth of the voluntary sector significantly accelerated after the "Compromise" of 1867. (The "Compromise" granted Hungary far-reaching independence from the Austrian Crown with the exception of financial, military and foreign affairs.) The dissolution of the guilds (Industry Act VIII/1872) also provided a great stimulus to this development. The law actually suggested that craftsmen could form voluntary organizations in order to protect their interests, to promote professional cooperation and to provide members with social services. Although the number of these newly created professional associations reached little more than one-third (only 1,247) of the dissolved guilds by 1878, their appearance still considerably increased the total number of voluntary organizations and changed the structure of the voluntary sector.

Table 2.1

Number of voluntary associations in 1878 by year of establishment

Year of establishment	Number of voluntary associations
Before 1800	55
1801–1830	52
1831–1850	202
1851–1855	50
1856–1860	126
1861–1865	278
1866–1870	554
1871–1875	1,753
1876–1878	925
Total number of voluntary associations in 1878	3,995

In fact, 31 per cent of the voluntary associations which existed in 1878 (almost half of those which were established between 1872 and 1878) cannot be considered really new, spontaneously created organizations. What happened can be interpreted as some kind of "modernization" because the completely obsolete guilds were substituted by more flexible professional associations organized on a voluntary basis, but we should not forget that the initiative came "from above". The growth of the voluntary sector and also its structural changes were partly an outcome of the changes in legal regulation.

Another law (the XVII/1884 Industry Act) probably had the opposite impact, when it stated that a special kind of association called "industrial bodies" could be established in any settlement with at least a hundred skilled craftsmen if more than two-thirds of them wanted to create such a body and they received the permission of the local and professional authorities. Once these "industrial bodies" were established, membership became compulsory to all craftsmen running businesses in the given settlement. The spread of these new organizations (which, of course, were not regarded as voluntary associations in contemporary statistics) obviously may have decreased the number of truly voluntary professional associations of the same craftsmen.

At any rate, with or without the professional associations, the number of voluntary associations augmented in a very spectacular way (see Table 2.2) from the Compromise of 1867 until World War II. The shock of the Treaty of Trianon (the loss of 67 per cent of the former territory and 58 per cent of the former population of Hungary after World War I) caused many distortions in the development of the Hungarian society and had far-reaching political consequences, but did not stop the development of the voluntary sector. Neither the legal regulation of the sector, nor policy towards it, nor the roles played by the voluntary organizations changed very much during this period.

The government attitude towards voluntary organizations was somewhat ambivalent, and this ambivalence was reflected in their legal regulation. Although many laws and decrees (e.g. Decree 9555/1863, Law V/1878, Law XV/1883, Decree 16.031/1886, Law XXI/1886, Decree 16.784/1900, Law X/1909, Decree 10.271/1924, etc.) contained clauses which stated how foundations or special kinds of foundations had to be established, managed, registered and controlled, these measures were only fragments of a possible legal framework, and their requirements were rarely and only partly met by foundations and by organizations managing foundations (Kovács, 1989). The only bill (prepared in 1928) which would have provided a comprehensive framework for the regulation of foundations has never been passed by Parliament.

Table 2.2

Number of voluntary associations, 1862–1993

Year	Number of voluntary associations
31 December 1862[a]	319
31 December 1878[b]	1,917
31 December 1932	14,365
31 December 1970	8,886
31 December 1982	6,570
31 December 1989	8,514
31 December 1990	11,255
31 December 1991	17,869
31 December 1992	21,528
31 December 1993	23,851

Sources: Publications of the Central Statistical Office in 1862–1982. 1862: *Magyarország különböző egyletei – Statisztikai Közlemények. A hazai állapotok ismeretének elmozdítására IV. kötet*, MTA Statisztikai Bizottsága, Budapest, 1862, pp. 246–69. 1878: *Magyarország egyletei és társulatai 1878-ban – Hivatalos Statisztikai Közlemények*, KSH, Budapest, 1880, pp. 516–17. 1932: Dobrovits Sándor: *Magyarország egyesületeinek statisztikája – Magyar Statisztikai Szemle 1935/1*, pp. 26–7. 1970, 1982, 1989: *Egyesületek Magyarországon, 1970, 1982, 1989 – KSH*, Budapest, 1972, 1984, 1991. The source of the 1990–1993 data is the computerized register of the Supreme Court. The figure for 1990 was revised on the basis of a survey carried out by the Research Project on Nonprofit Organizations.

Notes: [a] Number of voluntary associations located at the present territory of Hungary. The actual number of voluntary associations was 579 in 1862. [b] Number of voluntary associations located at the present territory of Hungary. The actual number of voluntary association was 3,995 in 1878.

The legal regulation of voluntary associations was much stricter. Decree 1394/1873 stated very clearly: "the government and the local authorities must be very tactful in order both to endorse the freedom of association and to reserve the right of government control over voluntary association activities" (Heller, 1923, p. 72). In practice this meant that the articles of newly established voluntary associations had to be approved by the authorities. New organizations were allowed to begin their activities only when they received this approval. The system of regulation became a bit more liberal in 1875, when Decree 5008/1875 stated that forty days after the submission of their articles to the authorities, newly created voluntary associations could start to work temporarily even if they had not yet received any response. The same Decree of 1875 also imposed some restrictions. It prohibited workers' associations and political associations from establishing local branches and from having foreign members. It also stated that ethnic minorities were allowed to create only cultural associations and literary societies. Another limitation of the freedom of association was that voluntary associations had to be "one purpose" organizations; establishment of associations having several different purposes was forbidden (Dobrovits, 1936, p. 9).

Under the threat of war, a new law (Law XLIII/1912) was enacted in 1912. This empowered the Ministry of Internal Affairs to forbid the establishment of new voluntary associations and to ban existing organizations in case of war. The law was put into force in 1914 by Decree 5735/1914. It was strictly forbidden to create new associations for two years. A government Decree (1442/1916) somewhat eased this prohibition in 1916, but new voluntary associations still had to seek the approval of the Ministry of Internal Affairs. The same ministry also assumed the right to limit and even to ban voluntary organizations if their activities were found detrimental to the state (Szabó, 1989, p. 5). With the exception of the brief interlude of democracy which guaranteed unlimited freedom of association in 1919 (Law III/1919), practically the same regulation remained in force until 1945. Laws XI/1922 and XVII/1922 simply affirmed that the rules, which originally had been introduced as emergency rules during World War I, were still in force (Dobrovits, 1936, p. 10).

Despite these strict conditions, almost all social, professional, religious and age-related groups formed voluntary organizations.

Even the worker and peasant movements and other political groups arousing the suspicions of the authorities found ways to create voluntary associations that the state could "tolerate". For instance, freemasonry, which was banned in 1920 by the Ministry of Internal Affairs, found a shelter in charitable organizations. Similarly, the Voluntary Association of Friends of Nature and Tourism was a relatively safe meeting place not only for freemasons, but also for social democrats and communists (L. Nagy, 1977, pp. 42, 47–8).

Voluntary associations played many different roles in this period in Hungary. Very many of them were a simple expression of civil society, of the greater cultural variation and growing social differentiation of a country on its way from feudalism towards capitalism. Besides (and most probably following the example of) voluntary organizations of nobles, intellectuals and members of the urban middle class, which had already been quite numerous before the 1848 revolution, thousands of voluntary associations created by the lower classes emerged in the last decades of the nineteenth and first decades of the twentieth century. In fact, this activity of the lower classes made the voluntary association a mass phenomenon in Hungary.

A special survey of 133 industrial firms (Rézler, 1943, pp. 77–9) found that a considerable number of the workers in these companies had formed voluntary organizations. Although the social network was less sophisticated and certainly much less institutionalized in the rural areas than in large cities, the most important social layers, ethnic and religious groups created their own voluntary associations in small towns and villages, too. According to the statistical survey of voluntary associations (Magyar statisztikai évkönyv, 1934, pp. 70–3), only 27 per cent of the voluntary organizations operated in the eleven largest cities in 1932, the rest of them being established in smaller communities.

In short, by the end of the interwar period all groups and levels of Hungarian society developed their voluntary associations. These voluntary groups were inherent parts of the everyday life and especially the leisure activities. They helped their members to satisfy the "need for belonging" (Scitovsky, 1990), to identify themselves as citizens, and provided everyone with a given level in society, with self-assurance and self-respect, thereby promoting the development of democracy.

Compared to this important cultural and political function, the service providing role played by the Hungarian voluntary organizations was much less prominent, at least in terms of actual numbers of service providing nonprofit organizations. Despite all its efforts in the direction of modernization, before World War II, Hungary remained a rural, traditional society. It is therefore not surprising to find informal systems of health care and other personal social services more important and larger than comparable systems in Western Europe or the United States. Particularly in rural areas, people in need received informal assistance from neighbours and family members, pre-empting the need for charitable organizations. The share of voluntary associations involved in health and social care reached about 20 per cent, but most of them were self-help income support organizations. Real charities represented only 6 per cent of all voluntary associations (*Magyar Statisztikai Évkönyv*, 1934, p. 70), and provided services primarily to the poor in urban areas. In the field of education the number of voluntary associations was negligible; their proportion actually decreased between 1878 and 1932 (See Table 2.3). It goes without saying that foundations (not being membership organizations) had somewhat closer connections to service provision, especially to its financial side, but the majority of them assisted other (mainly public) service providers rather than developed their own services. A great deal of foundation support and many private donations and bequests went to the public welfare institutions. There were "foundation beds" in several public hospitals, "foundation places" in numerous public orphanages, schools, and universities. We can say with certainty that, in terms of quantity, voluntary organizations as independent service-providers did not play a dominant role in pre-war Hungary. On the other hand, in terms of quality and in terms of innovation their role was enormous and essential. The first kindergartens, the first comprehensive schools, the first institutions of adult education and women's education, the first museums, libraries and exhibition halls, the first children's hospitals and orphanages, the first tuberculosis hospitals, and the first employment agencies were all established by or with the assistance of voluntary associations and foundations.

Several of the above mentioned examples seem to prove that the establishment of these "pioneer" organizations was not just an act of charity, but also a vehicle for policy advocacy. Voluntary organizations were quite successful in persuading successive governments to take the responsibility for providing health and social services.

Table 2.3

Composition of voluntary associations by fields of activity,
1862–1993 (%)

Activity	1862	1878	1932	1970	1982	1989	1993
Culture, religion	27.6	18.0	12.6	0.2	1.4	3.9	5.9
Sports	0.3	1.3	6.6	51.5	45.9	36.3	26.8
Leisure, hobby	27.3	14.4	32.6	16.1	26.3	23.8	20.8
Education, research	3.4	4.5	0.7	1.1	1.8	1.6	2.9
Health, social care	30.4	19.0	19.8	0.1	0.2	6.7	4.4
Fire brigades	–	6.2	9.3	30.4	22.5	13.9	5.6
Professional	6.6	31.9	16.4	–	–	7.6	18.5
Other	4.4	4.7	2.0	0.6	1.9	6.2	15.1
Total	100.0	100.0	100.0	100.0	100.0	100.0	100.0

Sources: 1862: *Magyarország különböző egyletei – Statisztikai Közlemények. A hazai állapotok ismeretének előmozdítására IV. kötet*, MTA Statisztikai Bizottsága, Budapest, 1862, pp. 246–69. 1878: *Magyarország egyletei és társulatai 1878-ban – Hivatalos Statisztikai Közlemények*, KSH, Budapest, 1880, pp. 516–49. Estimated breakdown of voluntary associations located in the present territory of Hungary. 1932: Dobrovits Sándor: *Magyarország egyesületeinek statisztikája – Magyar Statisztikai Szemle 1935/1*, pp. 26–7. 1970: *Egyesületek Magyarországon, 1970 – KSH*, Budapest, 1972, p. 11. 1982: *Egyesületek Magyarországon, 1982 – KSH*, Budapest, 1984, p. 8. 1989: Results of a survey carried out by the Central Statistical Office, reclassified by the Research Project on Hungarian Nonprofit Organizations. 1993: Data from the court register classified by the Central Statistical Office, Section on Voluntary Sector Statistics.

On the other hand, government authorities also laid claim to the sources available from private philanthropy and wanted to build a welfare system consisting of both public and voluntary service provision. This intention was clearly reflected in several decrees issued in the 1920s, which set rules and regulations for fund raising activities, then in the development of a sophisticated model of cooperation between private fund raisers, volunteers and authorities during the years of the Great Depression, when social problems became extremely serious in Hungary. The main idea was that the united efforts of churches, voluntary organizations and public authorities were more likely to solve poverty problems than their separate activities (Bartal, 1993).

This model of cooperation was developed in Eger, a medium-size Hungarian city. The initiative itself came from a local Catholic priest, the head of the Franciscan monastery (Petró, 1932). The leading force of the cooperation was a "Poverty Relief Committee" with members from the local authority, the local elite, the churches and the lay voluntary organizations. This committee was responsible for listing the people in need and preparing a complex plan of poverty relief. The plan had to give an overview of the tasks, the necessary costs and the possible resources. Private donations occupied a distinguished position among the possible resources. The fund raisers were volunteers (mostly female members of local "high society", often leaders and members of the local charitable organizations). They tried to raise not just occasional donations, but also pledges, and they regularly returned to collect the promised donations. (Later on, in some cities professional fund raisers were also employed by local government.) The decision on the use of these financial resources (both donations and public money) was made by the Poverty Relief Committee. Most of the services provided to the poor (e.g. shelters, food, personal and mental hygiene etc.) were delivered by or at least with the assistance of volunteers.

The new system of cooperation proved to be successful in Eger. Its success attracted the attention of the ministries which were responsible for the solution of social problems in the central government. They decided to promote the introduction of the Eger model (already called the Hungarian model) in other Hungarian cities, as well. Representatives of the government visited local communities, participated in meetings and argued for the introduction of the new model (Pálos, 1934, p. 110). Decree 172.000/1936, issued by the Ministry of Internal Affairs in 1936, actually obliged the cities and encouraged the bigger villages to apply the Hungarian model (Csizmadia, 1977, p. 95). Partly under this government pressure, and partly by their own choice, several big cities and small towns organized their social care in accordance with the principles of the Hungarian model.

Contemporary reports (Petró, 1932; Pálos, 1934) claimed that poverty relief following the Eger model was more efficient than the traditional methods, which involved much less cooperation between churches, voluntary organizations and public authorities. Criticism also appeared, especially at the later stage of development during World War II, when donations clearly could not cover the excessive costs which would have been needed to deal with the growing social problems. Some of the critics pointed out that the donations collected within the framework of the Hungarian model lost their voluntary character and this deprived the donors of the pleasure of giving. Others, on the contrary, emphasized that donations were "too voluntary", consequently did not offer a firm basis for social policy, and their replacement by taxes could be the solution (Csizmadia, 1977, p. 108). The debate on the merits of the different systems never was concluded, the supporters of mixed solutions and those of government dominated social policy never reached an agreement. The communist takeover determined the role of the Hungarian voluntary sector for the next couple of decades.

Post-World War II and state socialist period

The losses suffered in World War II affected the nonprofit sector in several ways. Voluntary organizations suffered from a shortage of skilled staff and managers. The holocaust reduced the Jewish population, whose charitable donations were particularly important for the support of foundations and voluntary associations. In the course of the Nazi occupation, some voluntary associations (especially those of the German population) became para-military organizations or part of the Nazi movement itself. These organizations were dissolved by Decree 529/1945 as soon as the German army had left (Szabó, 1989, p. 5).

The abolition of other voluntary organizations was a much slower, though more painful process. What we know about it is more from anecdotal than documentary evidence, not to mention the lack of genuine statistics. Communist governments were not eager to document how they demolished the voluntary sector, or to admit that they seriously limited freedom of association. On the contrary, most elements of the regulation were completely hypocritical. Everyday practice was in sharp contrast with the text of the laws. Before giving a short overview of the development of legal regulation, I shall give an example of what actually happened to Hungarian voluntary organizations during a period when freedom of association was "guaranteed" by Law I/1946; and when Law X/1946 even stated that public officials were liable to imprisonment if they infringed any human rights, including freedom of association (Szabó, 1989, p. 6).

The source of the following example is a collection of official documents (Magyar, 1986, Volume I: pp. 11–12, 95, 114, 182, 206, 207–11, 225; Volume II: pp. 344–6, 383, 397, 437; Volume III: pp. 660–1, 788, 811) from an ordinary Hungarian village, called Dunapataj. In 1941 it had 6,142 inhabitants, the overwhelming majority of whom were Hungarian. The proportion of Protestants and Catholics was 52 per cent and 42 per cent respectively. The population had established several voluntary associations. Some of them, namely the Shopkeepers' and Craftsmen's Reading Circle, the Farmers' Club, The 1848 Society (a voluntary association of "republican" members of the local elite) and the Gentlemen's Club had their own buildings. The Catholic Association and the voluntary associations of Catholic girls, Catholic boys, Protestant girls, Protestant women, Protestant boys and the Charitable Association of Women organized their meetings and cultural events in the Catholic and Protestant schools. There was also a Voluntary Fire Brigade, a Society of Hunters, a Beekeepers Club, an Association of Veterans, War-Widows and War-Orphans, a Funeral Society and a Sports Association in the village. The following fragments of their post-war history illustrate very clearly the fate of the Hungarian voluntary sector in the darkest years of the Stalinist regime.

- 15 February 1947: The local authorities report to the regional authorities that the religious associations (except the Catholic Association) were already dissolved. On the list of organizations in existence we can find the name of the Communist youth organization.
- 20 April 1947: The head of the local school reports that the school, in accordance with the authorities' instructions, has organized a local group of the National Pioneer Movement (a communist organization of children).
- 24 March 1948: The articles of the Society of Hunters were not approved by the Minister of Internal Affairs; a new version is

submitted. The formerly banned Reading Circle of Shopkeepers and Craftsmen also submits its new articles.

- 3 April 1948: The Minister of Internal Affairs dissolves the Voluntary Fire Brigade. (He refers to the Decree 7330/1946 which gives him the right to control every voluntary association.)
- 31 August 1948: The Minister of Internal Affairs dissolves the Farmers' Club.
- 8 October 1948: The Minister of Internal Affairs orders that the local authority shall take over the property of the dissolved Reading Circle of Shopkeepers and Craftsmen.
- 24 February 1949: The head of the school reports to the authorities that there are no religious associations in the village, and the only youth organization is the Pioneer organization.
- 26 April 1949: The 1848 Society asks the Minister's permission to continue its work and submits its modified articles.
- 11 August 1949: An ordinance of the Minister of Internal Affairs reminds the local authorities that there may be societies and self-help groups which do not declare themselves voluntary associations, do not have approved articles and still work. Since these organizations infringe the law, they must be dissolved, their property has to be confiscated, their leaders must be sued. The local authorities are obliged to seek out these illegal voluntary associations and report on them to both the Minister of Internal Affairs and the police.
- 28 September 1949: The 1848 Society is dissolved by the Minister of Internal Affairs.
- April 1951: The local authorities lead a campaign in order to convince the inhabitants that they have to join the international peace movement. (This means not only signatures, but also the purchase of "Peace-Loan bonds".)
- 14 August 1951: The regional authorities order the local council to report on the political behaviour of the Catholic priest.
- 4 February 1952: The public official who is responsible for the "education of the people" reports on the meetings and cultural events he organizes in cooperation with the Russian-type cooperatives.
- 18 February 1955: The local organization of the Communist Party (!) and the local authority give temporary permission to the effect "that – in order to develop agriculture – the working

peasants may educate and amuse themselves in the framework of evening meetings called the Farmers' Club, which can be held in the state school located on the fringes of the village".

- 3 January 1957: The leaders of the Farmers' Club established in 1955 apply for permission to recommence their activities.
- 16 January 1957: The regional authorities inform the Farmer's Club that "in principle" they don't object to the reorganization of the Club. In practice, the new articles must be submitted for approval to the regional authorities.
- 21 February 1957: A wall of the nationalized building which was originally constructed as the community centre of the Reading Circle of Shopkeepers and Craftsmen has fallen in. The whole building is on the verge of collapse.

The whole Hungarian voluntary sector was on the verge of collapse, too. Rooted in Leninist ideology, the Communist regime considered individuals as part of a potentially hostile, "bourgeois" mass that needed to be re-educated and re-oriented as socialists. Inherent in that concept was a fear that social movements might fall outside Party control, and voluntary organizations might follow political lines different from the official one. It was in order to counteract this fear that the government banned most voluntary associations. What remained of the voluntary sector was nationalized and brought under state control. The institutional effect of this far-reaching reorganization of the third sector was the establishment of "social organizations" such as the Adult Education Society, the Peace Council or the Patriotic Front. These pseudo-voluntary associations worked in close cooperation with the various organs of the Communist Party.

Foundations were considered even more suspicious and dangerous. The reasoning behind this suspicion and sometimes hostility towards foundations is common in every statist regime. As Tsyboula (1991, p. 28) points out, "the foundations represent a danger to the central government because they have endowments, and by using the revenues from these endowments they can significantly influence the very fields (e.g. culture, education, social policy) which the government itself would like to fully control". It is not accidental that foundations were liquidated, and that even the legal form for constituting a foundation was eradicated in Hungary, while some government controlled voluntary associations were tolerated, supported or sometimes even established by the government itself. The relative independence guaranteed by their ownership of property would have enabled foundations to develop alternative social and cultural policies and to challenge the state monopoly of decision making in the provision of welfare services. This danger was less in the case of state controlled voluntary organizations because they depended on the government for most of their income.

The Communist governments' hostility towards voluntary organizations was not explicitly reflected in the actual text of the legislation regulating them. Decree 474/1948 dissolved public law foundations and ordered that their properties become part of the state budget, but did not even mention private foundations (György, 1992, p. 25). Decree 2/1949, which provided the legal basis for the nationalization of private foundations was somewhat ambiguous. Although in articles 1–8 it provided for the dissolution of foundations, in articles 9 and 10 it still left one door open: private foundations could be established with the permission of the minister himself who headed the Ministry responsible for the services which the would be foundations wanted to deliver or support. (I have not found any trace of any foundation which received such a permission in the late 1940s or in the 1950s.) The Decree ordered that foundations had to be dissolved if

- they could no longer achieve their aim;
- the public interest was damaged by their activities;
- they delivered services which it was considered should be exclusively provided by the government;
- they did not fit in with the new socialist system.

The property of the dissolved foundations was to be given to central state or local government agencies (Kecskés, 1988, p. 113).

The ministerial introduction to the new Civil Code enacted in 1959 (Law IV/1959) blamed Decree 2/1949 for "having maintained the 'fictitious' legal personality of foundations" (*A Magyar Népköztársaság Polgári Törvénykönyve*, 1959, p. 468). The legal form of a foundation disappeared from the Civil Code for decades, and nobody was allowed to establish foundations until 1987, another modification of the Civil Code. People who wanted to donate some money to support public purposes could only create small endowments under the auspices of some public institution which had the right to decide on the use of the endowment.

Similarly, the political aversion to voluntary associations and grassroots social movements was not explicitly reflected in the legislation. The foreign observer needs to have sharp eyes to notice the nuances in the legal texts. There was not much likelihood of Hungarians – as the above example of Dunapataj shows – misunderstanding the real intentions of the government. The Decree 7330/1946 which gave the Minister of Internal Affairs the right to control the activities of voluntary associations actually authorized him to ban these organizations, and he exercised this right widely. The Constitution of 1949 proclaimed freedom of association for "working people", which actually meant an extreme limitation (almost a complete lack) of this freedom. The Constitution of 1972 repealed this limitation. It declared that all citizens could enjoy freedom of association. But this happened two years after the issue of Decree 35/1970, which had stated that even preparations to establish voluntary associations should be reported to the proper authorities. The enactment of the new Constitution did not change this regulation. On the contrary, another decree (29/1981) authorized government bodies to ban such preparations if the planned activities of the voluntary associations under preparation were likely to endanger "the state, social and economic order" (Szabó, 1989, p. 6).

Legislation and governmental attitudes vis-a-vis voluntary organizations were somewhat contradictory. While the legal regulations became more strict and demanding, the state gradually loosened its control of voluntary associations in the 1960–1989 period. The 1956 revolution revealed that communist governments could nationalize industry, "collectivize" agriculture, develop a nationalized system of social services, and dissolve most of the voluntary organizations, but they could not completely eradicate citizens' autonomy, solidarity and private initiatives, even though they tried their hardest. The Communist Party, the government and the Kremlin understood that crude oppression was not the appropriate way of governing Hungary.

On the other hand, the failure of the uprising taught lessons to the citizens as well. The population learned that open revolt would most likely fail, and began to adopt more latent and subtle ways of resistance. These strategies created a curious atmosphere of distrust. Citizens pretended to form politically neutral voluntary organizations. The actual activities of these groups did not challenge the state socialist system, but their mood was clearly oppositional, their very existence expressed the society's antagonism towards the totalitarian regime. This more or less hidden oppositional character of the voluntary sector is probably explained by the oppositional attitude of the Hungarian society itself. Against their better judgement, most of the Hungarian citizens had to cooperate with the authorities after the suppressed 1956 revolution. This discrepancy between opinion and behaviour could have resulted in attitude changes (Aronson, 1978), but it did not because the cognitive dissonance was significantly decreased by two factors. First, most people, including political leaders felt that they behaved under pressure from a foreign superpower. Second, the "reward" for conformity was quite big (relatively high standard of living, freedom of travelling abroad, opportunities for small entrepreneurship, relatively free press, access to the Western cultural products, etc.). Under these circumstances both the individual citizens and their voluntary associations could preserve some autonomy of thinking and judgement (Kuti, 1992a). That is how they were able to survive and that is why they could take all the opportunities to develop their activity when the political climate became milder.

As Heit and Vidra Szabó (1992) pointed out, the motivation behind the establishment of the numerous local voluntary associations (generally engaged in cultural and hobby activities) in the 1970s and 1980s was mostly the desire of citizens to create "small circles of freedom", to ensure some autonomy, to protect their communities against the tendencies towards centralization, to strengthen local identity, to control and influence the local authorities, to promote cultural and ethnic diversity, to develop local information networks, to educate citizens and to encourage them to behave as citizens.

The government was worried, but did not dare to ban these voluntary associations. It merely persecuted them. Both sides understood what was happening, but it was more comfortable to regard voluntary associations as "only cultural organizations" (Jagasics, 1992, p. 143). It was characteristic of the political situation of the 1980s that the authorities rarely prohibited the creation of voluntary associations, nor did they very often attempt to do so, even though they had the legal means available to them.

They had to be all the more tolerant because they were slowly groping towards an understanding of their complete failure in the provision of welfare services, and consequently the necessity of nonprofit service provision and the need for private donations. Most of the educational, health and social services were provided by public institutions completely or almost free of charge in Hungary by the 1980s. In principle, every citizen had access to these public services as of right. In practice, it was mainly privileged social groups such as the party and managerial elites which could take advantage of subsidised state housing, higher education, and high quality health services. The inequalities generated by this unequal access to the public goods provided by the state became an important source of social and political tensions, but the further enlargement of public services was obviously impossible.

The state socialists promised too much. They wanted to create a comprehensive system of public institutions providing every citizen with the whole range of high quality public services free of charge. Even the rich developed countries would have failed to meet all these promises because the system did not include any demand side constraint, while the growth of the supply of public services was obviously limited by the economic potential of the country. Under these circumstances, not only did "the continuing neglect of many discrete groups and basic services produce a strong demand for third sector initiatives" (Wunker, 1991, p. 95), but the deep structural problems of public service provision also made changes inevitable. The state socialists not only failed to meet the elementary needs of some marginalised social groups, they also provided privileged groups with too many services and failed to guarantee equal access to basic public services.

By the time the collapse of the Soviet bloc made fundamental political changes feasible, the Hungarian government had already admitted that it could not solve every social problem and needed the assistance of nonprofit organizations. The "rehabilitation" of foundations by Decree 11/1987, which modified the Civil Code and introduced once again the foundation as a legal entity, came about under both social and financial pressures. Some influential people (first of all George Soros and Ernő Rubik) were ready to donate money for charitable purposes, but insisted on establishing independent foundations instead of giving the support to public institutions. The Hungarian government, which was facing many problems in financing welfare services, could not (and perhaps did not even want to) resist the pressures. Moreover, two years after the reconstitution of the foundation as a legal entity it also prepared the Law on Association (II/1989) which guaranteed the freedom of association. This law stated that every citizen and any groups or organizations of citizens had the right to create voluntary associations without any government permission or control. The Law on Association has been generally regarded as one of the very first and most important legal documents of the transition process.

Recent history

The recent history of the Hungarian nonprofit sector has been very short but extremely eventful. As I have already pointed out, the reconstruction of the voluntary sector started much before 1989. Hungarian society developed some measure of compromise, cooperation, and sometimes even complicity with the state in the social, economic and political spheres. This cooperation between state and society made the transition relatively smooth (a "controlled muddling-through" as Anheier and Seibel (1992) called it) after the unexpected collapse of state socialism and the breakup of the Soviet bloc in 1989, which was probably the most important turning point in Hungary's modern history. The skills learnt in "second society" (alternative society) and the gradually developed "relative autonomy" (Hankiss, 1989) helped people and their organizations to give pragmatic answers to challenges, to seize opportunities, to evaluate new institutional forms and to choose from them. The II/1989 Law on Associations has guaranteed the freedom of association, and many voluntary associations, which should have belonged to "second society" before 1989, can be created as institutions of "first society" since then.

The legalization of the political parties has significantly decreased the need for voluntary organizations of a political nature. At the same time, the abolition of the state monopoly on welfare services has opened the door for the nonprofit service provision in the fields of health, social care, education and culture. The whole system of welfare services is changing, foundations and other nonprofit organizations are accepted and sometimes even welcomed and supported as service providers.

The introduction of a market economy has changed the whole institutional environment for foundations and voluntary associations. The transition from the "one sector" to the "three sector" economy (Marschall, 1990) has represented a challenge and offered several opportunities to both the old and the newly created third sector organizations (Kuti, 1990, 1992a, 1993).

As Table 2.2 and Table 2.4 suggest, nonprofit organizations and their founders have been eager to take these opportunities. The number of voluntary associations almost tripled between 1989 and 1993. The development of the foundation sector was even more spectacular, the number of registered foundations was almost twenty-nine times higher at the end of 1993 than it had been in 1989.

Table 2.4

Number of foundations, 1989–1993

Year	Number of foundations
31 December 1989[a]	400
31 December 1990	1,832
31 December 1991	6,182
31 December 1992	9,703
31 December 1993	12,064

Source: Court registers. The figures for 1990 and 1992 were revised on the basis of surveys carried out by the Research Project on Nonprofit Organizations and by the Central Statistical Office, respectively.

Note: [a] Estimated figure.

Although the legal and economic regulations of nonprofit organizations have become gradually stricter, the government has imposed serious restrictions on their tax exemption and tax deductibility (Harsányi, 1992; Kuti, 1992b), voluntary organizations have continued mushrooming, only the rate of growth is decreasing.

The recent history of the Hungarian nonprofit sector seems to suggest that voluntary organizations play an important, but somewhat ambiguous, role in the transition process. Citizens use them as a vehicle for enforcing their rights and interests, for developing new kinds of welfare services and for institutionalizing democratic achievements, but it also happens that nonprofits serve as tax shelters or they are actually disguised for-profit enterprises. Government bodies and state authorities are also interested in the development of the nonprofit sector because it can help to alleviate social problems which cannot be solved by public authorities alone, but they tend to make efforts in order to (directly or indirectly) control nonprofit organizations. Both historical patterns and new constraints influence the behaviour of the social and political groups whose actions are responsible for the contradictory features of the recent nonprofit history. A thorough analysis of these historical patterns (the survival-oriented nature of Hungarian nonprofits, their genuinely lay character, and the profoundly ambivalent but still very close government–nonprofit cooperation) is the purpose of the next section of this chapter.

Key features of nonprofit history

The Hungarian culture is definitely a survival-oriented culture. Hungarians have lots of illusions about their national character, they like to think they are "chivalrous, brave, proud, full of enthusiasm, good in passive resistance, etc." (Bibó, 1984, p. II/574), but their actual behaviour does not always harmonize with this self-portrait. Alhadeff's (1986, p. 183) general statement rings particularly true in Hungary, where any citizen is "a member of a species shaped by evolutionary contingencies of survival, displaying behavioral processes which bring him under the control of a social environment which he and millions of others like him have constructed and maintained during the evolution of a culture".

This social (and political) environment has been anything but favourable to the healthy development of either the Hungarian society as a whole or any part of it since the end of the fifteenth century. Foreign occupation or (in best case) limited independence, prolonged feudalism, delayed embourgeoisement, economic backwardness, etatist regimes, underdeveloped democratic institutions, social, religious and ethnic tensions have represented both the general conditions for the voluntary sector development and the challenges nonprofits must face.

The gap between the actual conditions and the aspirations of the Hungarian society has been permanently wide: the Western part of Europe, the political democracy, the modern, industrialized economy, the social welfare have been within sight, but out of reach. This has been a source of frustration and several, partly heroic, partly ridiculous, but equally desperate efforts. Failures of these efforts have traumatized the society, caused lots of personal tragedies and serious distortions in the national character, but have not completely paralysed the society and have not fully destroyed democratic values. A series of compromises and opportunistic "half-solutions" or specious solutions, a lot of illegal and semi-legal undertakings, a whole set of "second economy" and "second society" institutions have appeared. For lack of democratic institutions and legal guarantees, both individual and community behaviour are led by rather shortsighted pragmatism than by long-term strategies. Informal social networks play an extremely important role, borderlines between the official and unofficial, formal and informal are blurred. The "second society mentality" (Hankiss, 1986), which permeates the whole system, "is premodern in its preference for small-scale social and economic activity of the muddling-through style instead of rational action in larger-scale settings that involve trust in impersonal rules and public institutions" (Anheier and Seibel, 1992, p. 18).

This general distrust of public institutions (including not only state, but church organizations, as well) is an important explanatory factor of the impressive strength of voluntary movements and their potential for expansion in Hungary. Voluntary organizations learnt to survive prohibition and to wriggle out of government control, sometimes they could shelter social and political movements which were not tolerated by the authorities. The freedom of association was always endangered, the voluntary organizations often existed on the edge of illegality. Governments did not trust them at all, the most dictatorial ones even tried to completely eradicate them, but they were held in high esteem by citizens. They were considered to be a means of having a "voice" in "no-exit" situations.

The very first "benevolent entrepreneur" of the Hungarian nonprofit history was the Catholic Church, but – in contrast to many other European countries – it did not remain the dominating force in the initial development of the voluntary sector in Hungary.

Catholicism was something imported, it challenged not only the belief, but also the power of the traditional elite. The efforts the Church made in order to raise donations and bequests brought it into conflict with the feudal lords who worried about the integrity of their properties (R. Kiss, 1925). Kings themselves, who realized how important Christianity was as a vehicle for the country's integration into Europe, did not trust the Church too much, and did not give it a completely free hand in the care of the society's helpless. They tried to develop guarantees that the Church really use its revenues to relieve poverty, they played an active role in founding and supporting welfare institutions, and they granted numerous civic rights and privileges to the citizens in the "free royal cities", thus they helped the development of a citizenry that was willing and able to create social institutions outside the arena of the Catholic Church.

Several documents on different lawsuits show that there were serious conflicts between Church authorities, monastic orders and city governments about the ownership and control of hospitals and almshouses in the fourteenth and fifteenth centuries (Hahn, 1960, p. 11; Csizmadia, 1977, p. 17; Somogyi, 1941, pp. 30–1, 35–7, 42–3, 84–5). City authorities accused the leaders of church hospitals and almshouses of misusing the donations and bequests which should have served charitable purposes. The outcomes of the litigation were various, but a large part of the new hospitals were already established as lay public or nonprofit institutions. With the expansion of the Reformation movement, the Catholic Church seemed to lose most of its interest in social care in the sixteenth century, it turned to education as a strategic field of gaining converts (or rather "reconverts" under the given circumstances).

The newly established Protestant Churches were also eager to develop their schools. According to a Protestant analyst:

> As Luther himself realized very soon the crucial importance of education for the purity of Christianity, the Protestant Churches, including the Hungarian Protestant Church, also made efforts to become first in the field of education at any price because they were well aware of the fact, that the strongest weapon of the denominations and the Evangelism itself is the real knowledge, the broad intellectual horizon. (Karner, 1931, p. 81)

The relatively peaceful cultural competition among religions was

quite short in Hungary. The Habsburg emperors even used military force from the 1670s in order to make Catholicism a state religion again. Protestant churches and schools were closed,
Protestant preachers were persecuted and the most recalcitrant of
them were sold into galley slavery in 1674. The freedom of religion
was restored more than a hundred years later, in 1781 by the
"Edictum Tolerantiae" (Edict of Tolerance) issued by Emperor
Joseph II, so the development of the Protestant schools (and other
Protestant institutions) could start again only at the end of the
eighteenth century.

The Catholic Church remained too close to the state in the next
centuries, as well; Protestant Churches also curried favour with
the government. The rest of their credibility was lost when they
were ready to cooperate with state authorities during communist
times. In contrast with their Polish counterparts, Hungarian citizens did not have an "oppositional" Church, which would have
preserved some basic values and would have represented and
protected their interests. Consequently, there was more room and
more need for lay voluntary movements.

Similarly, very few (if any) of the Hungarian governments were
completely trusted by citizens. Although the variations in number
and depth of conflicts between state and society were wide over
history, there was always some need and mostly also some opportunity for independent citizen action.

The state–nonprofit relationship changed a lot in the course of
the development of the Hungarian voluntary sector, and did it in
a fluctuating manner. We cannot identify a clear tendency of
developing or shrinking cooperation, its size varied according to
the nonprofit fields and to the ruling governments and ideologies.
Nevertheless, we can state that cooperation is an essential feature
of the history of the state–nonprofit relationship in Hungary. Several examples of this cooperation have already been mentioned,
here I am trying to list its typical forms, typical problems and to
quote some typical opinions about its necessity and limitations.

The following excerpts from two speeches delivered at a meeting of the Széchenyi Society in Szatmár County on 12 September
1885 clearly express the position of the voluntary leaders. Lőrinc
Schlauch, honorary president of the Society said: "To support or –
if it is necessary – even force the government to make efforts in
order to strengthen the national identity; but avoid even the

appearance of being just the creatures or tools of the government: these are the two principles cultural associations, including the Széchenyi Society must follow if they don't want to paralyse themselves" (Gerlóczy, 1887, p. 85). Count István Károlyi, one of the leaders and most important supporters of the Society suggested. "Voluntary donations cannot ensure an appropriate financial basis any longer ... Let's turn then to our zealous county government and ask it to levy a 1 per cent additional tax in order to promote culture and education" (Gerlóczy, 1887, p. 87).

In other words, voluntary organizations were ready to cooperate with the government in order to achieve common goals, but they also wanted to take part in the formulation of these goals, and claimed the right to influence government decisions. Independence was all the more a great concern for them because they were aware that government assistance was inevitably needed in raising the necessary funds for their programmes.

Motivations and arguments for state–nonprofit cooperation are very clear on the government side, too.

> Besides the social services provided by public authorities, there is another, historically more deeply rooted, but much less bureaucratized form of social care: the private philanthropy of voluntary associations, foundations, charitable institutions, etc., which is the outcome of either humanism or religious conviction. Since volunteers are motivated by compassion and sympathy, charitable institutions are not bound by strict organizational rules, their services can be prompt, intensive and highly personalized. That is why we see them extremely active in the fields where there is a need for originality, genuine initiative, innovation, experimental actions, new methods and openness towards new experience (e.g. social work in railway stations or in prisons, home care for sick persons, etc.). This charitable work can be especially useful when there is a need for personal care, when the problems to be solved are of rather ethical, psychological, religious than of financial nature. In fact, the voluntary work serves not only the concrete individuals in need, but also the community as a whole; thus it must be treated as equal to the social care provided by government authorities and public institutions. Both sides are interested in some cooperation because this division of tasks and exchange of experiences and methods can help them to save work and money, to avoid overlaps and to build a comprehensive system of poverty relief. (Csorna, 1931, pp. 19–20)

The above quotations come from the late nineteenth and early

twentieth centuries, but the practice of state–nonprofit cooperation had started to develop much before; its first examples can be
found in documents from the Middle Ages. It is somewhat surprising that not only the idea, but almost all forms and techniques
of this cooperation have their roots in the first centuries of the
Hungarian history. Roughly speaking, there were four different
fields (or aspects) of the state–nonprofit cooperation, namely

- policy making;
- service provision;
- financing services; and
- development of the regulatory framework.

The state has never been the only policy maker in Hungary
(although it tried to become at least the dominant one in some
periods). In the beginning, welfare policy and education policy
were jointly formed by the main service providers, the voluntary
(mostly Church) institutions and the representatives of the state,
including kings and city governments. Already the first kings
were among the important founders of hospitals and universities.
The developing cities also made efforts to shape social policy.
Since the position of the state authorities gradually strengthened
over the centuries, voluntary organizations had to change methods in order to keep their role in policy making. Lobbying government and initiating the provision of new, innovative services
became bit by bit the crucial means of influencing government
decisions. Paradoxically enough, this does not necessarily mean
that the policy making role of the voluntary sector became less
important than it had been before. The decisions of the primary
service providers had made an undoubtedly more direct and
more immediate policy impact in the Middle Ages than the lobbyist organizations' actions did in the nineteenth and twentieth
centuries, but their scope had been also much narrower, and
"philanthropic insufficiency" (Salamon, 1987) had seriously limited the ability of nonprofits to develop a comprehensive social
policy. What nonprofits as primary service providers could have
never dreamt about, civic associations could at least try: as representatives of the civil society, they claimed their right to influence
and control the use of public properties and government funds.
A good example of these aspirations is the resolution adopted by
the general assembly of the Hungarian Royal Society of Natural

Sciences in 1844. The resolution declared that civic associations must have their voice in decisions on the use of the mineral wealth of the country (Kátai, 1868, p. 45). Although these efforts of the voluntary organizations generally were not welcomed by the authorities, the government was not always against sharing the responsibility for decisions, either. Sometimes it even happened that the initiative came from the government side. For example, during World War I the municipality of Budapest created a committee (chaired by the mayor), which was responsible for the distribution of financial aid to the people in need. The leaders of the major charitable associations were invited to become members of the committee. They played an active role in both the preparation of decisions and the decision making itself (Csorna, 1931, pp. 146–7).

In their lobbyist role, voluntary associations could (and did) also try to promote the development of public solutions to the commonly recognized social problems, the public provision of services, which would have been too expensive for the nonprofit service providers. (As an illustration, we can mention the campaign run by the National Association Against Unemployment. Its aim was to persuade the government to establish public employment agencies. The campaign was successful: Law XVI/1916 obliged cities of a certain size to create employment agencies which were supposed to provide clients with services completely free of charge (Heller, 1923, pp. 185–6).)

These changes in the policy making roles were paralleled by the changes of the roles played in service provision. Originally the overwhelming majority of welfare services were provided by nonprofit (mostly Church run) organizations, although the kings played an active role in establishing charitable organizations. The evolution of the cities brought about important changes: they either took over Church run institutions or established their own welfare organizations and started to develop public service provision. This was a slow, uneven process, but still resulted in deep structural changes. The public sector of welfare services became significantly bigger than the nonprofit service provision by the twentieth century.

Nevertheless, cooperation between the state and nonprofit service providers did not disappear at all. On the contrary, as we have already seen, the formerly *ad hoc* government–nonprofit partnership even became an institutionalized, officially supported pattern of cooperation in the model of Eger.

State–nonprofit cooperation in service provision took various forms over the whole history of the Hungarian nonprofit sector. Sometimes private donors chose city authorities as trustees of nonprofit organizations (Somogyi, 1941, pp. 54–6), sometimes city hospitals (Hahn, 1960, p. 11) or city owned community centres (Csorna, 1931, pp. 215–16) were run by volunteers or voluntary organizations. Nonprofit service providers enjoyed several types of "in-kind" state support from the assistance of public employees (Csizmadia, 1977, p. 14) till the appropriation of raw food for soup kitchens during World War I (Csorna, 1931, p. 182). It was quite frequent that state authorities took over the provision of welfare services formerly delivered on a voluntary basis (Csizmadia, 1977, p. 24), but it also happened that an originally public institution (e.g. the Count Albert Apponyi Outpatient Clinic) was taken over by a voluntary association (Béry, 1929, pp. 327–8).

Cooperation was even more common in financing the provision of welfare services. On the one hand, the use of private donations was a long-standing technique of covering the operating costs of public welfare institutions (Csizmadia, 1977, p. 44; Hahn, 1960, p. 16). On the other hand, the tradition of public support to voluntary organizations was born as early as the voluntary organizations themselves appeared in Hungary. Both direct and indirect forms of state support were already known in the Middle Ages. Royal donations, statutory transfers and tax exemptions all contributed to the financing of nonprofit service provision. Generous donations of the first Hungarian king (István I) secured the financial basis for the first Church run almshouses and hospitals. King Béla IV exempted all the hospitals and shelters from payment of the wine-tithe about 1240. In 1437 another king (Zsigmond) authorized the first hospital of Buda to get the tithe revenues of two monasteries (Zolnay, 1975, p. 124). Basically the same supporting techniques were (and still are) used in more recent times, too, only the actual forms of support have become more varied and some elements of regularity and guarantee have appeared.

Individual state donations (Balázs, 1991, p. 85; Béry, 1929, p. 330; Csorna, 1931, p. 129) have been complemented by regular and sometimes even guaranteed state support (Kohut, 1971, p. 129; Kuti and Somogyvári, 1993, pp. 4–7). This was an important development in the late nineteenth century and again in the early 1990s: the regular state support significantly contributed to the very impressive growth of the Hungarian nonprofit sector in both periods. Some new forms of the indirect state support also appeared: state lottery revenues were ordered to be distributed among charitable institutions and voluntary associations by the Minister of Welfare in 1867; foreign gifts to charities were exempted from customs duty by Law XIX in 1924 (Csorna, 1931, pp. 81–2). Both methods have reappeared again in the 1990s. The only really new form of state support is the tax deductibility of donations to foundations which was introduced in 1990.

State subsidies to nonprofits are usually coupled with some degree of government regulation and control. As the above overview of the history of nonprofit regulation shows, Hungarian governments tended to control even (or especially) voluntary associations, which they did not support at all. Civic associations suffered a lot from the repeated prohibitions and restrictions on their activities. At the same time, some of the service providing charities were complaining about the lack of consistent regulation and coordination in the nonprofit sphere. The General Association for Public Charity even submitted a memorandum to the Minister of Internal Affairs in 1909, which suggested some unified regulation and coordination of the activities of charitable associations (Csorna, 1931, pp. 214–15).

Unfortunately, the lack of specific and comprehensive regulation seems to be a chronic disease of the Hungarian nonprofit sector. Transparent, impersonal rules have been missing for a long time. The co-existence of unconditional advantages tempting into abuse, gaps in regulation, unreasonably sharp government reactions, capriciously imposed restrictions and repeated government attempts to gain control over voluntary organizations has made the deeply rooted and (at least potentially) mutually advantageous nonprofit–government cooperation much less fruitful than it could be if it were based on a comprehensive regulation. To understand this point more fully, however, it is necessary to examine the legal treatment of the nonprofit sector in Hungary more closely.

Chapter 3

THE LEGAL REGULATION OF THE NONPROFIT SECTOR IN HUNGARY

Legal principles shaping the nonprofit regulation in Hungary

The most fundamental legal principle in Hungary that shapes the way in which the nonprofit sector is dealt with is the *freedom of association, opinion and religion*. The freedom of association is a basic human right guaranteed by the Constitution and – in more detail – the II/1989 Law on Association. People must be free to form voluntary organizations for any purpose which does not explicitly contradict fundamental human values and does not endanger the democratic political order. Organizational aims like racism, violence or discrimination cannot be tolerated, but any particular or even eccentric purpose can be accepted if the organizations following these aims respect other people's freedom and dignity.

There are also some other, less basic legal principles which have significant influence on the legal and economic regulations of the Hungarian nonprofit sector.

The main *criteria* which lead the decisions on *granting legal personality* to organizations are as follows:

- The organization must become independent from its founders. In case of membership organizations, the relationships of the organizations themselves with third parties must be separated from the relationships of their individual members with the same third parties. In the case of foundations, the endowments donated to the foundations must become completely and definitively separated from the private properties of the founders or donors.
- Organizations need legal personality if their activities make property rights and other economic rights and responsibilities necessary.

- Legal personality can be granted to organizations which have durable purposes and permanent existence. Ephemeral associations of people do not need to get legal personality.
- Organizations having legal personality must be reasonably institutionalized, formal organizations. They must develop their internal governing bodies and decision making procedures. Informal groups with little durability and uncertain internal structure cannot get legal personality.
- Legal personality cannot be given to organizations which have aims explicitly prohibited by law. (Kozma and Petrik, 1990, pp. 63–4)

More recently, some principles intending to shape the decisions on direct and indirect public support have also appeared in the debates of legal experts and in some proposals prepared for the government and parliament. The most important of them is that any tax advantage or direct public support to the nonprofit organizations can only be justified by their social importance and usefulness. The social importance and usefulness of nonprofit organizations may derive from different social, political, cultural and economic roles they play in economy and society. Both legislators and government authorities must consider this social usefulness when they decide on support. Even voluntary groups not serving public interest at all must be tolerated by right of freedom of association, but they should not be supported from taxpayers' money.

Another legal principle, that of "sector impartiality" of supporting "public benefit" organizations, also seems to have developed. Most of the legal experts and legislators agree that state support to service providing organizations serving generally accepted public purposes must not depend on the sector to which the organizations belong. In practice, this means that nonprofit service providers have their right to get exactly the same per capita government support which is given to similar public institutions or church organizations. The "sector impartiality" of this per capita state support does not mean that the support is completely automatic. Nonprofit institutions have to prove that they are able to meet the official quality requirements.

As we shall see, these basic legal principles are mostly followed, while many of the internationally accepted principles are rather neglected in the legal regulation of the Hungarian nonprofit sector.

Legal forms of nonprofit organizations

There were only two legal forms provided for nonprofit organizations in the Hungarian law in 1990, which is the base year of our international comparison. These are:

- the voluntary association form; and
- the foundation form.

Both are private law organizations.

Membership organizations are not necessarily called voluntary associations, but the basic legal regulation of voluntary associations applies to all membership organizations (e.g. societies, clubs, self-help groups, federations, unions, chambers, trade unions, mass organizations, social organizations, etc.), even if there are special laws and government decrees on some of them setting detailed rules of their functioning.

Primary definitions of these two forms of nonprofit organizations are given by articles 31 and 71 of the Civil Code, which defines all the existing legal forms available for Hungarian organizations.

Voluntary associations are defined as autonomous organizations formed voluntarily for a purpose decided by their members and stated in their founding articles. They have registered members (unlike foundations) whose activities are organized in order to reach the associations' aims.

Foundations are legal personalities with an endowment to accomplish their public purpose. They can only be established for a durable public purpose. Their founders can be both private persons and organizations having legal personality.

Both legal forms are used by a wide range of nonprofit organizations.

The *main types of the voluntary associations* are as follows:

- associations, clubs and circles of private persons having the same hobbies (e.g. fishing, hunting, gardening, singing, sports, travelling, etc.);

- associations, self-help groups of people having the same personal problems (e.g. people with disabilities, drug addicts, unemployed persons, etc.);
- mutual benefit insurance and pension funds;
- clubs of people of the same age (especially young and elderly persons);
- associations of people belonging to the same social layers, religious or ethnic groups;
- clubs of people of the same political opinion;
- associations of people having common interests (e.g. home owners', renters' or consumers' advocacy organizations);
- societies of people supporting institutions or settlements (e.g. friends of schools, museums, theatres, towns, villages, etc.);
- neighbourhood organizations;
- environmental groups;
- associations of people protecting civil rights and promoting independence;
- associations of people providing others with social services;
- federations of nonprofit organizations;
- professional associations;
- employers federations;
- trade unions.

The *main types of foundations* are as follows:

- operating foundations (e.g. foundations running schools, nursing homes, health and cultural institutions, providing social services; publishing books and journals, managing cable television networks and local radio stations, etc.);
- "fund raising" foundations exclusively supporting the public institutions (e.g. libraries, theatres, museums, schools, universities, hospitals, research institutes, etc.) that established them;
- "fund raising" foundations exclusively supporting the voluntary associations that established them;
- grant seeking foundations having particular aims or projects (e.g. creation of monuments, organization of festivals, development of art collections, etc.);
- grant making foundations which support either projects or organizations;
- corporate foundations mostly supporting the present or former employees of the company.

Regulation of nonprofit status

Nonprofit organizations (either voluntary associations or foundations) cannot be established so that they run *mainly* for-profit business. Organizations of which the primary purpose is business cannot be registered as nonprofit organizations. (However, nonprofits serving public purposes are allowed to own and operate businesses in order to increase their revenues for use to achieve their charitable aims.)

Voluntary associations achieve nonprofit status (and legal personality) through their registration. Registration is the duty of the county and capital courts. Conditions for the registration of voluntary associations having legal personality are as follows:

- They must have at least ten members declaring the establishment of the organization.
- Their basic regulation must be stated in their articles.
- Their administrative and representative organs must be elected.

Voluntary associations can apply for registration after their statutory meeting. Registration cannot be refused if the founders fulfilled all the requirements of law. Applications for registration must contain the articles of the association and the minutes of the statutory meeting.

Similarly, *foundations* achieve nonprofit status when they are registered in the county or capital courts. Conditions for the registration of foundations with legal personality are as follows:

- durable public purpose;
- founding statute;
- an endowment which is large enough to reach the foundation's goal.

In contrast with voluntary associations, foundations have to pass a "public benefit" test during the registration process. While the II/1989 Association Law states that voluntary associations can be established for any purpose their members wish to have, except for-profit business activities and activities explicitly prohibited by the Constitution (e.g. racism, violence, armed attack against the constitutional order, etc.), foundations must have some durable public purpose if they want to be registered.

The administrative and control mechanisms which are supposed to grant, and ensure compliance with, nonprofit status are
very weak in both cases. At the time of registration the courts have
only the information they can acquire from the founding statutes.
They do not know anything about the actual plans and activities
of the nonprofit organizations. If the documents presented to
them are in accordance with the requirements of the law, the
courts don't have the right to refuse the registration. Later on, they
can dissolve the foundation at the attorney's request if

- its purpose cannot be fulfilled any longer;
- its registration ought to be refused because of changes in law;
- the trustee's activity does not comply with the foundation's
  aim, and the founder does not appoint another trustee. (Article
  74/E of the Civil Code)

Voluntary associations can only be dissolved by the court if they
break the law or infringe upon other people's rights and freedom
(Article 20 of the II/1989 law on associations).

In the founding statute the founder can set rules on joining the
foundation and on its operation. A trustee organization can also be
named by the founder in the founding statute. If the founder does
not make any arrangement, it is the court's duty to name the trustee
of the foundation. If the trustee's activity does not comply with the
foundation's purpose, the founder (in case of the founder's death,
the court) can appoint another trustee. This is practically the only
legal means public authorities have if they want to ensure foundations' compliance with the nonprofit status. In practice, the courts
are also trying to prevent founders from having a majority on the
boards of foundations established by them, but there is nothing in
written law which would authorize the courts to do so.

Two concepts of public benefit are present in the legal regulation of nonprofits in Hungary. The broader one appears in the
association law (II/1989) which reflects the conviction that voluntary associations are essential elements of a democratic society.
The minister's introductory explanation, which accompanied the
law proposal, explicitly stated that voluntary associations provide
the basis for the self-organization of the society and their presence
is a necessary condition of the healthy development and functioning of any community either at the local or at the national level
(Kozma and Petrik, 1990, p. 15).

Similarly, one of the lawyers who had been responsible for the development of the very liberal foundation regulation (I/1990 law on the modification of the Civil Code) asserted that the reason for the preferential treatment of foundations had been the conviction that foundations could and should play an important role in the democratization of decisions, and the denationalization and deregulation of the Hungarian economy (Sárközi, 1991). That is why foundations received really generous and practically unconditional tax advantages in the first period of their development. (For more details see the section on taxation.)

A much narrower concept of public benefit appeared later on in the economic and tax regulations of nonprofit organizations. When the legislators decided to limit the tax exemption of nonprofits' business income, the Ministry of Finances considered it necessary to differentiate between the related and unrelated business activities of nonprofit organizations. The 114/1992 and the 115/1992 government decrees about the economic activities of voluntary associations, other social organization and foundations presented a list of services which are regarded as closely related to the public purposes served by the nonprofit organizations. These are as follows:

- health care,
- social services,
- education,
- social tourism and recreation,
- research and development,
- environment protection,
- sports,
- libraries,
- museums, exhibitions,
- archives,
- theatres,
- music, dance,
- protection of the monuments,
- amateur arts,
- employment procurement for unemployed people.

The preparation of this list and similar ones in the tax laws is a clear sign of government efforts to develop a relatively narrow, well-defined concept of public benefit which would make decisions much easier for both the courts and the tax authority.

For the time being, only extremely clumsy and unskilful founders produce founding statutes which cannot pass the very loose "public benefit" test. As we have seen, in the case of voluntary associations there is not a public benefit test at all. What the court is supposed to test is only the nonprofit character of the newly created voluntary organizations. Kozma and Petrik (1990, pp. 20 and 21) mention two applications for registration which were rejected because one of the would-be voluntary associations intended to publish a newspaper, the other wanted to supply transportation services.

In principle, all foundations have to pass the public benefit test because only foundations serving public purposes can be registered in the court. In practice, most of the founders are able to formulate their purposes in a very sublime and solemn way, consequently the majority of the founding statutes can pass the public benefit test of the courts. As we shall see, failures are more frequent in the second round, at the Tax Authority.

The tax treatment of nonprofit organizations

Tax privileges for nonprofit organizations appeared as elements of the process of democratization, denationalization and deregulation. The reasons and principles on which the system is based are mostly political and economic. Even the legal experts (Kecskés, 1988; Kovács, 1988; Sárközi, 1991) elaborating on the topic prefer the political and economic reasons to the legal rationale for granting preferential treatment to nonprofit organizations. When the state wants to leave more room for citizens' actions in solving social problems, when it realizes that the state monopoly of social service provision cannot be maintained, tax privileges to nonprofit organizations seem to be reasonable vehicles for promoting the development of the nonprofit sector.

The tax treatment of nonprofit organizations follows the same principles throughout the whole country. There are no regional or local differences in the application of tax rules.

The tax treatment of nonprofit organizations was regulated by a government Decree issued in 1989 (16/1989), a law on the system of taxation enacted in 1990 (Law XCI/1990), and the tax laws yearly passed by the Hungarian parliament. The latter laws could have changed the rules of taxation year by year, but they did not. The tax advantages to nonprofits remained constant until January 1992.

This tax regulation guaranteed a multitude of privileges and exemptions to foundations. In contrast with the American regulation, in Hungary the tax treatment of foundations was more favourable than that of other nonprofit organizations. Their business activity was not limited at all, and their whole business income was tax exempt if it was used directly for the charitable purpose laid down in the founding statute. Registered foundations were automatically eligible for tax deductibility.

In the case of other nonprofit organizations, only voluntary associations engaged in scientific and technical research, culture, environment protection, sports, health care, social help, child and youth care were exempt from corporate income tax if all their profit was spent on their charitable purpose. The tax deductibility of membership fees and donations to voluntary associations was not guaranteed by law at all, but it could be (and sometimes was) approved by government authorities.

The tax laws which came into force in January 1992 (Law LXXXVI/1991 and Law LXXXVII/1991) have brought about changes of utmost importance.

Registration does not guarantee foundations' eligibility for either tax exemption or tax deductibility any longer. Their business income is tax exempt only if it does not exceed 10 per cent of their whole income (but not more than HUF 10 million).

Registered foundations can apply for tax deductibility of donations at the Tax Authority. This tax deductibility status is awarded if

- the foundation is engaged in preventive medicine, health care, scientific and technical research, environment protection, protection of the cultural heritage, education, culture, sport, religion, public security, care of the elderly, the poor, the national and ethnic minorities, the refugees, and the Hungarian minorities in foreign countries; and
- the donors do not get any (either direct or indirect) compensation for their donations.

The tax regulation of voluntary associations has also changed. The tax treatment of the business income of such organizations is the same as that for foundations. Donations to voluntary associations are still not tax deductible, except if the deductibility of some concrete donation is approved by the Tax Authority.

These changes in the tax law clearly created a second "public benefit" test for the foundations. The legal rationale of this measure has been heavily discussed in the Hungarian foundation community. There are many foundation leaders who consider it to be irrational that every foundation has to serve a public purpose, but that only some of them are considered of "public benefit" and are thus eligible for tax deductions on donations. In addition, some very important fields of nonprofit activitiy (e.g. the care of children and young people, services to unemployed persons, neighbourhood development programmes, promotion of the new entrepreneurs, etc.) are missing from the list of the preferred activities. This is not only injurious for some really prestigious foundations, but strange as well, because there are some large foundations in these fields which were established by state authorities and still get enormous grants from the government. This suggests that they are useful, "of public benefit" and important enough to be directly supported from the state budget, but not enough to get tax deductible private donations.

The application of the "public benefit" criterion was mechanical in the first year (in 1992). The Tax Authority only checked if the activities of the foundations were on the list of the preferred fields. If they were not, the tax deductibility was not awarded. The Tax Authority paid much less attention to the second requirement, especially because it had only the founding statutes as a basis for its decisions. These written documents evidently do not report on the compensations for donations even if they are part of the foundations' services. This requirement could be enforced only if the Tax Authority had enough energy (and staff) to supervise the actual activities and relationships of foundations. For the time being, this kind of control is quite rare: it happens mostly as a consequence of press reports, scandals or denunciations.

The tax deductibility of donations is equally available to all donors, including corporations. There were no limits for the deductibility of donations on the donors' side until 1993. The sole restriction for companies was that only their profit could be the source of deductible donations. Companies with no profits cannot claim tax advantages if they support foundations.

The tax laws passed in December 1993 have limited the tax deductibility of donations. The limit they have imposed is 50 per cent of the taxes actually payed by the donors in the former year: that is, individual and corporate donations can be deducted from taxable income only if they do not surpass the tax paid in the previous year. Although this limit (as a result of a compromise between the nonprofit umbrella organizations and the Ministry of Finances) is not too low, the tendency to cut the tax advantages is still alarming and raises serious worries in the nonprofit community.

There are serious debates on the tax deductibility of "in kind" donations, as well. The tax laws do not give any hint that they would like to differentiate between cash and "in-kind" donations. The XVIII/1991 Law on Accountancy mentions only the tax deductibility of cash donations. In the beginning nobody realized this. A whole book (Aćsné Molnár and Fodor, 1992) was published by the Tax Authority itself on the provisions of the new law on accountancy for nonprofit organizations, but it did not make any allusion to "in-kind" donations. More recently, some of the regional tax authorities did not approve the tax deductibility of "in-kind" donations. The main issue of the legal debate is whether a more or less technical law on accountancy can produce an interpretation of another law which significantly changes a major provision of the original law.

Recipients of tax deductible gifts do not incur special obligations. They are not obliged to refrain from any types of activity. They simply have to meet the "non-distribution" and the "public benefit" requirements.

Legal trends and debates

The three major legal developments and issues facing the nonprofit sector in Hungary today are as follows:

1 the problems of efficiency, independence and public control in the tax treatment of nonprofit organizations;
2 the emergence of public law organizations among the legal forms in the nonprofit sector;

3 The development of a government–nonprofit partnership in the provision of welfare services: legal guarantees of public support and contracting out services.

1 The number one development in the legal regulation of the Hungarian nonprofit sector is that most of the legal experts and some of the government officials, legislators and nonprofit sector leaders are aware of the problems to be solved and the pitfalls to be avoided in the direct and indirect support to nonprofit organizations. A number of preparatory documents, law proposals, polemical essays, declarations and alternative law proposals prove that the main dilemmas of nonprofit regulation, the possible consequences of some critical decisions have become clear by now. The decisions are still to be made, but this consciousness of the problems is a remarkable achievement in itself, especially if we take into consideration the extremely short history of the post-socialist nonprofit regulation in Hungary.

The main dilemma comes from a double requirement: the government should respect the independence of the supported nonprofit organizations, but at the same time it also should control their nonprofit and public benefit character in order to ensure the efficient use of the taxpayers' money.

In the case of tax allowances to nonprofit organizations, decisions on the use of public money are left at the supportees' discretion; consequently, their nonprofit and public benefit character becomes extremely important. Without the imposition of the non-distribution constraint, government subsidies can be transformed into private profit of the owners or founding members of the supported organizations.

The imposition of the non-distribution constraint is far from easy. There are many nonprofit organizations which do not produce (and consequently cannot distribute) any profit in the classical sense of the word, but do provide their members or supporters with services at a low price or completely free of charge. Since most of these services can be bought at a much higher price in the market, members of the nonprofit organizations take advantage of the preferential treatment of their organizations even if they do not distribute profit. In some cases (e.g. self-help groups of alcoholics or drug abusers) this is completely justified by the fact that these organizations alleviate commonly recognized public problems, and do it sometimes more efficiently than the public or for-profit service providers.

This public benefit character of the nonprofit organizations can be (and must be) thoroughly considered by the decision makers when they decide on the distribution of lump-sum subsidies, but such a due consideration is hardly possible in the case of tax allowances.

The system of decision making on tax allowances has significant consequences which must be analysed very carefully when thinking about a reform of this system. The main dilemma of the preferential tax treatment of nonprofit organizations derives from the fact that the definition of the public benefit character and its criteria is always difficult and somewhat subjective. Either legislative bodies or public authorities must take the responsibility for defining what or which nonprofit organizations are of public benefit.

Tax laws can set up a list of fields and activities (e.g. culture, education, health care, social help, child and youth care, etc.) and can guarantee that organizations involved in these fields will enjoy tax exemption or even tax deductibility if they meet the non-distribution requirement. This solution excludes arbitrary decisions. Nonprofit organizations are given preferential tax treatment as of right and not at the mercy of authorities, but the system is open to abuse. It is relatively easy to find a way of formally meeting all the requirements, but still gaining personal advantages from the nonprofit form instead of serving the public interest.

The other possible solution includes more arbitrary decisions on the part of the authorities. In this system the public benefit character of the nonprofit organizations is acknowledged by competent authorities (e.g. governmental bodies, local governments, tax authorities, etc.) which have the right to grant or refuse the tax exempt and/or tax deductibility status. Their decisions are based on the evaluation of individual applications. If the probability of tax evasion is somewhat smaller in this system, the danger of abuse of power is significantly bigger.

The first solution can be a bit expensive and harmful to the state budget, a very important consideration right now in Hungary. The second may constitute some danger to both social innovation and democracy. All these dangers and advantages must be carefully considered before any final decision. The choice between the two solutions depends on the traditions, political culture, social and economic conditions of a given society.

One would expect that in Hungary, where state control over the economy and society is traditionally strong, the development of the second solution is more probable. Actually, there were some government initiatives which would have led in this direction. In the autumn of 1992 when the Ministry of Justice suggested introducing new, more state-controlled nonprofit forms (such as the public law foundation, public law association and a special kind of nonprofit company) into the Civil Code, it also proposed to prohibit all other nonprofits from business activities. (This would have abolished their tax exemption automatically.) The proposal provoked indignation and hostile reaction from the advocacy organizations, the Ministry of Finance and some other ministries which are responsible for culture, education, research, health care and social services. This revealed that recentralization tendencies are quite strong in some government offices, but some others are in favour of contracting out services and developing the nonprofit sector. The threat of government control challenged the newly established nonprofit umbrella organizations to develop coalitions and a common strategy. Under this pressure the Ministry of Justice had to repeal the part of its proposal which would have prohibited private foundations and voluntary associations from business activities.

In fact, the present Hungarian regulation is closer to the first, more liberal, more normative and less arbitrary solution than to the second one. The limits on tax exemption and tax deductibility are quantitative limits; there is no room for arbitrary bureaucratic decisions about them. The parliament decided which fields of activities make the foundations eligible for the tax deductibility of donations if they also pass the "non-distribution" test. This list of activities cannot be revised by any public authority, but the final decision is taken by the Tax Authority which has to check the public benefit character of foundations.

In the first year of application of this system the Tax Authority did not really evaluate the applications. All foundations whose activities corresponded with the list got the tax deductibility status if they declared that they did not and would not distribute profit to their donors or founders. The validity of these declarations was promised to be regularly controlled in the future at least on a sample basis.

This type of control is more acceptable for the Hungarian non-profit organizations than the direct government control would be. The Tax Authority's fight against fraudulent behaviour is not likely to threaten democratic rights and freedom of either citizens or their voluntary organizations.

2 Although Hungary is a Roman law country and its legal experts work under strong German influence, the American experience and nonprofit theories provided more inspiration for the early development of the Hungarian nonprofit regulation than the German model. The American economic theories are very popular among Hungarian economists, especially among experts dealing with financial and fiscal problems. Almost the whole literature pertaining to the nonprofit regulation was born in the United States. Most of the foreign advisers came from America, most of the Hungarian experts and many of the nonprofit leaders either studied in the United States or participated in training workshops, seminars or briefings designed by American experts.

The simultaneous preparation of two very different regulation measures in two ministries has been quite indicative. While the Ministry of Justice was working on the inclusion of the legal forms of the public law foundation and public law association in the Civil Code (the bill was passed by the Parliament in 1993), the Ministry of Finance prepared the tax law which listed the preferred nonprofit activities and gave the Tax Authority the right to decide on the tax deductibility status of foundations.

The very emergence of the two public law organizations in the nonprofit regulation seems to be extremely important because this has broken the homogeneity, the clearly "private" character of the Hungarian nonprofit sector. Although some of these private non-profit organizations have never been completely independent from state support, their "private law" status was – if not a guarantee – at least some demonstration of their legal independence from the government and its institutions. The public law foundations and the public law associations will be definitely closer to the government than their private law counterparts. Otherwise there would not be any reason to create these legal forms. The official reasoning for their creation is that both public law foundations and public law associations will serve as structures for privatizing some functions that are currently performed by the state. It is to be seen how this will work in practice, how many and what kinds of public law foundations and associations will be created, how severe their government control will be, how these public law bodies will be treated by the tax laws. The umbrella organizations of the private nonprofits are most concerned about the danger that public law organizations may become the privileged part of the sector, to the detriment of the private nonprofit bodies. (The government's efforts to limit the tax advantages enjoyed by private foundations seem to prove that these concerns are quite plausible.)

On the other hand, the emergence of the public law associations and foundations is also explained by the public accountability problems of the sector. Private nonprofits' activity reports and financial accounts are not open to the public. The lack of this openness together with some scandalous cases of political and tax abuse considerably blemished the reputation of the private nonprofits (Wunker, 1991; Research Project on Hungarian Nonprofit Organizations, 1992).

Nonprofit organizations getting either direct or indirect public support must work under social control and their accounts must be open to the public. It is self-evident that some public control of the use of public funds is necessary. This control can be provided by the boards of nonprofit organizations if the general social climate and moral conditions are favourable enough, which is probably the case in most of the developed democratic countries, but it is not in Hungary. Another important component of the public accountability of nonprofit organizations can be the openness of their activity reports and financial accounts to the public at large. If private nonprofits decide to meet this requirement voluntarily, or if the forthcoming economic regulation makes it obligatory for them, this can weaken again the motivation to create easily controllable public law associations and foundations.

In short, the emergence of the public law associations and foundations in the nonprofit regulation represents some danger of a new "nationalization" of the nonprofit sector or at least a part of it. In the same legal debate there appeared some other signs of centralization efforts, too. In the autumn of 1992 when the Ministry of Justice suggested introducing the two public law nonprofit forms, it also proposed to create another legal form, that of the service providing nonprofit company, and to prohibit all other non-profits from business activities. The establishment of any service providing nonprofit company would have been subject to the approval of public authorities. As an answer to the first draft of the law modifying the Civil Code (Előterjesztés etc., 1992), the nonprofit umbrella organizations produced an alternative law proposal (Alternatív etc., 1992) which was heavily supported by the substantive ministries and became partly accepted by the Ministry of Justice.

The second draft of the new law was some kind of compromise. It did not suggest major changes in the former regulation of private foundations and voluntary associations, nor would it prohibit them from business activities. It did not propose any longer that service providing nonprofit companies could only be established with special permission from government authorities.

These developments seem to suggest that the impact of the German model on the Hungarian nonprofit regulation has grown somewhat, although this impact cannot really be distinguished from another influence: that of the renaissance of the pre-war legal tradition (Magyary, 1988).

It is not easy to foresee how strong and far-reaching the German influence will be. The German example shows that the intensive use of the legal form of public law foundations characterized the period of privatization, but then the importance of these foundations started to decrease. Recently, even the government itself prefers to establish private foundations (Schindler, 1991, p. 33).

The impact of the American model seems to remain quite strong in the economic and tax regulation of nonprofits. This is all the more probable because several groups of American lawyers have already declared their interest in helping the legislation on nonprofits in the East European countries.

At this crossroads of different models, the Hungarian legislators, nonprofit lobbyists and experts should be extremely cautious: a hybrid of different models can combine not only their strengths, but also their weaknesses. This risk is known, we shall see if this knowledge is enough to avoid the dangers.

The regulation task would become even more complicated, if the European Community developed its unified nonprofit regulation (6 and Kuti, 1993). The adjustment to the European norms is generally at the centre of the Hungarian efforts, thus any

European regulation in this field may significantly influence the Hungarian nonprofit regulation.

3 Purchasing and contracting out services were almost unknown methods under state socialism. Public institutions literally monopolized the provision of government financed welfare services. This monopoly was broken by a parliament decision in December 1992. According to this decision, nonprofit organizations providing basic social, education and cultural services have their right to get exactly the same per capita subsidies which are given to the state-owned institutions. This state support to the nonprofit sector is of vital importance because the income level is extremely low in Hungary, which limits any significant growth in the private giving.

The parliament decision accomplished a break-through: service providing nonprofit organizations became emancipated, the practice of purchasing and contracting out services could start to develop. Another step towards this emancipation was the XXXVIII/1992 Law on Public Finances which officially stated that the provision of public welfare services was not the monopoly of public institutions. Unfortunately, it did not say anything about the "non-public" service providers which are the possible contractors of the state authorities.

The development of contracting out will probably be slow and difficult at least for two reasons. First, very few individuals and organizations have enough money to establish new nonprofit schools, hospitals, nurseries without significant government support. Second, the procedures of setting quality standards for the nonprofit service-providers have not developed yet. This makes the bargaining about standards intricate and full of conflicts. The first experiences suggest that both central and local governments try to enforce quality and availability considerations when they decide on contracting out welfare services, but there are a lot of arbitrary elements in these decisions.

It seems to be reasonable that quality and availability must be the important considerations, when public authorities decide on purchasing or contracting out services. Both purchasing and contracting out are practically market transactions between public authorities and service providers. Government agencies deciding on these transactions must carefully consider the offers of the possible suppliers (nonprofit and for-profit organizations). They should reconcile the quality requirements with the requirement of ensuring the general availability of the services in question. They may prefer (in accordance with Hansmann's (1980) contract failure theory) the nonprofit service providers to the for-profit suppliers, but the aim of this transaction is not to subsidize nonprofits but to provide citizens with services.

These principles are generally accepted, but there are serious uncertainties about how to put them into practice. Neither the legal nor the economic regulation of nonprofits says anything about the conditions and requirements which should be met by the contractors and the rights and contractual obligations of the public authorities contracting out services to the nonprofit service providers.

The main problems to be solved concerning contracting out services are as follows:

- The list of services entitling nonprofit organizations to a per capita state support and determining the actual amounts of the support is settled every year in the law on the state budget. The list is always controversial, not only because of the missing items (e.g. health services in 1993), but also because of the lack of exact definition of the preferred services. For lack of generally accepted professional standards, there is too much room for the arbitrary decisions of the public authorities which always can (and sometimes do) decide that alternative and innovative service providers are not eligible for the per capita support.
- The competence of different public authorities is far from clear. The central and local government bodies, the Social Insurance Fund and the professional authorities all interfere in contracting out services. The consequence is described by a proverb in Hungarian: When there are too many midwives, the baby is likely to be lost. The clarification of responsibilities and competencies could help the development of the contract culture in Hungary significantly.
- The procedure of contracting out is not transparent. To get government contracts, an informal bargaining process takes place at the moment, mostly initiated by the would-be contractors. There is no open competition for the funds intended for contractors. The offers of applicants are not openly compared, some of the possible contractors may not even hear about the

services to be contracted out. It can easily happen that the most appropriate service providers are not considered at all, or they are declined for personal reasons. Neither the impartiality nor the efficiency of contracting out is guaranteed.

- There are no standards for the applications. Public authorities can decide what kind of documentation they use to judge the applications. Both extremes are possible. Important decisions can be made without basic information on the contractors. In other cases, other public authorities may request extremely and unnecessarily detailed applications from the future contractors.
- Similarly, there are no standards for the reports on the contractors' activities and achievements, either. Again, some authorities may accept superficial reports, others may ask for too detailed information. In fact, the result can be the same: the lack of substantial control of the contractors' performance.
- Another problem is the term of the contracts, the duration of the engagement. The position of the contracting parties is very unequal in this matter. The long term engagement of the contractors is often unavoidable because most of the services need massive investment. In contrast, the public authorities tend to be extremely cautious, they prefer short term contracts in order to be free to choose other contractors if they are not satisfied with the quality of services. Short term contracts endanger the independence of the nonprofit contractors which are in economic terms at the mercy of public authorities.
- The sanctions of breaking contracts between public authorities and nonprofit service providers have not been developed, yet. The lack of clear norms results in many conflicts and tensions and makes the whole development of contracting out extremely fragile.

A lot of these problems are emerging mainly because the contract culture is underdeveloped in Hungary. The improvement of the legal regulation evidently cannot be an exclusive solution to these problems, but may significantly contribute to alleviate them.

The missing items of the legal agenda

There are two important issues which are still missing from the legal agenda. These are as follows:

- *The problems of political commitment and campaigning activities of nonprofit organizations.* There is nothing in the nonprofit regulation in Hungary which would prevent voluntary organizations from political activities. The possible conflicts between independence and political roles, tax deductibility and participation in election campaigns have become clear quite recently. Both the nonprofit umbrella organizations and some government bodies are working on the development of their positions and strategies in these questions, but the issue has not appeared yet in the legal debates. Until now, competent authorities have been averse to considering possible restrictions on the political activities of nonprofit organizations.
- *The ethical problems.* There are neither laws nor restrictions on the "ethical" behaviour of nonprofit organizations. The questions of executive salaries and compensation of board members have already been raised by some experts and officials dealing with the preparation of a new nonprofit regulation, but the many other ethical problems (fund raising costs, insider training and self-dealing, discrimination in the selection of clients, etc.) have not even been faced yet in legal documents.

A group of foundation leaders recently started to develop an ethical code for foundations (but not for the whole nonprofit sector). Their work will hopefully influence the preparation of the legal regulation as well.

The above overview of the changing nonprofit regulation clearly shows that most of the important changes occurred in or after 1990, which was the base year of the international comparison. Thus the nonprofit sector we mapped in 1990 in Hungary bore marked resemblance to what existed immediately before 1989. The impact of the new legal and economic conditions on its size and structure can be tracked more recently.

Chapter 4

SCOPE AND STRUCTURE OF THE HUNGARIAN NONPROFIT SECTOR IN 1990

The challenge: how to explain the renaissance of the voluntary sector in Hungary

Recent developments indicate that the nonprofit sector must be of some importance in Hungary if so many private and government figures pay significant attention to its promotion and regulation, and spend time and money on creating and supporting voluntary organizations. The "nonprofit explosion" in a declining economy needs a complex explanation. I have presented two elements of this explanation in the previous chapters. The rich, long-standing tradition of voluntary activities and the encouraging legal regulation undoubtedly created a very favourable environment for the development of the nonprofit sector. However, even the best conditions would not have produced similar growth of the sector without some strong motivations on the side of the actual actors: the citizens, government, public and private institutions.

In Chapters 4 and 5 I will discuss what social and economic roles nonprofit organizations play, what activities they engage in, how their activities are financed, how they spend their money, what the main characteristics of the Hungarian nonprofit sector are in an international perspective, and what the most important tendencies are in its development. What quickly becomes clear is that the reality analysed here is embarrassingly rich and varied. In order to understand it, I have to gather all the available information including anecdotal evidence; narratives, statements and interpretations of recent developments given by other social scientists (Anheier and Seibel, 1992; Hankiss, 1989; Kolosi and

Róbert, 1992; Konrád and Szelényi, 1991; Kornai, 1992; Les, 1994; Salamon, 1993; Siegel and Yancey, 1993; Tóka, 1992; Wunker, 1991); and empirical data both from official statistics and from our own survey of the nonprofit sector.

Based on all this evidence, I tentatively suggest that the roles played by nonprofit organizations in Hungary are as follows:

The role of the voluntary sector in building civil society

A number of Hungarian voluntary organizations square with Arató's description of the main agents of civil society: "modern civil society is constituted and developed by various forms of civic initiative and self-organization, and is institutionalized by a legal system (especially of basic citizens' rights) respecting social diversity" (Arató, 1992, p. 55). These organizations mediate between the citizen and the state, and between the citizen and economic power; they fulfil the essential functions of civil society:

- They provide means for expressing and actively addressing the varied complex needs of society.
- They motivate and help individuals to act as citizens in all aspects of society rather than bowing to or depending on state power and beneficence.
- They promote pluralism and diversity in society, such as protecting and strengthening cultural, ethnic, religious, linguistic (and other) identities.
- They establish the mechanisms by which government and the market can be held accountable by the public. (Siegel and Yancey, 1993, p. 15)

It goes without saying that not all nonprofit organizations are necessarily institutions of civil society. Voluntary groups can be agents of the totalitarian state (Anheier and Priller, 1991; Bauer, 1990); the nonprofit form can be chosen as the second best institutional form by private entrepreneurs under the conditions of contract failure (Hansmann, 1980). The first model was widespread under state socialism, and the second has been emerging since the political changes, but still many Hungarian nonprofit organizations act as institutions of civil society.

The political role of voluntary organizations

A lot of voluntary organizations were also tempted to play some role in the political changes of 1989–1990. The opportunity to build a multi-party political system and a real political democracy came unexpectedly in Hungary. Even the clearly oppositional voluntary organizations, which practically acted as substitutes for the non-existing political parties (Kuti, 1993), were taken somewhat by surprise by the sudden crash of the Soviet empire. A new political society had to be developed within a very short time. The leaders of voluntary organizations were among the prominent target groups when political parties tried to recruit leaders and activists. Many of the nonprofit organizations had to face the dilemma of becoming active supporters of the newly emerging political parties or remaining neutral and independent; taking part in the election campaign or withdrawing from politics.

Both the case studies (Jagasics, 1992) and the statistical data (Farkas and Vajda, 1991) suggest that Hungarian voluntary organizations were very active in the preparation for the local elections in 1990. (More than 600 voluntary associations entered their own candidates in the local elections, and more than 400 other associations had common candidates with political parties.) Their political role was less important, but still significant, during the parliamentary elections.

The role played in the reorganization of the social structure

The recent political changes have brought about fundamental changes in all parts of society and the economy. Wealth, political power and economic positions are being redistributed. Individuals and whole layers within society are exposed to many dangers and at the same time many exceptional opportunities are open to them. The political changes were accompanied by an economic shock. The real income of half the population decreased between 1989 and 1991, and the real income of another 13 per cent stagnated. Even the nominal income of 40 per cent of households decreased in the period between 1988 and 1990 (Kolosi and Róbert, 1992), when the inflation rate was 50 per cent (Magyar Statisztikai Évkönyv, 1991). On the other hand, a small group from the old political elite (Hankiss, 1989), the old managerial elite and some new entrepreneurs (Kornai, 1991, 1992) are on their way to becoming extremely rich, and another group from the intelligentsia have occupied dominant political positions (Konrád and

Szelényi, 1991). Whether they want to protect themselves or to seize these opportunities, Hungarians have to form alliances, action groups and advocacy organizations. The mushrooming of advocacy groups in the period of transition is only the initial phase of an evolutionary process, which is probably a necessary condition for the selection of viable organizations.

People changing their social and economic positions often feel that they have to leave their old organizations and find new ones where they can meet the members of their new class. This "need to belong" cannot be easily satisfied when the social changes are too rapid and social mobility is too intensive. The newcomers are not always welcomed by the already existing groups. It very frequently happens that they have to establish their own organizations, which compete with the more traditional ones. Nevertheless, voluntary organizations play an important role in the process of social restructuring. Membership of voluntary associations, participation and volunteering are essential elements of status-seeking behaviour (Douglas, 1987; Collins and Hickman, 1991), even if their integrating effect is weaker than it might be under a relatively stable social order.

The service providing role of the nonprofit organizations

There were some fields of service provision, especially the sports, recreation and fire protection, which were considered to be the "territory" of voluntary organizations even under state socialism. There is no reason to expect that their service-providing role will decrease in these spheres.

On the other hand, state socialist governments monopolized the provision of welfare services (e.g. health care, social services, education, etc.) and promised to provide their citizens with all kinds of such services free of charge. Given the institutional and economic conditions in Hungary, the consequence of this arrangement could not be anything other than a chronic shortage and unequal accessibility of these services (Manchin and Szelényi, 1986; Kuti, 1990). Individuals have always tried to enlarge this market (for lack of better opportunities, mostly towards the second economy and the black market). Recently they have come to feel that this is more and more necessary because of cuts in the public welfare services. According to a survey carried out in 1991

(Tóka, 1992), 75 per cent of the adult population think that the state does not care enough about the social security of its citizens.

Since nonprofit service provision and the establishment of foundations became legal, numerous nonprofit organizations have been created in order to meet the unsatisfied demand or at least to alleviate the shortage. Most of these new organizations are fund-raising agencies or foundations supporting service-providing public institutions, but some service-providing nonprofit organizations have also been established.

Until recently, it was quite rare for private entrepreneurs to establish service-providing nonprofit organizations. The initiatives I know about are either disguised profit-making bodies or attempts by enthusiastic professionals (teachers, librarians, social workers, artists, etc.) lacking both managerial skills and sufficient money to invest.

Very few Hungarian consumers have enough money to pay the market price of welfare services, or enough capital to start new nonprofit welfare institutions if they are not satisfied with the quality and quantity of services delivered by the state run organizations. However, most of them are ready to support "voluntarily" the improvement of these services. The majority of Hungarian public hospitals, clinics, universities, colleges, and many schools, libraries and other cultural institutions have set up foundations in order to encourage and facilitate this voluntary contribution. These foundations are formally and legally independent, but are more similar to the fund raising departments of Western health, educational and cultural institutions than to real grant-making foundations. Their establishment was practically forced by the circumstances. There were serious cuts in the budget of public services, and public institutions had to look for additional resources if they wanted to survive. But – not being non-profit organizations – they were neither tax exempt nor tax deductible. That is why it was in their best interest to create foundations assuming their fund raising and business activities. They did not consider it a tax abuse (nor did their donors), but rather a kind of correction of the regulations.

The founders of these grant-seeking foundations can be the clients or the institutions themselves, but representatives of the clients and other supporters can nearly always be found among the board members. Consequently, the emergence of these "satellite foundations" not only improves the financial position of the public service providers, but also imposes some consumer control on their professional activities, which may bridge or at least decrease the gap between the supply and demand for welfare services.

The role played in restructuring the economy

The "one sector economy" failed in every field, including the provision of welfare services. In accordance with Weisbrod's (1986) theory, the government was not able to provide discrete groups (such as minorities, disabled people, etc.) with the services they needed. The overwhelming majority of the state run service providers also proved to be actually harmful to the public as a whole. Neither the quantity, nor the quality of their services were adjusted either to the limited resources or to consumer demand. Their functioning was far from efficient and flexible. The distribution of the welfare services they provided was perceived as unequal and unjust. These problems have made changes inevitable. The resources which are available cannot be dramatically increased (in fact, they are decreasing if anything), but social control of their use seems to be feasible. Clients want and can be allowed to influence the provision of welfare services. The emergence of nonprofit and for-profit service providers is clearly a step towards the institutionalization of this consumer control.

Public authorities are well aware of the necessity of modernizing and restructuring the provision of welfare services, and of a new partnership between public, nonprofit and for-profit organizations. It is common knowledge that this restructuring will not be possible without public assistance because most of the assets are publicly owned and the purchasing power of private consumers is very limited. The intensive government participation in funding the nonprofit organizations and the indirect support to the sector through the tax laws are based on an ideology which regards the nonprofit organizations as constituent parts of the modern three sector economy. In some economic programmes they are also mentioned as possible means for the denationalization of state property.

Nonprofit organizations as "life belts" and "tax shelters"

People active in the nonprofit field can also have their personal motives. Government officials, artists, professionals, and private entrepreneurs are all fighting for survival under the new conditions. They are eager to seize all possible opportunities including those which are offered by the relatively generous government support and the very liberal tax regulation of the nonprofit sector.

These personal motives range from the most respectable to pure profit ones. There are many professionals who simply want to continue or develop their activities (and retain their jobs) in the arts, education, social care, health care, environmental protection, etc. Nonprofit institutional forms and the additional resources (donations, government support, tax advantages) available through them serve as a life belt for several organizations endangered by recent political and economic changes. The same is true of some individuals in precarious positions. Members of the political elite seem to realize that becoming presidents or board members of the large grant-making foundations created by the government is one of the best ways to preserve their redistributive power if political changes happen. The motivation of some private entrepreneurs is much simpler: they establish nonprofit organizations in order to avoid paying taxes and to make their enterprises viable or more profitable. Many of the foundations created by public institutions or by their clients are also tax shelters: one of their roles is to disguise service fees as (tax deductible) donations.

The composition of founders (Table 4.1) of the nonprofit organizations surveyed by the Hungarian research team seems to largely support the above analysis. Only about 70 per cent of voluntary associations and 27 per cent of foundations were established exclusively by private individuals, the rest of the nonprofits had organizations among their founders.

Table 4.1

Composition of nonprofit organizations by founders in 1990 (%)

Founder	Foundations	Voluntary associations	Total
Private individual	26.8	69.7	47.2
Organization	53.2	11.8	33.5
Individuals and organizations together	20.0	18.5	19.3
Total	100.0	100.0	100.0

Table 4.2 shows that business firms (mostly state owned in 1990) represented about one-third of all the founder organizations mentioned by our respondents. This suggests that corporations regarded nonprofit organizations as an appropriate institutional form of their welfare policies and, most probably, also as a vehicle for shielding revenues from taxation. Government bodies and public institutions also represented relatively high shares (21 per cent and 16 per cent, respectively) of the organizations which took part in the establishment of nonprofit organizations. This seems to prove that state institutions were also willing to use the nonprofit forms in order to achieve their aims or to protect themselves against the dangers and financial difficulties raised by the transitional period. Even several nonprofit organizations, churches and political parties found it reasonable to establish foundations or participate in the establishment of voluntary associations. The share of foreign organizations among the founders also reached 10 per cent.

Table 4.2

Composition of founder organizations of foundations and voluntary associations in 1990 (%)

Founder	Foundations	Voluntary associations	Total
Central government	10.7	9.3	10.3
Local government	9.0	12.1	9.9
Public institution	14.8	17.9	15.6
Business firm	36.1	32.1	35.0
Nonprofit organization	7.7	12.1	8.9
Church	1.6	2.1	1.8
Political party	1.6	2.1	1.8
Other organization	6.8	5.2	6.2
Foreign organization	11.7	7.1	10.5
Total	100.0	100.0	100.0

The above list of the roles played by nonprofit organizations in Hungary is just a summary of "conventional beliefs" about the sector. Unfortunately, both analysts and decision makers tend to pick only some of these roles and thus overrate them when considering the overall importance of the Hungarian nonprofit sector.

Personal feelings and subjective judgements frequently result in bias in the way the media report and politicians decide on the sector. This bias has been almost unavoidable for lack of reliable information on the nonprofit organizations. We should not expect considerable improvement in the conventional wisdom until we have sufficient data to say exactly what nonprofit organizations are doing, where their revenues come from, how they use their money and how they compare to their counterparts elsewhere.

The main purpose of our participation in the international comparative project was to fill this information gap; to replace vague personal impressions by internationally comparable statistical estimates in the analysis of the roles, size, structure and finances of the Hungarian nonprofit sector.

Methodology: estimating the Hungarian nonprofit sector

Systematic information on the Hungarian nonprofit sector is much less well established than that in the Western countries because the sector itself is also less established. The need for statistical information about the newly emerging nonprofit organizations is quite recent and the changes in the sector are extremely rapid, which is why existing data sources are very poor. We can find very few figures on nonprofits in national accounts and other national statistics. Hungary was a one sector economy when the traditional population surveys, employment surveys and national income statistics were developed. The economic importance of voluntary associations was not significant. Statisticians did not even suppose that they should have differentiated between the government sector and the largely state-controlled voluntary sector. (They did not differentiate either between the very small private for-profit sector and the government sector.) Although the reform of the whole statistical system has already started, the market sector–government sector–private nonprofit sector classification has not been fully developed yet. A new classification drawing a distinction between the three sectors was introduced only in January 1995.

The results of the former surveys of voluntary associations have become completely outdated. They can no longer be used as proxies to represent the whole nonprofit sector. The last two surveys of voluntary associations were carried out in 1983 and in 1990. They collected information on the 1982 and the 1989 situation. The 1982 survey covered the whole nonprofit sector because the voluntary association was the only possible legal form for nonprofits at that time. Although foundations had become legal in 1987, there were only about 400 of them in 1989, so the 1989 survey of voluntary associations still represented almost the whole nonprofit sector. (It found 8,514 voluntary associations. The number of registered organizations was 9,760.)

Since then, the structure of the sector has changed dramatically. By the end of 1990, which was the base year of our comparative study, the number of foundations had reached 1,832. The number of registered voluntary associations was 13,833. The results of our survey showed that about 10 per cent of the registered organizations did not really exist. The estimated number of voluntary associations actually in existence was 11,255. Both the 50 per cent change of the population of nonprofit organizations and the emergence of the foundation form prevent us from using the data produced by the 1989 survey.

Consequently, the Hungarian project could not work on the premise on which the Comparative Project was based:

> A central premise of this project is the belief that existing national income data systems and subsector surveys, at least in the advanced industrial societies, contain far more data on the nonprofit sector than is commonly recognized … By systematically assembling the results of these surveys, making various estimates to break out the nonprofit sector, and using the best-available statistical methods to estimate key relationships (e.g., between numbers of employees, the total wage bill, and total expenditures), it should be possible to assemble at least a rough estimate of the scope and scale of the nonprofit sector in each country (Salamon and Anheier, 1992a, pp. 13–14)

Most of the statistical information on the Hungarian nonprofit sector comes from the official register of nonprofit organizations and from a sample survey carried out by the Research Project on Hungarian Nonprofit Organizations.

Since the base year of the Comparative Project was 1990, we used the population of nonprofit organizations which had been registered before 31 December 1990 as a sampling population. It was fortunate that – in accordance with a government decree – all existing foundations had to be re-registered in the Budapest or local county courts by the end of 1990. Foundations not applying for the re-registration were considered to be abolished. This means that the list of foundations we received from the High Court largely reflected the real size of the foundation sector.

The court register of voluntary associations was less up-to-date. The list we received contained many of the typical "social organizations" of the communist regime. A great deal of them had already been dissolved, but their closure was not reported to the court. That is why we decided to scale down the number of registered voluntary associations by 10 per cent (proportion of organizations which could not be found by the interviewers) when we estimated the actual size of the voluntary sector after our survey.

Unfortunately, the court register did not offer any classification of the registered nonprofit organizations. The structure of the nonprofit sector was known from other information sources.

The Federation of Hungarian Foundations produced a directory of foundations in December 1990 which used a slightly modified version of NTEE, the Independent Sector classification system (Hodgkinson, 1990). The basis of classification was a short description of the field of activity of every foundation. The directory contained 1,518 of the 1,832 foundations registered up to the end of 1990. We knew only the names and addresses of the rest of the foundations. Their classification was based on this very poor information. We must admit that the result (see Table 4.3 and Table 4.4) is not necessarily a perfect structural estimate, but it is definitely the best we could produce under the circumstances.

The structure of the sampling population of voluntary associations was known from two different information sources. The whole range survey of voluntary associations produced detailed activity and financial data about the 1989 population of voluntary associations, but this was much smaller than our 1990 sampling population. The number of registered voluntary associations had been only 9,760 in 1989, but it reached 13,833 by the end of 1990. We cannot assume that this increase did not change the structure of the voluntary sector. The breakdown of the 1990 population by ICNPO (International Classification of Nonprofit Organizations) groups was estimated with the help of the information collected by the Research Project on Hungarian Nonprofit Organizations in order to publish a directory of voluntary associations (Harsányi

and Kirschner, 1992). Voluntary associations were asked for information on their activities by the editors of the directory, but only
10 per cent returned the questionnaire. For lack of other information, the editors had to classify the rest of them using only the
names of the organizations. Although this method of classification
is anything but satisfactory, the results seem to be reassuring. The
1990 structure is not strikingly different from the one estimated
from the 1989 statistical survey of voluntary associations. All the
changes fitted in with our expectations. (The share of the newly
emerging service-providing organizations, advocacy groups,
civic, neighbourhood and environmental associations increased,
that of organizations, e.g. sport clubs, hobby circles, voluntary fire
brigades, which had existed traditionally, declined.)

Table 4.3

Number of foundations and voluntary associations by
subsectors in 1990

Subsector/field	Foundations	Voluntary associations	Total
Culture	343	936	1,279
Sports, recreation	150	5,215	5,365
Education, research	485	337	822
Health	115	75	190
Social services	397	1,759	2,156
Environment	36	247	283
Development and housing	121	408	529
Civil and advocacy associations	49	342	391
Philanthropic intermediaries	9	82	91
International activities	38	160	198
Business and professional associations, unions	32	1,469	1,501
Other	57	225	282
Total	1,832	11,255	13,087

Sources: Alapítványi almanach, 1990; Egyesületi címtár. Data from the two
directories were revised on the basis of the court register of nonprofit
organizations and of the results of our sample survey.

Table 4.4

Breakdown of foundations and voluntary associations by
subsectors in 1990 (%)

Subsector/field	Foundations	Voluntary associations	Total
Culture	18.7	8.3	9.8
Sports, recreation	8.2	46.3	41.0
Education, research	26.4	3.0	6.3
Health	6.3	0.7	1.4
Social services	21.7	15.7	16.5
Environment	2.0	2.2	2.2
Development and housing	6.6	3.6	4.0
Civil and advocacy associations	2.7	3.1	3.0
Philanthropic intermediaries	0.5	0.7	0.7
International activities	2.1	1.4	1.5
Business and professional associations, unions	1.7	13.0	11.5
Other	3.1	2.0	2.1
Total	100.0	100.0	100.0

As Tables 4.3 and 4.4 show, the structure of the Hungarian non-profit sector differs significantly from that of its counterparts elsewhere. Almost all of the voluntary organizations tolerated by the state socialist regime (2,324 hobby circles, hunters' and fishermen's associations, 2,891 sport clubs, 920 voluntary fire brigades, 1,469 professional associations) belong to 3 ICNPO groups. Their proportion (about 58 per cent of the whole sector in 1990) is so large that the different structure presented by the newly established foundations and voluntary associations can change the structure of the sector only very slowly.

In addition, most of the newly emerging foundations are not foundations in the classical sense of the word. Even the grant making ones are closely connected to very limited professional fields (if not to concrete institutions). Their legal form would qualify them to be considered philanthropic intermediaries, but their actual character is closer to that of the operating nonprofits. Our decision to classify them according to their fields of activities has resulted in having a very small group of philanthropic intermediaries.

Our limited financial resources and the fact that the structure of the nonprofit sector is so unbalanced prevented us from selecting a simple random sample. We had to stratify the sample using all the available information on the structure of the sampling population. We decided to select two subsamples. This was not necessary for the purposes of the international project, but we needed separate information on the foundation sector and on the voluntary associations because these two parts of the Hungarian nonprofit sector differ too much to be analysed together.

The sample of foundations (See Appendix A) was relatively large, 15.5 per cent of the whole population. We stratified the sample by major ICNPO groups. Organizations within the ICNPO groups were chosen at random.

The sample of voluntary associations was much smaller, only 2.3 per cent of the whole population. Fortunately, we knew much more about the structure of this part of the sector than about the foundations. The breakdown of voluntary associations by income categories was known from the 1989 survey. We could reduce the size of the sample using this additional information. The subsamples of the hobby circles, hunters' and fishermen's associations, sport clubs, etc. were stratified by income categories, as well. Organizations within the income categories were chosen at random. In the case of the newly emerging and – in terms of size – therefore unknown voluntary associations such as environmental groups, social service providers, civil and advocacy organizations, etc. we selected a random sample at the level of the ICNPO groups.

The survey was carried out in May 1992 by a professional opinion poll company. It was a personal interview survey. The interviewers had to complete the questionnaire included in Appendix A. When answering the financial questions, interviewees were asked to use the balance sheets and tax reports of their organizations in order to give precise answers. The mechanical data processing tasks were conducted by the opinion poll company and by a computer expert.

I trust the survey provides us with reasonably reliable information on the 1990 size, structure, organizational and economic conditions of the Hungarian nonprofit sector. A bigger sample would naturally have been better, but the double stratification helped us to produce a sample which largely represents the sector even though it is not representative in the strict mathematical sense of the word.

The stratified sample made the process of estimation somewhat complicated. The sample values had to be multiplied in accordance with the sampling principles in order to get results reflecting the original structure of the nonprofit sector. I did this myself, very carefully, because I wanted to avoid the problems which can emerge (especially in the very small groups) if the estimation is mechanical and there are some markedly divergent figures among the sample values.

In short, the 1990 figures are as reliable as the sample survey and our preliminary knowledge of the sector made possible. The definition, the concept, and the classification we used are those of the international project, so the comparability of the data is quite high.

The 1980 figures are more problematic. The voluntary sector was surveyed in 1970 and in 1982, but not in 1980. The classification used was very different from ICNPO, and a great deal of information that would be necessary for the comparison was simply not gathered. The actual content of some of the categories is rather obscure. Nevertheless, for lack of other information sources we had to use these survey results when trying to estimate the size and structure of the Hungarian nonprofit sector in 1980.

Methods used, assumptions made, and problems met in the estimation process are described in more detail in Appendix A.

Size and structure of the Hungarian nonprofit sector in 1990

According to nonprofit theories and existing explanations of the scope of the sector, Hungary could be expected to have a very small nonprofit sector in 1990. The degree of cultural and ethnic heterogeneity of the country is extremely low. The level of government social welfare spending is much higher than would be expected given the overall level of economic development. The country is traditionally centralized, and the role of the state and public institutions is very important. The decades of state socialism were likely to even strengthen the tradition of "etatism" and to weaken, if not destroy, the also existing tradition of voluntary action. The newly developed legal and economic regulation favouring nonprofit organizations did not have enough time to exert its influence until 1990.

As Table 4.5 and Table 4.6 show, the Hungarian nonprofit sector was much smaller than those of the other project countries in 1990, but against all expectations the difference was not very large.

Table 4.5

Third sector employment and expenditures in Hungary in relation to total employment and gross domestic product in 1990

	Expenditures (billion HUF)	Employment
Third sector	25.9	32,738
Total economy	2,080.9	4,168,701
Third sector as % of total economy	1.24	0.79

In fact, the gap between Italy and Hungary proved to be surprisingly narrow. This is probably explained by the fact that most of the sport and recreation services were delivered by voluntary organizations in Hungary even in communist times. The state socialist regime tolerated and sometimes even supported voluntary associations engaged in sports, recreation, disaster prevention and control, namely sport clubs, hunters' and fishermen's associations, hobby circles (included in "Sports, Recreation") and voluntary fire brigades (included in the "Social Services" category of ICNPO). Voluntary associations of the elderly and handicapped people were also tolerated, and some part of the completely state-financed social services were actually delivered by the Red Cross. The share of services provided by these voluntary organizations in the whole service sector was not very important, but their existence still meant that the development of the Hungarian nonprofit sector did not have to start from zero after the political changes.

As Table 4.7 and Table 4.8 show, operating expenditures of these traditionally existing organizations represented more than half of the sector's expenditures in 1990.

Table 4.6

Nonprofit sector operating expenditures as % of GDP and nonprofit sector employment as share of total employment and service employment in 1990, Hungary and selected other countries

Country	NPS operating expenditures as % of GDP	NPS employment as % of total employment	service employment
France	3.3	4.2	10.4
Germany	3.6	3.7	10.0
Hungary	1.2	0.8	3.0
Italy	2.0	1.8	5.5
Japan	3.2	2.5	8.6
UK	4.8	4.0	9.4
USA	6.3	6.8	15.4
7-country average	3.5	3.4	8.9

Source: Salamon and Anheier, 1994, pp. 32, 33 and 35.

Table 4.7

Operating expenditures in major fields of the third sector in 1990 (million HUF)

Subsector/field	Foundations	Voluntary associations	Total
Culture	597.3	750.0	1,347.3
Sports, recreation	165.5	13,053.7	13,219.2
Education, research	653.5	383.0	1,036.5
Health	130.2	102.6	232.8
Social services	284.7	6,163.4	6,448.1
Environment	271.1	117.7	388.8
Development and housing	273.6	91.3	364.9
Civil and advocacy organizations	96.5	7.6	104.1
Philanthropic intermediaries	93.9	82.4	176.3
International activities	13.7	17.5	31.2
Business and professional associations, unions	42.6	2,396.9	2,439.5
Other	84.2	48.8	133.0
Total	2,706.8	23,214.9	25,921.7

Table 4.8

Breakdown of third sector operating expenditures by fields in 1990 (%)

Subsector/field	Foundations	Voluntary associations	Total
Culture	22.1	3.3	5.2
Sports, recreation	6.1	56.2	51.0
Education, research	24.1	1.6	4.0
Health	4.8	0.4	0.9
Social Services	10.5	26.5	24.9
Environment	10.0	0.5	1.5
Development and housing	10.1	0.4	1.4
Civil and advocacy associations	3.6	0.0	0.4
Philanthropic intermediaries	3.5	0.4	0.7
International activities	0.5	0.1	0.1
Business and professional associations, unions	1.6	10.4	9.4
Other	3.1	0.2	0.5
Total	100.0	100.0	100.0

Almost 90 per cent of nonprofits were voluntary associations in 1990, and two-thirds of them had already existed before the political changes. In terms of expenditures these "old" voluntary organizations were still dominant, they determined the structure of the nonprofit sector. The composition of the newly emerging foundation sector was dramatically different, but its economic importance was not large enough to significantly change the structure of the whole nonprofit sector, yet.

It is worth noting that the composition of capital expenditures was significantly different from the breakdown of operating expenditures (Table 4.9).

The share of capital expenditures in the total expenditures was definitely higher in the fields where the share of foundations is also relatively high among the nonprofit organizations, namely in health care, culture and education (Table 4.10). This is probably explained by the fact that 1990 was just the beginning of an accumulation period in the foundation sector. Foundations which were established in order to develop service providing institutions (e.g. schools, museums, clinics, etc.) had to create buildings and develop facilities. Therefore, their investment activity was seemingly more intensive than that of the voluntary associations (Table 4.11).

Table 4.9

Operating and capital expenditures in the third sector in 1990 (%)

Subsector/field	Capital expenditures	Operating expenditures	Total expenditures
Culture	17.8	82.2	100.0
Sports, recreation	7.0	93.0	100.0
Education, research	11.2	88.8	100.0
Health	56.3	43.7	100.0
Social services	6.8	93.2	100.0
Environment	5.6	94.4	100.0
Development and housing	0.1	99.9	100.0
Civil and advocacy organizations	9.4	90.6	100.0
Philanthropic intermediaries and voluntarism promotion	0.4	99.6	100.0
International activities	0.0	100.0	100.0
Business and professional associations, unions	3.2	96.8	100.0
Other	29.4	70.6	100.0
Total	8.4	91.6	100.0

Nevertheless, the relatively higher share of capital expenditures in some formerly less developed fields could not significantly change the structure of the nonprofit sector in 1990, yet. The picture is roughly the same if we describe the structure of the Hungarian nonprofit sector with the help of employment figures (Tables 4.12 and 4.13) instead of using expenditure data.

The most important field of the nonprofit sector both in terms of operating expenditures and employment was "Sports and recreation" in 1990. Sport clubs accounted for 38.5 per cent of the nonprofit sector's expenditures, and employed 53.5 per cent of the sector's employees. Hunters' and fishermen's associations and hobby clubs spent another 12.5 per cent and employed 6.8 per cent of the sector's "total".

Table 4.10

The share of foundations among nonprofit organizations and the share
of capital expenditures in total expenditures in 1990 (%)

Subsector/field	Share of foundations among nonprofit organizations	Capital expenditures as % of total expenditures
Culture	26.8	17.8
Sports, recreation	2.8	7.0
Education, research	59.4	11.2
Health	60.5	56.3
Social services	18.1	6.8
Environment	12.7	5.6
Development and housing	22.9	0.1
Civil and advocacy organizations	12.5	9.4
Philanthropic intermediaries and voluntarism promotion	9.9	0.4
International activities	19.2	0.0
Business and professional associations, unions	2.1	3.2
Other	20.2	29.4
Total	14.0	8.4

Table 4.11

Share of operating and capital expenditures of foundations and
voluntary associations in 1990 (%)

Expenditures	Foundations (n= 3,427.0 million HUF)	Voluntary (n= 24,859.4 million HUF)	Total (n = 28,286.4 million HUF)
Operating expenditures	79.0	93.4	91.6
Capital expenditures	21.0	6.6	8.4
Total	100.0	100.0	100.0

Voluntary organizations engaged in social care (including
disaster prevention and control) represented the second largest
group of nonprofits. They accounted for one-quarter of the expenditures and 16.3 per cent of the employment in the sector. The
third group of significant importance was that of the business and
professional associations and unions (9.4 per cent of expenditures,
14.2 per cent of employment).

Table 4.12

Third sector employment in 1990 (full time equivalent employment figures: number of employees)

Subsector/field	Foundations	Voluntary associations	Total
Culture	155	1,065	1,220
Sports, recreation	188	19,555	19,743
Education, research	396	283	679
Health	14	61	75
Social services	142	5,195	5,337
Environment	41	206	247
Development and housing	23	30	53
Civil and advocacy associations	–	–	–
Philanthropic intermediaries	25	61	86
International activities	–	–	–
Business and professional associations, unions	186	4,455	4,641
Other	36	621	657
Total	1,206	31,532	32,738

Table 4.13

Breakdown of third sector employment by subsectors in 1990 (%)

Subsector/field	Foundations	Voluntary associations	Total
Culture	12.9	3.4	3.7
Sports, recreation	15.6	62.0	60.3
Education, research	32.8	0.9	2.1
Health	1.2	0.2	0.2
Social services	11.8	16.5	16.3
Environment	3.4	0.7	0.8
Development and housing	1.9	0.1	0.2
Civil and advocacy associations	0.0	0.0	0.0
Philanthropic intermediaries	2.1	0.2	0.3
International activities	0.0	0.0	0.0
Business and professional associations, unions	15.4	14.1	14.2
Other	2.9	1.9	1.9
Total	100.0	100.0	100.0

The relative importance of these groups of nonprofit organizations inside the nonprofit sector largely corresponds with their relative importance in the respective fields of services (see Table 4.14). Besides the three most important groups of nonprofit organizations (sports and recreation, social services, business and professional associations) there are two more fields where nonprofits account for a significant part of employment in Hungary. One is, of course, philanthropy; and the other is environmental protection.

Table 4.14

Third sector employment in relation to total employment by subsector in 1990

Subsector/field	Number of employees		Third sector employment as % of total employment
	Third sector	Total economy	
Culture, recreation	20,963	71,394	29.36
Education, research	679	354,258	0.19
Health	75	217,983	0.03
Social services	5,337	45,037	11.85
Environment	247	1,439	17.16
Development and housing	53	495,450	0.01
Civil and advocacy associations	0	15,702	0.00
Philanthropic intermediaries	86	86	100.00
International activities	0	4,939	0.00
Business and professional associations, unions	4,641	58,664	7.91
Other	657	2,903,749	0.02
Total	32,738	4,168,701	0.79

The relatively large share of nonprofit employment in the field of environment is explained by the fact that environmental movements started to develop quite early, much before the political changes in Hungary. They dealt with relatively simple, concrete problems. Consequently, they did not have serious conflicts with the government and they belonged to the "tolerated" category of voluntary organizations. On the basis of this tradition they could develop and institutionalize rapidly in the late 1980s, especially because a large part of the foreign support given to the Hungarian nonprofit sector went to the environmental field (Siegel and Yancey, 1993). The Ministry of Environment and several local governments also supported some of the environmental groups.

This structure clearly reflected the "heritage" of the state socialist period. In 1990 the influence of this heritage was obviously stronger than the impact made by the establishment of several new organizations. At the same time, the differences between the composition of the mostly old voluntary associations and the structure of the completely new foundation sector heralded significant changes in the composition of the nonprofit sector as a whole. The fields (education and research, health, development and housing, civil and advocacy activities, international activities), which were definitely underdeveloped in Hungary compared to other project countries, represented much higher shares in the foundation sector than among voluntary associations. This can be interpreted as a sign that the structural changes in the Hungarian nonprofit sector were beginning to decrease the differences displayed in Table 4.15, which compares the structure of the Hungarian sector to that of the other countries included in the Johns Hopkins Comparative Nonprofit Sector Project.

The most striking of these differences is the almost negligible presence of Hungarian voluntary organizations in health and education, which are the most important fields of activities of nonprofit organizations in the developed countries. This difference is explained by the state monopoly of education and health care under state socialism. While voluntary organizations as service providers were tolerated in culture and social care, and even promoted in sports and recreation, they were not allowed to establish schools or hospitals. Although this state monopoly was broken by the political changes in 1989, nonprofit service provision could not rapidly develop because it would have needed a lot of investment and there was very little capital available for the possible nonprofit entrepreneurs.

Similarly (but at a much lower scale), the state monopoly of housing and urban infrastructural services prevented Hungarian nonprofits from playing a more active role in development and housing, and thus contributed to keeping their share relatively low in this field compared to other project countries.

Table 4.15

Structure of the Hungarian nonprofit sector in international perspective
(%)

Subsector/field	Operating expenditures		Employment	
	Hungary	7-country average	Hungary	7-country average
Culture, recreation	56.2	16.5	64.0	16.9
Education, research	4.0	24.0	2.1	22.1
Health	0.9	21.6	0.2	22.3
Social services	24.9	19.6	16.3	24.5
Environment	1.5	0.8	0.8	0.7
Development and housing	1.4	5.0	0.2	4.2
Civil and advocacy associations	0.4	1.2	0.0	1.0
Philanthropic intermediaries	0.7	0.5	0.3	0.3
International activities	0.1	1.2	0.0	0.8
Business and professional associations, unions	9.4	9.2	14.2	6.1
Other	0.5	0.8	1.9	1.0
Total	100.0	100.4	100.0	99.9

Source: Source of the seven-country average: Salamon and Anheier, 1994, pp. 126–7.

Mostly political reasons are responsible for the petty share of international and advocacy organizations among Hungarian non-profits. The state socialist regime tried to fully control international assistance and discourage open advocacy activities by voluntary organizations. Although the establishment of such organizations was already free in 1990, fewer voluntary groups decided to specialize either in international or in advocacy activities than in the developed countries. Moreover, even the very few existing voluntary organizations in these fields were not institutionalized enough to have employees.

In short, at the beginning of its renaissance, in 1990, the Hungarian nonprofit sector was significantly smaller than that of the developed countries, but its size was still beyond most expectations. The relatively liberal Hungarian version of state socialism had let "politically innocent" voluntary associations exist. Some services had been provided by state-supported voluntary organizations. Consequently, the development of the politically free nonprofit sector did not start from zero. In fact, the size and structure of the sector in 1990 reflected at least as much the "heritage" of the state socialist period as the new developments of the democratic era.

Revenue sources: support and earned income

Both Hungarian and foreign observers are somewhat puzzled by the dynamism of the voluntary sector in Hungary. We have already tried to identify the motivations behind this phenomenon and found several social, economic and psychological factors of explanation, but a series of questions still remains: How do nonprofit organizations finance their growing activities? What are the sources of support? Who pays for the development of the nonprofit sector in Hungary?

For the sake of comparability, Tables 4.16 and 4.17 use the terms and follow the structure developed by the international comparative project. However, we must note that the actual meaning of some of these terms, the actual content of some of these categories, were slightly different in Hungary in 1990, i.e. the year when the three sector economy started to develop.

First of all, the role of the state was more important in financing nonprofit organizations than is suggested by our data. The denationalization of the Hungarian economy only began in 1990. Therefore, most of the companies and all the large banks were still state owned at that time. Consequently, their expenditures on supporting voluntary organizations decreased the revenues of the state budget, making these donations in some sense only semi-private contributions. The Hungarian government created several foundations that actually distributed government money. The decision making was more or less private in these cases, but the money itself came from government sources. Even the really private donations of individuals and private companies included indirect state support through tax-deductibility of both individual and corporate donations to foundations. (This indirect state support is naturally present in other countries' figures for private giving, as well, but its share is probably higher in Hungary than elsewhere because of the very high Hungarian tax rates and the unlimited tax deductibility of donations.)

Table 4.16

Sources of third sector cash revenue in 1990 (million HUF)

Revenue sources	Foundation	Voluntary associations	Total
Government	2,382.5	4,812.5	7,195.0
Grants, contracts	2,315.8	2,425.5	4,741.3
Central government	2,230.0	1,766.2	3,996.2
Local government	85.8	659.3	745.1
Statutory transfers	9.5	375.4	384.9
Third party payments	57.2	2,011.6	2,068.8
Private contributions	2,507.8	3,579.2	6,087.0
Direct contributions	2,472.7	2,373.0	4,845.7
Individuals	1,206.3	429.5	1,635.8
Foundations	140.4	107.4	247.8
Corporations	1,126.0	1,836.1	2,962.1
State companies	817.6	680.0	1,497.6
Private companies	32.6	332.9	365.5
Cooperatives	42.6	386.5	429.1
Banks	233.2	436.7	669.9
Federated fund contributions	–	451.0	451.0
Other NGOs	35.1	755.2	790.3
Churches	32.3	3.0	35.3
Political parties	0.6	71.0	71.6
Federations	–	676.7	676.7
Trade unions	2.2	4.5	6.7
Private earnings	1,350.7	16,232.0	17,582.7
Sales	94.5	8,765.3	8,859.8
Sale of products	2.7	2,451.0	2,453.7
Business income	91.8	6,314.3	6,406.1
Fees for service	72.9	2,467.3	2,540.2
Dues and assessments	4.1	3,668.4	3,672.5
Investment income	1,179.2	1,331.0	2,510.2
Other	166.0	339.5	505.5
Total	6,407.0	24,963.2	31,370.2

Table 4.17

Breakdown of the third sector income by revenue sources in 1990 (%)

Revenue sources	Foundation	Voluntary associations	Total
Government	37.2	19.3	22.9
Grants, contracts	36.1	9.7	15.1
Central government	34.8	7.1	12.7
Local government	1.3	2.6	2.4
Statutory transfers	0.2	1.5	1.2
Third party payments	0.9	8.1	6.6
Private contributions	39.1	14.3	19.4
Direct contributions	38.6	9.5	15.5
Individuals	18.8	1.7	5.2
Foundations	2.2	0.4	0.8
Corporations	17.6	7.4	9.5
State companies	12.8	2.7	4.8
Private companies	0.5	1.3	1.2
Cooperatives	0.7	1.6	1.4
Banks	3.6	1.8	2.1
Federated fund contributions	–	1.8	1.4
Other NGOs	0.5	3.0	2.5
Churches	0.5	0.0	0.1
Political parties	0.0	0.3	0.2
Federations	–	2.7	2.2
Trade unions	0.0	0.0	0.0
Private earnings	21.1	65.0	56.1
Sales	1.5	35.1	28.3
Sale of products	0.1	9.8	7.8
Business income	1.4	25.3	20.5
Fees for service	1.1	9.9	8.1
Dues and assessments	0.1	14.7	11.7
Investment income	18.4	5.3	8.0
Other	2.6	1.4	1.6
Total	100.0	100.0	100.0

Second, some part of the private contributions to voluntary associations was mixed with membership dues and therefore hidden in the category of earned income in Hungary. Since membership dues paid by corporations to voluntary associations were tax deductible (donations to voluntary associations were not), it was worth choosing this way of supporting these organizations. In fact, many companies did so, but we don't know anything about the proportion of these "donation-like" contributions among membership dues. The interpretation of membership dues as earned income can be problematic in other cases, as well. Even individual membership fees paid by the patrons of voluntary associations supporting museums, libraries, sports clubs, etc. are sometimes more similar to donations than to fees for services.

Third, for lack of a developed stock market, nonprofit organizations could not invest their endowment and savings in stocks and shares in 1990, yet. The relatively large proportion of their unrelated business income was not necessarily the outcome of their entrepreneurial zeal, it was partly the consequence of the very limited investment opportunities. Nonprofit organizations which did not want to confine themselves to depositing their money in a bank, had to start some business. Despite all the reservations expressed above, we must admit that the composition of the third sector revenues (Table 4.18) is quite surprising, especially when compared internationally.

Table 4.18

Revenue sources of the Hungarian nonprofit sector in international perspective (%)

Country	Private contributions	Government support	Earned income
France	7	59	34
Germany	4	68	28
Hungary	20	23	57
Italy	4	43	52
Japan	1	38	60
UK	12	40	48
USA	19	30	51
7-country average	10	43	47

Source: Salamon and Anheier, 1994, pp. 128–30.

Although private giving was the least important source (about 20 per cent) of the third sector revenue in Hungary in 1990, its share proved to be the highest in an international comparison. At first glance, the figures in Table 4.18 do not look conceivable, but on closer examination we can find some explanation for this strange phenomenon. No doubt, among the project countries Hungary is the one where private giving operates from the smallest base, but relative poverty does not necessarily prevent people from philanthropy. One of the most important findings of several surveys of charitable giving carried out in different countries was that poor people are not less generous than the rich. Having more personal experience of struggling with financial difficulties and being more endangered themselves, Hungarians seem to be sensitive to other people's need for help. On the other hand, under the circumstances of denationalization and shrinking public services they can be sure that their problems won't be solved by the government, so they must contribute both work and money if they want to increase the consumption of collective goods.

As I have already mentioned, the tax deductibility of donations to foundations was not limited at all in 1990. This represented a serious temptation in a country where the personal income tax was just levied. Several service-providing foundations raised donations among their clients instead of charging fees for their services, thus some part of private contributions were simply disguised service fees. (Fortunately, this bias in our data is likely to more or less counterbalance another bias: the one caused by the registration of some part of donations as membership dues among the private earnings of voluntary organizations.) The importance of the tax incentives for charitable contributions seems to be confirmed by the fact that the share of private contributions was much higher among the revenues of foundations than in the income of voluntary associations in 1990 (39 per cent and 14 per cent respectively). Both individuals and corporations preferred to address their contributions to foundations, that is, nonprofit organizations which were authorized to receive tax deductible donations.

Another element of the explanation can be that foreign donations (like the ones from Mr Soros or the Rockefeller Brothers Fund), which were also put into the category of private giving, significantly increased the share of private contributions. Although these donations would not have been considered enormous in other countries, the limited scale of the overall nonprofit income "revalued" them in Hungary. These foreign donations represented almost 5 per cent of the sector's revenues and about 20 per cent of the private contributions.

Finally, accumulation efforts may also have to do with the relatively high proportion of private contributions in Hungary. The base year of our comparison represented the very beginning of the development of foundations. These newly established organizations were trying to increase their endowments, and did not have much investment or business income, yet. Their fund raising efforts were probably more intensive than usual at a later stage of development. On the donors' side, the willingness to contribute to the establishment and consolidation of the newly emerging foundations (especially the ones providing new services) probably did not mean that donors were ready to keep supporting foundations at the same level. As far as companies were concerned, many of them simply converted their "welfare funds" (financial assets which served as a basis for the quasi-obligatory corporate welfare policy in communist times) into foundations. These kinds of donations were extremely beneficial for the early development of the foundation sector, but did not give any guarantee that the corporate support to foundations would be permanently high in Hungary.

In contrast with private contributions, the proportion of government support to Hungarian nonprofit organizations was surprisingly low (far the lowest among project countries) in 1990. The share of government support was about 23 per cent in the nonprofit sector as a whole, but 37 per cent among foundations and only 19 per cent among voluntary associations revenues came from government sources.

The forms taken by government support in the foundation world also proved to be significantly different from those which were widespread among voluntary associations. The overwhelming majority of the government support to foundations came from the central budget and took the form of grants. The share of these central government grants was much lower in the case of voluntary associations. The support of the latter organizations depended more closely on their actual performance and on the number of their clients. Support from the local governments and statutory transfers were practically negligible in both parts of the nonprofit sector.

Third party payments generally mean "per capita support" of nonprofit organizations in Hungary. The system of "vouchers" and consumer subsidies has not developed yet. When the government wants to support the provision of some service, it often decides to give a per capita subsidy to the service providers. The consumers do not get the money either in a direct or in an indirect form. Hence, they cannot buy the services in question. But they can preserve their consumer autonomy: they can choose the service provider. The per capita subsidy is given to the organizations chosen by the consumers, its actual amount depends upon the number of clients of the particular institutions. This "per capita technique" of government support had been in existence for a long time, but it was significantly changed when the law on the state budget (passed by the parliament in December 1990) gave nonprofit organizations providing basic social, education and cultural services the right to get the same per capita subsidies that are given to the state-owned institutions. The impact of this guaranteed per capita support, of course, could not be reflected in our 1990 data. Consequently, the share of third party payments was quite low (only 8 per cent) among the revenues of voluntary associations and close to zero in the foundation sector.

The relatively low government support to nonprofit organizations is all the more surprising because it does not seem to be consistent with the official ideology. What politicians said about the importance of civil society and the possible role of voluntary organizations in the denationalization and decentralization of service provision did not correspond with what they actually did (or rather did not do) in order to help the nonprofit sector in 1990. While the legal regulation and the indirect support of the sector suggested that the government favoured the sector, nonprofit organizations were not treated really generously in terms of direct state support.

For lack of other resources, Hungarian voluntary associations relied on earned income even more than their Western European and American counterparts in 1990. (This was not true for foundations, which received almost 40 per cent of their income from private contributions and 37 per cent from government support. Remarkably, the most important source of voluntary associations' earned income was not the sale of their products or the fees charged for their services (they represented only 9.8 and 9.9 per cent of the revenues, respectively), but their unrelated business income (25.3 per cent). This entrepreneurial character of the voluntary associations was probably a consequence of their growing political independence and deepening financial problems. The umbilical cord between voluntary associations and government authorities was cut in 1989, when the freedom of association and the independence of voluntary organizations became legally guaranteed. The state renounced its claim to control voluntary movements, but at the same time it also stopped feeling responsible for financing them. Sometimes this happened in the opposite way: public institutions realized that they were not able to cover the costs of some activities and persuaded their clients into establishing voluntary associations in order to continue providing the endangered services. This is how many dance groups, choruses, orchestras, theatre groups originally run by public cultural institutions were transformed into voluntary associations (Kuti, 1989a). Since their clients were hardly able to pay prices which would have covered production costs, voluntary associations could not completely rely on sale income and service fees. Many of them had to start for-profit business (usually not related to their nonprofit activities) in order to fill the gap between their revenues and expenditures.

As Tables 4.19 and 4.20 show, although in-kind donations surpassed 10 per cent of the total cash revenue, they were significant only in two fields: in sports and recreation and in international activities. This suggests that, here again, the supporting patterns developed in the state socialist period had a major impact on the behaviour of donors. (Forty-six per cent of the in-kind donations was corporate support, another quarter came from government sources and the rest from private individuals.)

There developed a strong tradition of in-kind corporate and state support to the sports clubs in the state socialist period. Most of the sportsmen were "employed" (actually paid without working) by either state-owned enterprises or public institutions. Office space, accounting and administrative services, training, recreation and transport facilities were offered free of charge; dresses, shoes, sporting goods were donated by the supporters of the sports clubs. This routine was strong enough to survive the political and economic shock of 1989–1990.

Similarly, a large part of the international exchange programmes were traditionally financed by corporations and local governments through in-kind donations: mainly through offering transport facilities to the Hungarian groups travelling abroad and accommodation to the foreign guests. This kind of support remained quite stable, probably because many of the international friendship societies were firmly embedded in "twin-towns", "twin-regions" schemes.

Table 4.19

Total cash and in-kind revenue in 1990 (million HUF)

Subsector/field	Total cash revenue	In-kind revenue	Total cash and in-kind revenue
Culture	1,469.7	51.3	1,521.0
Sports, recreation	12,032.6	3,001.9	15,034.5
Education, research	2,187.8	4.3	2,192.1
Health	657.0	4.5	661.5
Social services	4,319.1	101.7	4,420.8
Environment	1,777.2	3.5	1,780.7
Development and housing	759.4	8.2	767.6
Civil and advocacy organizations	177.6	7.7	185.3
Philanthropic intermediaries and voluntarism promotion	591.9	19.2	611.1
International activities	28.6	6.4	35.0
Business and professional associations, unions	6,671.0	37.2	6,708.2
Other	698.3	1.1	699.4
Total	31,370.2	3,247.0	34,617.2

Table 4.20

In-kind revenues as a share of total revenue by subsectors in 1990

Subsector/field	In-kind revenues as % of the total revenue
Culture	3.4
Sports, recreation	20.0
Education	0.2
Health	0.7
Social services	2.3
Environment	0.2
Development and housing	1.1
Civil and advocacy organizations	4.2
Philanthropic intermediaries and voluntarism promotion	3.1
International activities	18.3
Business and professional associations, unions	0.6
Other	0.2
Total	9.4

Table 4.21 shows that mostly the voluntary associations bene-fited from the in-kind donations, which also suggests that a signi-ficant part of this support went to the old voluntary organizations. The newly established foundations were almost exclusively recip-ients of cash donations. As reflected in Table 4.22, not only the share of in-kind support, but also the structure of cash revenues was dramatically different in various fields of the Hungarian non-profit sector in 1990.

Table 4.21

The share of cash and in-kind revenues of foundations and voluntary associations in 1990 (%)

Revenues	Foundations	Voluntary associations	Total
Cash revenues	98.3	88.8	90.6
In-kind revenues	1.7	11.2	9.4
Total	100.0	100.0	100.0

Table 4.22

Breakdown of income by subsectors and revenue sources in 1990 (without revenues from unknown sources reported as "Other")

Subsector/field	Source of revenue (%)			
	Private support	Govern-ment	Private earnings	Total
Culture	32.7	25.8	41.5	100.0
Sports, recreation	17.7	32.0	50.3	100.0
Education, research	17.7	7.5	74.8	100.0
Health	60.6	19.4	20.0	100.0
Social services	21.7	11.9	66.4	100.0
Environment	0.3	94.6	5.1	100.0
Development and housing	56.5	15.9	27.6	100.0
Civil and advocacy associations	31.3	52.5	16.2	100.0
Philanthropic intermediaries	71.0	25.4	3.6	100.0
International activities	73.4	–	26.6	100.0
Business and professional associations, unions	11.8	1.5	86.7	100.0
Other	21.8	24.8	53.4	100.0
Total	19.7	23.3	57.0	100.0

Nonprofit organizations engaged in international activities, philanthropy, health care, development and housing received more than half of their income from private contributions. This sounds quite logical in the case of philanthropy and international aid which are among the traditional fields of charity. The high proportion of private donations among the revenues of nonprofits engaged in health care is explained by the fact that in 1990 these organizations were mostly foundations which had been established in order to raise funds for hospitals or for the treatment of either individuals or groups of people. (For example, the foreign treatment of several children and famous sportsmen, artists, TV stars was financed through foundations. There existed foundations which raised funds for the treatment of people from the neighbouring countries in Hungary. The aim of other foundations was the improvement of facilities used for the therapy of special diseases.) Private contributions in the field of development and housing mostly served the development of the urban infrastructure in cities and villages where the donors lived, thus they can hardly be interpreted as charitable donations in the classical sense of the word.

There were only two fields where more than 50 per cent of revenues came from government support in 1990. One of them was environmental protection, a field which is clearly considered to be almost exclusively the responsibility of voluntary organizations by the Hungarian government. In accordance with this approach, the government is ready to subsidize environmental movements despite the sometimes latent, sometimes open, conflicts between green groups and public authorities. Another factor of the explanation is that environmental nonprofits received substantial aid from the European Community in 1990. We had to classify it as government support because it came from EC governments and was distributed through Hungarian authorities. Nevertheless, it is worth mentioning that 1990 was not an ordinary year for the environmental organizations in Hungary, therefore our data are not really comparable in this field.

Strikingly enough, civic and advocacy organizations also enjoyed exceptionally high state support in 1990. This was anything but expected in the second year of the newly developing democratic system. One could suppose that more time was necessary to change government attitude towards civic associations. I still think (but cannot prove) that the very impressive proportion of government support to civil and advocacy organizations is somewhat misleading. It reflects intensive financing of a limited number of organizations politically close to the government and hides the negative attitude towards oppositional advocacy groups.

Private earnings were the most important source of income for business and professional associations and for the nonprofit organizations engaged in education and research, social services, sports and recreation, that is, practically in all fields where the service providing role of nonprofits was sizeable. Despite the different circumstances, Salamon's and Anheier's observation (1994, p. 59) seems to apply to Hungary as well: "The heavy reliance of nonprofit organizations on fees and sales reflects the market context within which nonprofit organizations operate … Where services are provided to clients who can pay, collecting fees becomes a matter of organizational necessity." In addition, increasing business and investment income was also an economic necessity in Hungary in 1990, when the cuts in public spending endangered the provision of several, formerly state-financed services.

Table 4.23 suggests that the revenue structure of the Hungarian nonprofit sector was quite different from that of the other project countries. (The signs "+" mean that the share of the given kind of revenue is also higher than 50 per cent in the given country, just like in Hungary. The signs "-" show that this proportion is lower than 50 per cent.)

There was only one country (France) where private giving was the main source of income in the fields of international activities and philanthropy in 1990. The proportion of charitable contributions did not amount to 50 per cent of nonprofits' revenues in the health care, development and housing fields anywhere else but Hungary.

Although government support to the nonprofit sector as a whole and to most of its subsectors was much more important in every other project country than it was in Hungary, in other countries its proportion happened to be lower than 50 per cent just in the field of environment, where it was the dominant revenue source of the Hungarian nonprofit organizations. The picture is less clear in the case of civic and advocacy organizations. Their major revenue source was government support not only in

Hungary, but in Italy and the United Kingdom, as well. The average share of government support to civic and advocacy associations in the seven countries also amounted to 50 per cent, which raises important questions about the independence of these kinds of voluntary organizations.

Table 4.23

Similarities and differences between the income structure of the Hungarian nonprofit sector and the third sectors in France (F), Germany (G), Italy (I), Japan (J), the UK and the USA

Fields receiving more than 50 % of their income from	F	G	I	J	UK	USA	7 country average
Private conributions							
International	+	−	−	−	−	−	−
Philanthropy	+	−	−	−	−	−	−
Health	−	−	−	−	−	−	−
Development, housing	−	−	−	−	−	−	−
Government sources							
Environment	−	−	−	−	−	−	−
Civic, advocacy	−	−	+	−	+	−	+
Private earnings							
Business, professional	+	+	+	+	+	+	+
Education, research	−	−	+	+	−	+	+
Social services	−	−	−	−	−	−	−

Source: Salamon and Anheier, 1994, pp. 128–30.

Private earnings were unquestionably dominant income sources of business and professional associations in every project country. The dependence on earned income was considerable among nonprofits engaged in education not only in Hungary, but in Italy, Japan and the United States, too. On the contrary, the Hungarian nonprofit organizations providing social services were unique in their dependence on private earnings. Except for the United Kingdom, government support was the major revenue source of nonprofit organizations in the field of social care in developed countries.

To be sure, a distorted structure of the Hungarian nonprofit sector was only to be expected after forty years of state socialism.

If I analyse how it differs from the structure of the nonprofit sectors in more developed, traditionally democratic, countries, I do so not only for piquancy's sake, but also in order to detect what are the likely ways and directions of the sector's development in Hungary in the near future.

Chapter 5

GROWTH AND CHANGES OF THE HUNGARIAN NONPROFIT SECTOR SINCE 1990

The growing size and economic importance of the nonprofit sector in Hungary

The development of the nonprofit sector has been strikingly dynamic in 1990–1992 in Hungary. There has been a leap both in the number of voluntary organizations (see Tables 2.2 and 2.4) and in the economic importance of the sector (Tables 5.1, 5.2 and 5.3).

Table 5.1

Change in actual operating expenditures in the third sector, 1980–1992

Year	Third sector expenditures (billion HUF)	GDP (billion HUF)	Third sector as % of GDP
1980	3.0	721.0	0.42
1989	16.4	1,706.0	0.96
1990	25.9	2,080.9	1.24
1991	51.6	2,346.0	2.20
1992	89.9	2,805.1	3.20

Table 5.2

Change in inflation adjusted expenditures in the third sector, 1980–1992

Year	Third sector expenditures (billion HUF)	GDP (billion HUF)	Third sector as % of GDP
1980	3.0	721.0	0.42
1989	8.0	828.6	0.96
1990	10.0	801.8	1.24
1991	16.2	738.0	2.20
1992	22.6	704.8	3.20

112

Table 5.3

Change in third sector employment, 1989–1992 (full-time equivalent employment figures)

Year	Third sector (thousand employees)	Total economy (thousand employees)	Third sector as % of total
1989	19.4	4,459.8	0.43
1990	32.7	4,168.7	0.78
1991	35.2	3,672.6	0.96
1992	46.2	3,118.6	1.48

This growth of third sector expenditures and third sector employment is all the more impressive because the economy itself is clearly declining. The emergence of a flourishing nonprofit sector in a declining economy can only be explained by the fact that the patterns of problem solving offered by nonprofits are equally acceptable and attractive for citizens and government. The nonprofit institutional form is generally considered to be an appropriate means of facing the social and economic challenges of the transition period.

Unfortunately, we have very little empirical information about the sources of this extraordinary growth. While we are sure (on the basis of anecdotal evidence) that all kinds of nonprofit revenues increased significantly, we have more or less reliable data only about two items: individual donations to foundations, which were deducted from personal income; and government support, which was separately recorded in the state budget.

As far as individual donations are concerned, we positively know that there is a large gap between the actual amount of donations and the one indicated in the tax files. In the questionnaire of a statistical survey carried out in 1993, nonprofit organizations reported that they had received HUF 4,579 million as individual donations in 1992 (Bocz, *et al.* 1994, p. 38). The overwhelming majority of this support (HUF 4,051 million) went to the foundations. As Table 5.4 shows, less than half (only 44 per cent) of these donations were deducted from taxable income.

Consequently, the figures displayed in Table 5.4 do not necessarily represent the real dynamism of the individual donations. Their growth is extremely impressive, but we cannot be sure about the tendencies in the background. It is highly possible that the tax deductibility of donations became widely known in the early 1990s and the share of the donations deducted from the taxable income increased within the total individual support to foundations. In this case, the growth rate of total donations was probably lower than the one indicated in Table 5.4.

Table 5.4

Growth of the number of private donors and the amount of their donations as reported in the tax files, 1988–1992

Year	Number of donors	Amount of of donations (million HUF)	Average size of donations (thousand HUF)
1988	25,457	54	2.1
1989	45,682	177	3.9
1990	56,674	425	7.5
1992	96,605	1,789	18.5
1992/88 %	379.5	3,313.0	881.0

Source: Bocz *et al.*, 1994, p. 52.

Not only did the number of donors and the amount of donations increase extremely rapidly, but also the number of foundations increased very quickly at the same time. Since the citizens were obviously very active in establishing these new foundations, we don't have much reason to suppose that the growth displayed in Table 5.4 was only the outcome of a shift towards deductible donations. It is more likely that the total amount of donations also increased, even if at a lower rate than that of the donations deducted from the taxable income.

Another deficiency of our data is that they do not reveal the motivation behind this phenomenon. Unfortunately, there are no survey results on donors' behaviour (the very first survey on charitable giving was carried out in Hungary only in 1994 and its results are not available yet), so we can only guess that both the sense of solidarity and the personal interests influence private donations.

The solidarity-motivated donations of Hungarians are probably very similar to donations of this kind anywhere else in the world. The private donations motivated by pure self-interest are more special. Most of the service providing nonprofits (schools, nurseries, clinics, cable television networks, etc.) have been established as foundations, and urge (tax deductible) donations instead of charging service fees. Authorities are well aware of this anomaly and (as we have already seen) try to limit it, but the change of this practice is quite difficult because – according to former government promises – the vast majority of the services provided by these operating foundations should be available free of charge for all Hungarian citizens. The clients ("donors") of the "member-serving" foundations feel it just that their contribution must be tax deductible if they pay for services which are free for other (privileged or simply more lucky) people.

Impressive as it is, the growth of the private donations cannot be a sufficient financial basis for the nonprofit sector. The level of personal income is so low, the share of the income centralized in the state budget is so big (about 60 per cent) in Hungary, that the state support is indispensable for the development of the nonprofit sector. As Table 5.5 suggests, the government does not hesitate to increase its contribution to the nonprofit organizations, but, here again, we have only very fragmented information about the changes in state support to the nonprofit sector.

Comparing the 1990 figures in Table 5.5 with those reported in Table 5.4 it can be ascertained that less than one-third of the state support to nonprofit organizations was separately reported in the state budget in 1990. We have every reason to suppose that the share of these separately reported grants and subsidies has significantly increased since then, and therefore the "visible" part of the state support has grown more rapidly than its actual amount. Nevertheless, the growth shown in Table 5.5 proves that the supportive government attitude towards the nonprofit sector has been manifested not only in fine speeches, but also in financial support. Especially the foundations and the service-providing nonprofit organizations have enjoyed increasing state support. The growth rate of grants to voluntary associations has been lower than the inflation rate.

Despite all reservations about the reliability of the available data, we can state that both government and individual donors have made considerable efforts to help the third sector in the early 1990s. The nonprofit organizations themselves must have also increased their earned income because, roughly speaking, the growth of their total revenues has kept pace with that of the individual donations and state support. However, the comparison of growth indicators (Table 5.6) suggests not only the growing importance, but also the fragility of the voluntary sector in Hungary. The growth of the number of employees has been much slower than that of the sector in terms of revenues, expenditures and organization numbers.

Table 5.5

Direct state support to the nonprofit organizations (items which are individually mentioned in the central budget) not including local and regional government support, 1990–1993 (million HUF)

Year	Grants to foundations	Grants to voluntary associations	Per capita support to nonprofits	Total
1990	295.4	1,775.9	–	2,071.3
1991	761.3	2,000.5	1,195.9	3,957.7
1992	2,521.3	2,254.5	2,376.9	7,152.7
1993	5,273.3	2,343.3	3,449.2	11,065.8
1993 as % of 1990	1,785.1	131.9	–	534.2

Source: Bocz *et al.*, 1994, p. 51.

Table 5.6

Indicators of third sector growth between 1990 and 1992

Indicators	1992 as % of 1990
Number of nonprofit organizations	238.6
Inflation adjusted third sector revenues	236.9
Inflation adjusted government support[a]	225.1
Inflation adjusted individual donations[b]	274.4
Inflation adjusted third sector expenditures	226.0
Number of third sector employees	141.3

Notes: [a] Only items separately reported in the state budget. [b] Only donations to foundations which were deducted from the personal income tax.

It is extremely difficult to solve the staff payment and personnel recruitment problems because their origin is the lack of appropriate funds in the nonprofit sector. In order to attract well trained, talented employees, the nonprofit organizations should offer decent salaries, and this brings us back to the financial problems, which – of course – cannot be solved without the assistance of well-trained professionals.

Changing structure of the nonprofit sector

The growth of the size of the nonprofit sector has naturally resulted in structural changes as well. As Table 5.7 shows, the number of nonprofit organizations has increased at an uneven rate in different subsectors. The growth rate was much higher than the average in the fields of health, education and philanthropy; significantly below the average in social care, sports, recreation, environment; and slightly above the average in all the other subsectors. Some of these differences can be explained fairly easily, but some others represent a bit of a puzzle. The analysis I am trying to give here is tentative: a special survey focusing on the subsectors in question would be necessary in order to scrutinize the factors influencing their development potential.

Table 5.7

Changes in the structure of the nonprofit sector between 1990 and 1993 (%)

Subsector/field	1993/1990	Subsector growth as % of sector growth
Culture	297.3	108.3
Sports, recreation	231.9	84.5
Education, research	438.8	159.9
Health	593.2	216.2
Social services	185.1	67.5
Environment	248.4	90.5
Development and housing	323.8	118.0
Civil and advocacy associations	322.3	117.5
Philanthropic intermediaries	411.0	149.8
International activities	343.9	125.3
Business and professional associations, unions	298.4	108.7
Other	616.3	224.6
Total	274.4	100.0

Source: *Court register.*

One of the explanatory factors is probably the "myth" of foundations. Establishing a foundation was generally considered to be a panacea for all financial problems in Hungary in the early 1990s. "The foundation" as a legal entity was quite new. The name itself filled several people (especially the elderly) with nostalgia; based on the pre-war experience, the word "foundation" had absolutely positive connotations. Grants received from, fellowships, events, projects financed by foundations before 1945 were not completely forgotten. The very fact that foundations had been banned under state socialism also strengthened their myth.

As we have seen, the tax treatment of foundations was also very favourable. Both private donors and government authorities seemed to be willing to support the newly created foundations, mostly in the hope that their efforts will be joined by other supporters, too. The expectations towards the fund raising potential of foundations were clearly excessive. The result was a mushrooming of the foundations and a striking, though rather uneven, growth of their share among nonprofit organizations (Table 5.8) in all but two fields of the nonprofit sector.

Table 5.8

Growth of the share of foundations among nonprofit organizations between 1990 and 1993 (%)

Subsector/field	1990	1993
Culture	26.8	62.6
Sports, recreation	2.8	8.9
Education, research	59.4	81.2
Health	60.5	78.8
Social services	18.1	46.2
Environment	12.7	34.7
Development and housing	22.9	54.6
Civil and advocacy associations	12.5	24.7
Philanthropic intermediaries	9.9	9.4
International activities	19.2	40.2
Business and professional associations, unions	2.1	1.5
Other	20.2	60.9
Total	14.0	33.6

Source: Court register.

It is noticeable that the two fields (health and education) which have grown at the highest rate are also the fields where the share of foundations is the highest. I do not want to say, of course, that simply the growth of the foundation sector caused the development of the nonprofit sector or some parts of it. I only state that founders of the new nonprofit organizations tended to choose the foundation form when they did not have a special reason to adhere to the legal form of the voluntary association. In most cases this special reason was probably the member-serving character of the nonprofit organizations (e.g. nonprofit umbrella organizations, business and professional associations, sports clubs, recreational associations, service clubs, etc.).

In order to get a bit closer to the explanation of the structural changes, it is worth inquiring into the internal structure of some nonprofit fields of growing importance. One of them is the field of education where the development started almost from zero in the late 1980s. The monopoly of education was extremely important for state socialist governments. The state control of education was a question of power, a vehicle for influencing the citizens' philosophy of life, opinion and way of thinking. This political importance helped education to come into the limelight right after the political changes, to declare freedom of education, and to get guaranteed per capita subsidies to a wide range of its nonprofit institutions.

Despite these helpful changes in the general environment, the actual development of services was quite difficult because a lot of investment would have been needed in order to establish new nonprofit schools. Table 5.9 clearly shows that the population of educational nonprofits is dominated by foundations which have been established for the last couple of years mainly in primary and secondary education, and in the field of "Other education" (mostly language teaching, computer training and "do-it-yourself" courses). The majority of the foundations involved in primary, secondary and higher education are fund raising organizations helping the development and everyday operation of state run schools and universities, but there are some operating foundations (new nonprofit schools) among them, as well. The foundations involved in "Other education" are partly service-providing organizations, partly multipurpose organizations giving grants at different educational levels.

Table 5.9

Composition of nonprofit organizations in the field of education
in 1993 (%)

Field of activity	Foundations	Voluntary associations	Total
Primary and secondary education	57.7	5.6	63.3
Higher education	5.7	1.1	6.8
Adult education	5.1	3.0	8.1
Other education	18.1	3.7	21.8
Total	86.6	13.4	100.0

Source: Court register.

As Table 5.10 suggests, the picture is more complicated in the case of health services. The majority of nonprofit organizations are foundations here, too, but they are more dispersed all along the field of health care. As a result of a relatively slow erosion of the state monopoly of health care, and the much more rapid and dramatic deterioration of the financial conditions of the public service providers, the number of nonprofit organizations has increased a lot in health care for the last two years. Practically every kind of state run health institution established foundations in order to manage their fund raising activities. There are lots of foundations which serve simply the treatment of concrete diseases, or try to solicit donations in order to finance some special treatment of private individuals. The very first service providing nonprofit organizations have also appeared. Unfortunately, there are several foundations among them which provide their clients with naturopathic services of a rather dubious character.

The number of voluntary associations involved in health care is still very limited. Health institutions seem to be either unable or reluctant to recruit supporters' whose associations could help their work.

The provision of health and social services were equally considered to be state monopolies until ten years ago, but the demolition of this monopoly started earlier and is more advanced in the field of social care than in health services (Gayer *et al.*, 1992). Accordingly, the development of the nonprofit organizations was also somewhat different in social care.

Nonprofit organizations involved in social care represent a major puzzle for the researchers of the Hungarian nonprofit sector. The development of this segment of the sector is surprisingly slow. Since the transfer of significant corporate property into some foundations in 1990 (put mainly in the rows of "Self-help and other personal services" and "Other social services" in Table 5.11), the social sphere of nonprofits has been growing at a significantly lower rate than any other part of the nonprofit sector.

Table 5.10

Composition of nonprofit organizations in the field of health care in 1993 (%)

Field of activity	Foundations	Voluntary associations	Total
Hospitals	12.1	0.9	13.0
Emergency medical services	6.9	2.3	9.2
Outpatient and rehabilitative medical services	10.6	1.3	11.9
Mental health	4.7	5.8	10.5
Public health, wellness education	22.9	6.7	29.6
Other health services	21.6	4.2	25.8
Total	78.8	21.2	100.0

Source: Court register.

Voluntary fire brigades still represent one-third of the nonprofits involved in social care. Most of these voluntary groups are extremely small and very few of them have regular meetings. They exist because they have some role in disaster prevention and get some support from the local governments, but the citizen involvement is very weak in their case. Some of their members are not even aware that they are registered as members.

Other voluntary associations of the social field are much more active both in advocacy, lobbying and in service provision. This makes it even more difficult to understand why these kinds of organizations are less efficient in creating foundations than the institutions of education or health care. The only exception is the field of child and youth welfare, where a significant number of foundations try to raise funds in order to finance services for the children and young people in need.

Table 5.11

Composition of nonprofit organizations in the field of social care in 1993 (%)

Field of activity	Foundations	Voluntary associations	Total
Child and youth welfare	11.0	1.2	12.2
Family services	1.4	3.8	5.2
Services for the handicapped	4.9	3.9	8.8
Services for the elderly	5.0	4.9	9.9
Self-help and other personal social services	8.5	3.5	12.0
Income support and maintenance	1.2	0.1	1.3
Other social services	13.7	2.6	16.3
Emergency prevention, relief and control	0.6	33.7	34.3
Total	46.3	53.7	100.0

Source: Court register.

Environmental groups and their members also seem to be less enthusiastic about the foundation form than most of the other nonprofits. Only one-third of the environmental organizations are foundations. Half of these foundations have several different purposes, one-third of them are involved in the conservation and protection of natural resources. By contrast, the majority of the voluntary associations are involved in the environmental beautification of cities and villages. The share of organizations dealing with animal protection is insignificant both among foundations and among voluntary associations (see Table 5.12).

The new political regime does not like the environmental movement very much (probably no more than the former one), but – given its democratic character – it cannot afford to ban organizations, it has to compromise with them. In fact, the Ministry of Environment and several local governments even support some of the environmental groups (Pálfalvi, 1993. pp. 7–8). If there are more conflicts (Sólyom, 1985; Szabó, 1993) between the environmental movements and different levels of the government than is typical in health and social care or education (definitely not more than in the field of advocacy), it is partly balanced by the more significant foreign patronage which makes ecological nonprofits less dependent on domestic support. Despite the internal conflicts between different streams of the environmental movement, its organizations are hopefully on their way to becoming an integral part of the Hungarian nonprofit sector.

Table 5.12

Composition of nonprofit organizations in the field of environment protection in 1993 (%)

Field of activity	Foundations	Voluntary associations	Total
Natural resources conservation and protection	11.5	11.7	23.2
Environmental beautification	4.3	38.3	42.6
Animal protection	3.8	2.4	6.2
Other environmental organizations	15.1	12.9	28.0
Total	34.7	65.3	100.0

Source: Court register.

The shift of political regime was more important for the civic associations than for other institutions of the nonprofit sector. Under state socialism most of them could survive only by dis-guising themselves. Usually the declared field of activity (mostly culture, sometimes hobby or environment) served as the mask they wore to hide their real identity (Heit and Vidra Szabó, 1992; Jagasics, 1992). The political changes, the growing respect for the institutions of civil society offered a choice to these organizations (see Table 5.13). They could decide which of their activities were really important. Many of the formerly disguised civic associa-tions changed their self-definition. There are several organizations which were registered (for example) as ethnic dance groups or multipurpose cultural and arts organizations before 1989, and now describe themselves as civic associations, ethnic associations or even civil rights groups. (This does not necessarily mean that they don't dance any more: names and self-definitions change more easily than the mix of activities.)

Table 5.13

Composition of nonprofit organizations in the field of civil rights and advocacy in 1993 (%)

Field of activity	Foundations	Voluntary associations	Total
Civil rights	8.2	60.7	68.9
Consumer protection	0.6	4.7	5.3
Other civic and advocacy organizations	4.3	21.5	25.8
Total	13.1	86.9	100.0

Source: Court register.

Nevertheless, the growing number of civic associations can hardly be explained by these shifts of identity. There are hundreds of newly created organizations in this field. Their activities are not necessarily narrower than those of their predecessors (a great deal of them combine advocacy work with service provision), but they are much more self-confident and therefore probably more appropriate actors of the slowly developing civil society.

The overwhelming majority of nonprofits classified as civic and advocacy organizations are voluntary associations. Most of them are involved in the civil rights movement and try to protect the interests of ethnic or religious minorities and other groups of the population which think they are somehow discriminated against. Understandably enough, consumer protection is underdeveloped. During the honeymoon with the market economy Hungarians did not have the idea that they needed protection as consumers. More recently, they are starting to realize its necessity and to establish consumers' organizations.

In short, whichever special fields of the Hungarian nonprofit sector come under scrutiny, we always find that they have not fully developed yet. More than two-thirds of the voluntary organizations are below the minimum income level which would allow them to have at least one employee. Consequently, they are quite vulnerable, most exposed to the cuts of direct public support and tax allowances or other changes in their legal and economic regulation. This vulnerability greatly increases the responsibility of the government and the importance of government policy towards the nonprofit sector.

Chapter 6

GOVERNMENT POLICY TOWARDS THE NONPROFIT SECTOR

Overall posture of the government

If I had to characterize the overall posture of the Hungarian government towards nonprofit organizations with just one word, I would vacillate between ambiguous and ambivalent. There are several explicit and implicit government policies influencing the nonprofit sector and they definitely lack consistency. So does the general attitude of government authorities towards nonprofits.

After forty years of state socialism, Hungarian society (Fricz, 1990), the political parties (Heller *et al.* 1992), and consequently government declarations as well, set an exceptionally high value on individual rights, on the freedom of association and on the development of civil society. They all use the same terms, but the interpretation significantly varies throughout parties and government bodies. Although there is a general agreement concerning the importance of citizens' rights and citizens' autonomy, the political parties have different priorities. As far as the former government parties are concerned, the citizen as a patriot is favoured by the Hungarian Democratic Forum; church controlled citizens' movements are especially welcomed by the Christian Democratic People's Party; while the citizen is almost synonymous with the bourgeois in the ideology of the Smallholder Party. The position of the present government parties is somewhat different. While emphasizing the importance of citizens' rights, the Socialist Party expects citizens to respect collective interests. The Free Democrats provide a focus for human rights and the autonomy of citizens. (Heller *et al.*, 1992, pp. 30–6 and 39–40). These differences are only slightly reflected in the general vocabulary of political declarations, but they leave their mark on the practical policy developed by the parties and various ministries.

126

It is quite remarkable that the "associational revolution" (Sala-mon, 1993) does not seem to alarm the government. Although it is not always happy with the criticism coming from the voluntary sector (there are lots of conflicts about environmental issues, social security matters, legal and political questions, economic mea-sures, etc.), these conflicts have not led the government to deny the importance or to try to limit the scope of action of the civic organizations. There is a general agreement (at least in principle) that the voluntary sector has to fulfil a series of essential functions of the civil society. The head of the Parliamentary Committee for the Support of Voluntary Organizations (a member of the Hun-garian Democratic Forum, which was the ruling party at that time) met general agreement when he declared: "We all intend to promote the civil society, its development is in the centre of our efforts" (Naplótöredékek, 1993, p. 26).

Partial as it is (see Table 4.17), the information we have on direct government support still seems to prove that government funding of nonprofit organizations is in line with the generally supportive government posture towards nonprofits. The steadily growing subsidies show that in transparent situations, when they have to decide on direct support to nonprofits, both politicians and gov-ernment bureaucrats act in accordance with the considerations which were formulated at a meeting of the Hungarian Parliament:

> We attach great importance to the free initiatives of free citizens, to voluntary organizations and to the institutions of the civil society because we think they are essential elements of a fully developed democracy. Voluntary associations have to develop the organizational framework in which the voluntary work of citizens can solve social problems in cheaper and more efficient ways than the government could do. Therefore state support to these voluntary organizations – at least in the beginning – is absolutely necessary.

(Naplótöredékek etc., 1993, p. 26)

The institutional forms of promoting the civil society have not developed yet, but there are initiatives which aim to build the mechanisms of cooperation between the government and the civic organizations. In the above mentioned Parliamentary Committee for the Support of Voluntary Organizations one of the members (an MP of the Hungarian Socialist Party) suggested that the Parlia-ment should create a special body which would be a consultative forum for the representatives of the civil society and those of the government and the political elite (Naplótöredékek, 1993, p. 26). A similar body, a Consultative City Forum, has already been established by a city government in South Hungary (Füredi, 1993, p. 31). All the local civic associations are invited to participate in the work of the Forum which can develop recommendations for the city government, but its main function is to ensure the continuous communication and exchange of information between the local civil society and the political elite.

Of course, similar initiatives are much more usual on the part of the civic associations. Many of them expressed their intention to build regular communication with the public authorities and political decision making bodies. The newly elected Parliament has started to develop some "lobby-lists", i.e. lists of voluntary organizations which have to be consulted before decisions are made.

In short, on the surface, at the level of declarations the overall posture of the national government towards voluntary organizations is quite favourable, supportive and cooperative in Hungary. This general posture is based on two different reasons. One is the commitment to democratic principles and the conviction that the institutions of civil society are constituent parts of any democracy. The other is the complete failure of the overcentralized Hungarian welfare system and the need for any help from any social actor in solving social problems and meeting people's demand for welfare services.

The position of local governments towards nonprofit organizations does not diverge from that of the national government to a significant extent in Hungary. They welcome service providing nonprofits which help them to meet the needs of welfare services; appreciate the role played by voluntary associations in strengthening the local community, but dislike civic organizations which criticize them too sharply. The main difference between the positions of the national and local governments has its roots in the fact that local governments are not directly interested in increasing the tax revenues of the central budget. Their overall posture towards nonprofits is similar to that of the substantive ministries. They work under serious financial constraints, they have to solve lots of difficult problems. Therefore, it always represents some relief to them if some of their duties are undertaken (or partly undertaken) by the local nonprofits. As the mayor of a small town (who

donated half of his one year salary to a local charitable foundation) points out: "It's obvious that this foundation alone will not
solve all the social problems of the town, but can be of great help"
(Sebestyén, 1993, p. 12).

Given their critical budget situation, local governments desperately need additional funds, therefore they establish foundations
which seem to be appropriate means of fund raising. In one of his
interviews the deputy mayor of Budapest is very clear about the
role of these foundations: "The establishment of foundations by
ministries and local governments is reasonable only if these foundations can attract private, corporate and foreign donations"
(Gyergyói, 1991, p. 6). Local governments establish foundations
mainly in order to facilitate the fulfilment of their basic duties.
These foundations do not seem to be alternative or avant-garde
institutions. Their main role is to attract private funds to the local
government budgets.

The figures in Table 4.16 can lead us to a similar conclusion. The
local government support of the foundations is almost negligible
(less then 4 per cent of the total government support of foundations). These two facts, the obvious enthusiasm in establishing
foundations and the limited willingness to financially support
them, suggest that local governments want to (or need to) play the
role of beneficiaries and not that of patrons or donors.

The figures of the support for voluntary associations seem to
imply a somewhat different relationship. Voluntary associations
get about 13 per cent of their state support from the local governments. This share is not high, but still shows that local governments are willing to cooperate with the voluntary organizations of
the local community. The "civil society ethos" is present, then, at
least in this segment of the local voluntary sector, whereas the
pragmatic and utilitarian approach seems to be dominant in the
foundation–local government relationship.

Contradictions and divisions within the government on the policy towards the nonprofit sector

Public authorities are well aware of the necessity to modernize
and restructure the provision of welfare services (Ferge, 1989;

Gayer *et al.*, 1992), creating a new partnership between the public, nonprofit and for-profit organizations (Lévai and Széman, 1993). It is common knowledge that this restructuring will not be possible without public assistance because most of the assets are publicly owned and the purchasing power of private consumers is very limited. The intensive government participation in funding nonprofit organizations and the indirect support of the sector through tax regulation is based on the conviction that nonprofit organizations must play a very important role in the modern three sector economy. In some economic programmes they are also mentioned as possible means of the denationalization of state property.

One of the main problems of the East European privatization process is to find the possible owners and the feasible mechanisms of the distribution of the former state property (Major, 1992). The idea of donating some part of the state property to nonprofit organizations is not new in Hungary, but initially it was sharply opposed by the leading economists (Kornai, 1989). Thanks to a series of analytical debates and to a great deal of bitter experience of how privatization occurs if it is left at the mercy of market forces, a general agreement has been developing on the possible ownership role of nonprofit organizations. Even the most famous former opponent, Kornai (1991) argues that nonprofit organizations as shareholders of formerly state owned enterprises can meet both the efficiency criteria and the social requirements (the necessity of the "embourgeoisement", the distributive–ethical considerations). Some economists (e.g. Tardos, 1992) are fairly optimistic, others (e.g. Stark, 1991) are more sceptical about the future economic behaviour of the nonprofit shareholders, but the idea that they can play this owners' role has become generally accepted.

Unfortunately, the general understanding of the social, political and economic importance of nonprofit organizations does not necessarily result in a comprehensive government policy towards nonprofits. The explicit, publicly expressed policy of the Hungarian government is rather supportive, but the practical measures and the implicit policies are somewhat contradictory. This inconsistency is explained by several factors:

● Both democracy and liberal economic principles are relatively new in Hungary. The tradition of paternalism and centralized political structure is very strong. Although most of the Hungarian citizens (including government officials) are in favour of the democratic transition, only a few of them expect that these changes will solve the problems of the country in the short run (Bruszt and Simon, 1992). This distrust of democracy as a vehicle of problem-solving, the government proposals on the economic regulation of the nonprofit sector and many small elements of our interviews with politicians and government officials reveal that centralization tendencies are still alive, if not in government declarations, but definitely in the instinctive reactions of some politicians and public officials.

- The political tradition of centralization, coupled with the legal tradition originating from the German legal system makes public law institutions especially attractive for the Hungarian legislators. The euphoria of the political changes produced a very liberal nonprofit regulation, but there have been repeated attempts to regain control over the nonprofit organizations and replace really independent nonprofit forms by rigorously state controlled public law institutions since then.

- The Hungarian government is caught in a "fiscal trap" (Kornai, 1992) and faces a serious dilemma. The budget deficit is extremely high, the rate of economic growth is negative, the social problems (poverty, unemployment, etc.) are increasing. The government would need more tax revenues in order to finance public welfare services and to directly support non-profit service providers. At the same time, the tax burden should be decreased in order to encourage investment, foster economic growth and to give tax incentives to the nonprofit providers of welfare services.

- There are serious ethical problems in the nonprofit sector. The fraudulent behaviour of some foundations has come to light and ruined the reputation of nonprofit organizations. Some enterprises and private entrepreneurs have established non-profit organizations in order to avoid paying taxes. Many of the foundations created by public institutions or by their clients are also tax shelters disguising service fees as tax deductible donations. Due to the strong tradition of the second economy and the traditionally disharmonious state–citizen relationship (Anheier and Seibel, 1992; Kuti, 1993), public opinion is not

unanimous in the condemnation of tax avoidance and fraudulent behaviour. According to an opinion poll (Manchin and
Nagy, 1991a), 44 per cent of the interviewees think that tax
abuse is not immoral. Nevertheless, the government is supposed to do something about tax evasion. Fiscal authorities
which are most interested in increasing tax revenues can use
foundation scandals as a pretext for reducing or completely
abolishing tax advantages.

- On the other hand, the nonprofit welfare services are considered to be possible substitutes for the declining public services.
Since nonprofit service provision and the establishment of
foundations became legal, numerous nonprofit organizations
have been created in order to meet the unsatisfied demand or
at least to alleviate the shortage. Most of these new organizations are fund-raising agencies or foundations supporting the
service providing public institutions, but some service providing nonprofit organizations have also been established. These
services seem to be of crucial importance in solving the growing social problems. Additional resources which can be
attracted to the field of welfare services by the nonprofit organizations are desperately needed. Consequently, the government can hardly afford to renounce them, or to discourage
people from charitable donations by cutting the tax advantages. Our interviews show that most of the government bodies
which are responsible for the provision of public services
understand this aspect of the problem and try to act in order to
defend the preferential tax treatment of the nonprofit organizations against the financial authorities.

- Government officials playing some role in forming government
policy towards the non-profit field can also have their political
and personal motivations. They found the donation of state
property to nonprofit organizations close to the ruling parties
especially attractive in the second half of their rule when it was
quite probable that the representatives of the government would
loose their redistributive power and get into precarious positions
after the elections. Some "government foundations" literally
scandalized both the general public and the oppositional parties
(Soós, 1993). These scandals had several negative impacts on the
nonprofit sector. One of them was the strange development that
the leading liberal parties became fervent supporters of the intro-

duction of public law foundations into the Hungarian legal system. The Federation of Young Democrats even suggested that all foundations established by the government should be obliged to change their legal form and to become public law foundations (*Az Országgyűlés* etc., 1993, p. 40).

The above overview of the factors explaining the inconsistency of the government policy towards nonprofit organizations can also help us to specify the divisions within the national government on the question of the role of the nonprofit sector and the appropriate policy towards it in Hungary. These divisions are as follows:

Division between the economic approach and that of the substantive ministries

The conflict is very simple here: the substantive ministries are responsible for providing the citizens with welfare services. They do their best to get as much support from the government budget as possible, but they realize that this support is not enough, it is even decreasing, so they welcome the nonprofit organizations which are ready to provide services or to raise funds for the public institutions. (A large part of the Hungarian foundations were established by the government or by the public institutions in order to help public schools, universities, hospitals, nursing homes, shelters, research institutes, theatres, orchestras, museums, libraries, etc.)

Since the substantive ministries are interested in providing services, the quality and availability of these services have a clear priority for them over the economic considerations. They do not care too much about the overall costs (including the lost tax revenues of the central budget) or the efficiency of the nonprofit service provision.

On the other hand, government agencies responsible for the overall performance of the economy are more concerned about the lack of information on the size and efficiency of the direct and indirect support going to the nonprofit sector, and about the poor accountability of the nonprofit organizations. For lack of comprehensive data, they have the feeling that abuse is more frequent in the nonprofit sector than in other parts of the economy. Their reaction is a diffuse suspicion and sometimes even hostility towards the nonprofit organizations. Unfortunately, this suspicion very rarely raises intentions and efforts to really understand the nonprofit phenomenon and to develop a more comprehensive regulation of it. It is definitely simpler to say what was actually said by the director of the State Property Agency: "Nonprofit organizations can play only a marginal role because this kind of institution is a foreign body in the present Hungarian economy and society. It lacks just the merits (the well defined full responsibility and trustworthiness) which are most needed in the privatization process." The president of the Internal Revenue Service put it similarly: "I don't think that we can find solutions for the nonprofit organizations while the problems of the state run institutions are not solved." (Both of them were interviewed by Ildikó Gyergyói.)

Division within the economic approaches, inside the Ministry of Finances

The approaches of different departments of the Ministry of Finances are not uniform, either. There are "substantive" departments again which are responsible for the "expenditure side" of the state budget. The economists working on the problems of financing culture, education, health care, social care, etc. are well aware of the deep problems of these fields. They are in favour of supporting the nonprofit service providers because they think this is still the cheapest way to compensate (at least partly) for the shrinking public welfare services.

In contrast, the Taxation Department of the Ministry of Finances wants to increase the tax revenues at any price. After limiting the tax exemption of nonprofits' business income and having set conditions for the tax deductibility of donations, it is trying right now to seriously limit the tax deductibility.

The division between the substantive departments and the Taxation Department of the Ministry was very spectacular in the first case. The Taxation Department managed to pass a law changing the formerly very advantageous tax treatment of the nonprofit sector. The tax law which came into force in January 1992 ordered that the business income of nonprofit organizations would be tax exempt only if it does not exceed 10 per cent of their whole income (but not more than HUF 10 million). The tax law panicked the service-providing nonprofits because the share of their fee income was normally much higher than 10 per cent. They argued that the loss of tax exemption would prevent them from service provision. They could not convince the Taxation Department, but the substantive departments of the Ministry of Finances understood the problem. Their answer was a government decree which declared that the nonprofit service provision in the fields of preventive medicine, health care, scientific and technical research, environment protection, protection of the cultural heritage, education, culture, sport, religion, public security, care of the elderly, the poor, national and ethnic minorities and the refugees is not a business activity, thus the income from the service fees is not business income, consequently it is not subject to taxation.

Division between the Ministry of Justice, the substantive ministries and the Ministry of Finances

As I have already mentioned, the legal profession in Hungary is deeply influenced by the German legal system. In contrast, the American influence is quite strong among Hungarian economists, especially among experts dealing with financial and fiscal problems. The division between the two approaches is reflected in some competition between the Ministry of Justice and the Ministry of Finances in the regulation of the nonprofit sector. While the Ministry of Justice is eager to develop legal schemes in order to more closely control nonprofit organizations, the Ministry of Finances clearly prefers keeping a more liberal approach at the price of cutting the sector's tax advantages.

Besides these main divisions, one can detect a large variety of different policies towards nonprofits throughout the ministries. The means of these policies are mostly the different forms of direct supports, donations, subsidies and contracts. Political influence and personal motivations obviously play an important role in the formation of these policies, but it would be extremely difficult to analyse them because the process is very poorly documented. Decisions are frequently made by a limited number of ministry leaders, the minutes of government meetings which approve or reject ministry proposals concerning the establishment of foundations are not always open to the public (Harsányi, 1993; Soós, 1993).

The analysis of these more or less hidden policies towards nonprofits would be extremely interesting, but a special survey would have to be carried out in order to gather the necessary information. Since it would be far beyond the scope of the present study, I must confine myself to the general statement that the government policy towards nonprofits is a complicated set of particular and somewhat contradictory policies developed by different government bodies. This confused conglomeration of civil society rhetoric and tightening state control; liberal economic and etatist legal approaches; establishment of large government foundations, increasing direct subsidies and shrinking tax advantages leaves us with the impression that we are witnessing a learning process. The Hungarian government – just like the Hungarian society at large and the Hungarian nonprofit community itself – has to develop new strategies and new behavioural patterns which are appropriate in a democracy. It will take a lot of time and a great deal of effort. The development of a comprehensive policy towards the nonprofit sector can be expected only as a result of this learning process.

The philosophy and principles that lie behind government policy towards the nonprofit sector changed dramatically in 1989 when the "one party" political system and "one sector" economy collapsed in Hungary. Building political pluralism, democracy, civil society and market economy became the new aim of the society and its political leaders. Although sociologists (Anheier and Seibel, 1992; Hankiss, 1989; Konrád and Szelényi, 1991; Szelényi, 1992) are undoubtedly right when they point out the importance of the "status quo ante", the far reaching social consequences of the pattern of state–society relationship prior to the transformation, one can hardly deny the seriousness of the shift in philosophy and ideology.

The Hungarian society and government have to face major challenges, to repair severe errors, to find a way between deep abysses towards a politically democratic, economically efficient system. Both stakes and risks are enormous. Politicians and government officials may sometimes relapse into the old paternalistic and authoritarian habits, people may behave as subordinates or vassals instead of acting as self-confident citizens, but the major features of the government–citizen relationship have significantly changed. Hungary has a legitimate government now which is supposed to consider its citizens and their autonomous organizations as partners. None of the governing or oppositional parties would dare to openly question this principle.

After decades of mutual distrust and repeated conflicts, cooperation has become the leading principle in the government–nonprofit relationship.

Nonprofit organizations as vehicles of policy

Nonprofit organizations have been playing extremely important roles in introducing, shaping and implementing social policies in Hungary since the mid-1980s. We can differentiate roughly three approaches and methods used by nonprofits when they behave as actors rather than objects of policy formulation. They are as follows:

- *Problem-solving approach.* Provision of alternative and innovative or simply missing services; prosaic, everyday advocacy.
- *Responsive, reactionary approach.* Feedback on government proposals; defensive, protective advocacy.
- *Dynamic, creative approach.* Challenging, original initiatives; farsighted, provident advocacy.

The problem-solving approach

Foreign observers are often surprised and disappointed by the prevalence of the pragmatic, problem-solving approach in Hungary. It is worth citing a longer paragraph from 6 (1993, p. 31) who tries to compare the British and the Hungarian attitudes:

> I interviewed one executive of a large and influential British foundation ... who told me: A charitable foundation making a judgement on a particular application can clearly draw the line by asking, 'Are we replacing state funding? ... Has this been funded up till now by a local authority or central government?', because if it has, we ain't going to take over it ...
>
> While the sector in the UK devoted much of its energy available for anxiety to the problem that it is being pressed to substitute for the state, but lacks capacity to do so, the agenda of "privatization" (in a very broad sense of the word) of services in countries such as Hungary is creating concerns among foundations which are quite the reverse of these.
>
> I interviewed one foundation executive in Budapest in April 1993 positively trying to take over a service from a state hospital, who firmly

believed that the only chance for securing funding for a particular emergency service was for foundations to take it over, and to bring philanthropic money and contracts from other parts of the public sector. I raised the issue with him, that he might be giving signals to state treasury officials that large slabs of the health service could be closed down, and abandoned to their financial fate in the philanthropic sector. He shrugged and said, "Look, I'm just trying to help prematurely born babies, and this is the only way to do it." The risk of longer term negative consequences was simply not an issue for him.

The attitude of the interviewed foundation executive is quite typical in the Hungarian nonprofit sector, but does not necessarily reflect the neglect of long-term consequences. The same behaviour can be interpreted in a very different way, as well. Hungarian citizens and their organizations have learned that they have to be extremely active and pragmatic if they want to solve problems. The authoritarian regimes of the last centuries (and not just the last decades) left very little room for open policy advocacy. There were only very short periods in Hungarian history, when voluntary movements could freely and efficiently influence legislation and government policy. More often, the police and not the policy makers paid attention to these movements.

As a consequence, the relatively well tolerated and definitely more efficient pragmatic "problem-solving" approach is held in high esteem in Hungary. The underlying considerations are reflected in a frequently cited proverb: "Help yourself and God will help you!" (Significantly enough, there is nothing about government in the proverb.)

The conclusion citizens seem to draw from the history of welfare services and from the most recent experiences is that practical achievements are more convincing than petitions, demonstrations and theoretical arguments. They start to provide services even when they are aware that philanthropic sources will not be sufficient. One of their purposes is indeed to solve the problem at least partially, but they also have in mind that making needs explicit is a possible method of advocacy. When they face the government with a fait accompli, they know that it is much more difficult to let a service-providing voluntary organization go bankrupt and thus stop the provision of an already existing service than simply not to start providing new services.

Hungarians have learnt that their service-providing voluntary organizations can act as policy makers if they are able to smartly combine lobbying and service provision. An abundance of examples (nonprofit psychiatric hospital for children, shelters for homeless and for victims of family abuse, school for drop-out children, "job-exchange" for unemployed people, etc.) show that these service-providing nonprofits are able to attract significant government support. In the beginning it is sometimes only indirect state funding (through tax deductible donations), but in the longer run many of the nonprofit service providers can get government contracts and other direct subsidies, as well.

In short, one of the possible (and probably the most frequently used) methods of the nonprofits' participation in introducing, shaping and implementing policies is to act as "alternative policy makers", without paying much attention to the difficulties to be overcome. The Hungarian experiences (Gádoros, 1992; Gayer *et al.*, 1992) suggest that this "problem-solving" approach can be quite fruitful, can efficiently influence the decisions of the "professional policy makers", and can result in some kind of social control of the changes in the welfare mix. A great advantage of this method is that it can be used even in an underdeveloped democracy. This is very important in Hungary which is quite far from being a fully developed democracy.

Responsive, reactionary approach

Nonprofits as alternative policy makers naturally cannot substitute for voluntary organizations which are trying to control and influence government policy in a more direct way. This civil control of government action is of crucial importance. Voluntary organizations which engage in this kind of advocacy still take some risk in Hungary. Their activity was much more dangerous before the political changes. Nevertheless, one of the most famous examples dates back to the 1980s when the protest against the construction of a huge water plant on the Danube started (Szabó, 1993). This protest movement was called the Danube Circle, its members were called "Blues". The leaders and activists of the Danube Circle were fully committed to the issues of the movement and devoted a lot of their time to organizing it. They disseminated information materials to the wider public in order to gain financial support and signatures against the water plant.

They managed to convince a lot of people and used this mass support to influence public opinion and politics. The movement was successful in some sense: it could not convince the last communist government, but the newly elected democratic Parliament voted against the construction of the water plant in 1990.

Similar initiatives were extremely rare in Hungary before 1989, but they have become quite an ordinary phenomenon after the political changes. There are lots of protests organized by voluntary organizations, trade unions, interest groups, sometimes even by the business community against additional taxes, industrial–technological projects, pollution, discriminative government measures, etc. One can hear and read about single-issue movements based on local conflicts every day. The nonprofit umbrella organizations themselves are also involved in organizing a protest against the planned restrictions on the tax deductibility of donations.

Despite the numerous examples of this defensive, protective advocacy, there is a general feeling among nonprofits that they are not well informed enough, not organized enough, not prepared enough to be really successful in controlling government actions. The service-oriented, multipurpose character of most of the Hungarian voluntary organizations is becoming an obstacle to the professional advocacy work in some cases. Even the responsive, ensuing approach of shaping government policy is very demanding, time and money consuming. If nonprofit organizations want to influence government policy, they must follow the political debates, get access to the different proposals, be knowledgeable about the relationships, keep contacts with politicians, government officials and other nonprofit organizations, be prepared to analyse the newly emerging issues and to start action at any moment when it is necessary.

These considerations lay behind the decision of several nonprofit umbrella organizations when they created a nonprofit information centre which is supposed to be – amongst other things – a basis for the advocacy activities.

The dynamic, creative approach

Some of the nonprofit leaders also argue that the responsive, ensuing advocacy should be supplemented by a more dynamic, more creative approach. They think that the voluntary organizations should not wait for government initiatives in the fields where they can develop their own concepts and policy proposals. As the institutions of a developing civil society, nonprofits have their right not only to criticize and control government programmes, but also to raise questions, suggest solutions and strategies. If they want to be accepted as partners by the government they cannot afford to confine themselves to playing a passive, inferior role. They have to take the initiative in many fields where their members and supporters are knowledgeable enough and the citizens are likely to support the nonprofit proposals.

This approach is only feasible if nonprofit organizations are able to increase the professional level of their activities. Another necessary condition is the more stable and more efficient communication and cooperation within the voluntary sector. Some nonprofit leaders have serious doubts about the chance of success of similar initiatives at the present level of development of the Hungarian nonprofit sector.

Nevertheless, we can mention some examples of this dynamic, creative approach, as well, though their number is significantly smaller than that of the former two types of action. Two voluntary associations (the League for Civil Rights and the National Federation of Former Tenants who have bought their originally state-owned flats) initiated the preparation of a law on the rights of people's communities. They have undertaken responsibility for preparing the first draft of the law proposal. Another civic association called the "Magistracy of Budavár" decided to discuss the problems and developmental perspectives of their neighbourhood and to produce new concepts which can help in the formulation of local strategies.

In short, despite its relatively new independence, the Hungarian voluntary sector has made very impressive efforts in order to influence government policy. There is reason to believe that nonprofit organizations are on the right way, they are hopefully becoming a significant force in shaping government policy in Hungary.

Current policy issues

In order to identify the most important issues in the nonprofit sector, we interviewed twenty-nine leading experts of the nonprofit sector in Hungary, including representatives of government ministries and departments, representatives of major political parties, leaders of nonprofit organizations and their umbrella groups, journalists and researchers specialized in the nonprofit field. In selecting interviewees, we tried to cover the major policy actors as well as the central representatives of the nonprofit sector (See Appendix A for their list).

The interviews consisted of two parts: a rather informal discussion of the problems and challenges faced by the nonprofit sector and a more formalized part, when interviewees were asked to rank issues confronting the sector. The "informal" discussion was guided by the following set of questions:

1 How would you characterize the present social, economic and political roles played by the foundations and voluntary associations in Hungary? Are these roles important? Is their importance increasing? Is such an increase desirable?
2 What are the possible fields of activities of nonprofit organizations? Are there problems which should be solved exclusively by the nonprofit sector? Are there fields where only the government agencies are likely to be efficient enough in providing welfare services? Where is cooperation necessary between the nonprofit and government sectors?
3 How viable are the Hungarian nonprofit organizations providing services in the fields of education, health and social care, etc.? What is the market like for these services; is there enough demand for nonprofit services? Do nonprofit organizations need and deserve government support?
4 If yes, which are the most reasonable and most efficient ways of supporting them:
   - lump sum subsidies,
   - grants,
   - statutory transfers,
   - third party payments,
   - contracts,
   - donating property.
5 Should the nonprofit sector be among the beneficiaries of the denationalization programme? Would it be reasonable and desirable to give some part of the formerly state owned property to the nonprofit organizations? If yes, how much and in which way:

- Should service providing nonprofits get the buildings and facilities they need in order to develop their services?
- Should they also receive stocks and shares?

What would be the impact of the emergence of nonprofits as shareholders on the Hungarian stock market?

6 How important was the role of the citizens' organizations and associations in the political transition? Did they influence the results of the parliamentary and the local elections? What do you expect – will this impact increase or decrease on the next elections?

7 What do you think about the present state of the Hungarian nonprofit sector? What are its main problems? How can these problems be solved?

8 The new legal and economic regulation of the nonprofit sector is under preparation. How do you feel about this process? Do you think it is all right? Is there any element of the law proposals you are worried about? What would you change in the present nonprofit regulation?

9 Does your organization have any policy towards the nonprofit sector? Do you think it should develop such a policy?

10 Can you identify any foreign influence on the development of the Hungarian nonprofit sector?

11 The growth of the nonprofit sector has been amazing for the last couple of years in Hungary. The number of its organizations has almost quadrupled since 1989. How can you explain this really fast development? What do you think about the future of the sector?

The answers we have received from the interviewed politicians, government officials, foundation leaders and heads of the nonprofit umbrella organizations are summarized in Table 6.1.

However, there is an important problem which cannot be listed in our tables: this is the general level of awareness about the nature, characteristics, problems and difficulties of the nonprofit sector.

The experiences of the interviews suggest that this level is shamefully low among the politicians and government officials who do not deal directly with the nonprofit sector. They don't really understand the differences between the nonprofit and the public sectors, don't have any understanding of the boundaries between the third sector and the world of politics, show very limited sensitivity to the delicate nature of the present situation of nonprofits. This ignorance was accompanied by apologies, arrogance or embarrassment according to the personality of the interviewees. The answers they gave to our open questions were not much help for the policy analysis.

Table 6.1

Ranking of issues confronting the nonprofit sector in Hungary based on twenty-nine interviews with political, government and nonprofit leaders (%)

Issue	Low			High		N/A
			Importance			
	1	2	3	4	5	
A Government policies						
1 Tax treatment of private giving	7	3	24	17	49	0
2 Legal status of nonprofit organizations	3	17	17	28	35	0
3 Reductions in government support	7	3	28	24	35	3
4 Changes in forms of government support	10	10	32	24	24	0
5 Extent of government control	14	17	31	14	17	7
6 Policies on nonprofit/ for-profit competition	21	14	10	14	24	17
7 Government social policies	3	0	21	24	49	3
8 Regional integration (EC)	28	14	17	14	7	20
B Other funding						
9 Extent of private giving	0	14	17	24	45	0
10 Extent and character of corporate giving	0	7	27	38	28	0
11 Competition from for-profits	38	14	21	3	0	24
12 Fee income	10	24	14	28	14	10
13 Sales and other business income	3	3	21	38	28	7
14 Other funding problems	10	3	32	17	24	14
15 Volunteer recruitment	7	7	38	24	21	3
C Management and personnel						
16 Personnel recruitment/ management	7	14	14	24	38	3

Issue	Low			High		N/A
			Importance			
	1	**2**	**3**	**4**	**5**	
17 Staff compensation	7	0	38	17	38	0
18 Professionalization	14	10	20	28	21	7
19 Staff training	7	3	24	31	35	0
20 Tension between advocacy and service provision	7	14	20	24	11	24
21 Legal problems (e.g. liability)	10	3	35	21	24	7
22 Accountability within the nonprofit sector	14	3	14	28	38	3
D Other						
23 Regional, religious and ethnic conflicts	41	14	21	10	7	7
24 Political instability	17	24	17	28	11	3
25 Ideological/political attacks on nonprofits	17	17	24	35	4	3
26 Independence from churches	28	14	37	14	7	0
27 Independence from business	14	21	27	17	14	7
28 Extent of service to the poor	7	3	38	14	31	7
29 Ethical issues	14	21	13	28	24	0
30 Research	14	3	25	41	17	0
31 Independence from political parties and labour unions	0	10	24	21	38	7
32 User and client control	31	21	13	10	11	14

This ignorance is all the more dangerous because these government officials have significant impact on the proposals and government measures influencing the nonprofit sector, these MPs will vote on the bills which are likely to be decisive for the near future of the nonprofit sector. The main benefit of the interviews they gave us is probably that they had to think about the issues confronting the nonprofit sector.

On the other hand, the other half of our interviewees were the people (nonprofit leaders, government officials working on the forthcoming nonprofit regulation or closely cooperating with nonprofits in their field) who are best informed and most sensible about the problems of the nonprofit sector.

Table 6.2

Ranking of issues confronting the nonprofit sector in Hungary based on a sample survey of nonprofit organizations (%)

Problems	Not important	Somewhat important	Very important
Inadequate private funding	9.7	37.7	52.6
Inadequate government support	9.1	22.6	68.3
Reliance on fee income	25.3	30.1	44.6
Reliance on business income	36.8	28.4	34.8
Decreasing interest rates	70.5	12.8	16.7
Excessive dependence on government	74.4	14.1	11.5
Difficulties recruiting able staff	67.1	13.2	19.7
Low salaries and benefits	33.9	25.9	40.2
Excessive professionalization of staff	63.0	19.2	17.8
Difficulties recruiting volunteers	20.8	42.5	36.7
Difficulties managing volunteers	54.4	31.2	14.4
Tax laws do not encourage enough giving	9.5	26.0	64.5
Excessive government regulation	17.0	27.1	55.9
Political pressure	69.4	15.3	15.3
Dealing with supra-national governments	83.6	11.9	4.5
Lack of clear policy direction	37.0	21.6	41.4
Restrictions on policy advocacy	37.1	33.6	29.3
Competition from for-profit businesses	47.4	23.7	28.9
Limited public awareness of the agency	27.2	38.7	34.1
Ethics issues	45.0	26.4	28.6
Political instability	69.0	17.2	13.8
Minority problems	75.0	10.4	14.6
Prejudices	42.8	27.5	29.7

To analyse these two sets of answers together raises a methodological question which I cannot solve because the sample is not large enough for the separate analysis. What I can do is to be extremely careful and cautious about the interpretation of the results. Fortunately, in our sample survey of the nonprofit sector we also asked the opinion of nonprofit leaders and managers about the issues confronting the nonprofit sector. Although both the lists of problems and the methods of ranking were different, the survey data (Table 6.2) still can help us to verify the interview results and to explore the differences and similarities between the evaluation of the problems by the "ordinary" nonprofit managers and by the most influential policy makers and top leaders of the nonprofit sector.

Private giving

Both the share of the "very important" answers and the average scores show that the number one issue confronting the Hungarian nonprofit sector is that of private giving.

The growth of the Hungarian nonprofit sector has come about for many reasons, but independent citizen action has been of crucial importance, especially in the establishment and support of nonprofit organizations as alternatives to the state-run institutions. Poor as they are, Hungarians are unexpectedly generous with donations to nonprofit organizations. As we have already seen in Chapter 5, both the number of donors and the amount of donations have increased steeply for the last three years. Nevertheless, the low and stagnating income level is likely to limit the further increase of private donations seriously. Our interviewees think (and nonprofit managers agree with them), that the planned restrictions on the tax deductibility of donations would discourage citizens from supporting foundations and this would represent a severe danger for the future of the Hungarian nonprofit sector. The score of the issue of corporate giving is almost as high as that of the individual giving for the same reasons (see Table 6.3).

Social policy

Surprisingly enough, the issue of the government's social policy hits exactly the same score as the problems of private giving. I tend to think that this is a bias which is explained by the fact that most of the politicians and government officials were unable to really evaluate the issues from the nonprofit sector's point of view. I don't mean, of course, that the social policy, or rather the lack of a comprehensive, far-sighted social policy is not important for the nonprofit sector, but I seriously doubt that it would be the most serious problem.

Table 6.3

Average score on issues confronting the nonprofit sector in Hungary
based on twenty-nine interviews with political, government and
nonprofit leaders and on a sample survey of nonprofit organizations

Issue	Average score	
	Survey	**Interviews**
A Government policies		
1 Tax laws do not encourage enough giving – tax treatment of private giving	4.1	4.0
2 Excessive government regulation – legal status of nonprofit organizations	3.8	3.7
3 Inadequate government support – reduction in government support	4.2	3.7
4 Changes in forms of government support	–	3.4
5 Excessive dependence on government – extent of government control	1.7	2.8
6 Policies on nonprofit/for-profit competition	–	2.6
7 Government social policies	–	4.0
8 Dealing with supranational governments – Regional integration (EU)	1.4	2.0
B Other funding		
9 Inadequate private funding – extent of private giving	3.9	4.0
10 Extent and character of corporate giving	–	3.9
11 Competition from for-profits	–	1.4
12 Reliance on fee income – Fee income	3.4	2.8
13 Reliance on business income – sales and other business income	3.0	3.6
14 Other funding problems	–	3.0
15 Volunteer recruitment	–	3.3
C Management and personnel		
16 Difficulties recruiting able staff – personnel recruitment/management	2.1	3.6
17 Low salaries and benefits – staff compensation	3.1	3.8
18 Excessive professionalization of staff – Professionalization	2.1	3.1
19 Staff training	–	3.8
20 Tension between advocacy and service provision	–	2.4

Issue	Average score	
	Survey	Interviews
21 Legal problems (e.g. liability)	–	3.2
22 Accountability within the sector	–	3.6
D. Other		
23 Minority problems – regional, religious and ethnic conflicts	1.9	2.1
24 Lack of clear policy direction – political instability	3.1	2.8
25 Ideological/political attacks on nonprofits	–	2.8
26 Independence from churches	–	2.6
27 Independence from business	–	2.8
28 Extent of service to the poor	–	3.4
29 Ethical issues	2.7	3.3
30 Research	–	3.4
31 Political pressure – Independence from political parties and labour unions	1.9	3.7
32 User and client control	–	2.1

Staff

The third highest score is that of the staff compensation and staff training issues. The score of the personnel recruitment/management problems is somewhat lower, but still quite high. This suggests that the professionalization of the nonprofit organizations is considered to be very important by politicians and top leaders of the sector. It is interesting that the nonprofit managers interviewed during the sample survey attached much less importance to the staff problems.

While nobody sees appropriate sources to improve staff compensation, the training issue is likely to be resolved in the short run. There are lots of different initiatives. The foreign help is exceptionally intensive in this field. The Hungarian nonprofits themselves and many for-profit entrepreneurs are also organizing training courses. Regular nonprofit management training has also started at all universities of economics of the country and at some other universities, too.

It is much more difficult to solve the staff payment and personnel recruitment problems because their origin is the lack of appropriate funds in the nonprofit sector. In order to attract well-trained, talented employees, the nonprofit organizations should offer decent salaries, and this brings us back to the financial problems.

Government support

The chronic shortage of funding produces a strange phenomenon among our interviewees. They attach great importance to the issue "Reductions in government support" (its average score is 3.7) although most of them are in the position to know that the overall government support of the nonprofit sector has been increasing. The high score here probably means that more government support would be necessary. The results of our sample survey seem to confirm this interpretation. The formulation of the question was different there, and 68 per cent of the interviewed nonprofit managers said that "inadequate government funding" was a very important problem of the nonprofit sector. Another 23 per cent found this problem important, and only 9 per cent thought that it was negligible. In contrast with politicians and top leaders, the nonprofit managers regarded the government support problem as the most important issue confronting the nonprofit sector.

The awareness of the importance of forms and mechanisms of government funding is also notable. Our interviews showed that many of the decision makers are considering the possible impacts of the different financing mechanisms. This awareness itself of the problems and contexts seems to be an important development, maybe even more important than the actual changes which have occurred in the forms of government support to nonprofits. Our interviewees do not always agree with each other, they may prefer different financing mechanisms, but they are trying to overview aims, methods and consequences, and to choose the methods which are adequate for the purposes. This new approach is critical in a country where problem-solving has been characterized by the system of "collective irresponsibility", the "negative social contract" (Hankiss, 1986) for decades.

Legal status and political independence

There are two other issues which received the same score as the government support problem from politicians and top nonprofit leaders. One is the legal status of the sector, the other is the independence from political parties and labour unions. In some sense both are hot issues, the legal regulation because of the debate on the development of a comprehensive law on nonprofit organizations, the political independence as a consequence of the establishment of some government foundations with boards absolutely dominated by the governing parties. The solution of these problems can only be some correct and careful legal and economic regulation. Sooner or later it will probably occur because comprehensive regulation has its advocates both in the government and in the nonprofit sector. The survey results show that nonprofit managers also attach great importance to the nonprofit regulation. The low score of the political pressure problem given by them is probably explained by the fact, that the survey had been carried out before the scandals of government foundations broke.

Accountability and ethical issues

Nonprofit regulation is also supposed to solve the problem of accountability within the nonprofit sector. It is a bit surprising that the ethical issues which are widely known all over the country and even outside Hungary have a relatively low score. So do the problems of the volunteer recruitment, the extent of services to the poor and nonprofit research. All the other issues on our list have scores which show that their importance is lower than medium.

Information sharing and cooperation within the nonprofit sector

There was one more issue mentioned by several interviewees which seems to be important. This is the problem of information-sharing and cooperation within the nonprofit sector. Both individual nonprofits and their advocacy groups suffer a lot from the lack of structured information on the sector and their foreign counterparts, and from the shortage of facilities for networking.

There is not an appropriate meeting point for the leaders and activists of nonprofit organizations and umbrella groups. Their letters and faxes are sent by their employers' offices (hospitals, universities, research institutes, ministries). Information gathered during their foreign trips or through personal and organizational contacts is accumulated in their private libraries. Students or practitioners interested in nonprofit matters cannot find any public library which would have even the basic literature and periodicals. They must call nonprofit leaders or researchers who may or may not have relevant materials for them. A huge amount of information comes to and is produced in Hungary without becoming generally available for people and organizations that would need it.

This last problem is hopefully getting closer to a solution. The newly created nonprofit information centre is supposed to merge the umbrella organizations' information stocks. This pool of information could be the basis of a well organized library and information service which would be completely open, available for private persons, national and foreign organizations, grant-makers and grant-seekers, students, researchers and practitioners. The centre could also play advisory and mediatory roles and could host management training programs.

Internationalization of the nonprofit sector

The prospect of Hungary opening its borders to the Western institutions on accession to the European Union provokes varied opinions. The government and the political parties are publicly welcoming the future EU membership. Intellectuals are more sceptical, and willing to identify costs and risks of membership. Some speak of the EU as an empire, some others even suspect that leading forces within the EU would prefer the three Central European states to remain outside the Union, as Napoleonic-style buffer states against a renascent Eastern threat. The business community is disappointed by the limited inflow of foreign direct investment, by some experiences of exploitative "partnership" with West European firms, and by the arrogance and self-seeking of some Western consultants.

The nonprofit community does not yet seem to realize either the dangers or the opportunities of full EU membership. Ninety-eight per cent of the 542 nonprofit managers interviewed in our sample survey last year answered that dealing with supranational governments would not raise serious problems. (More exactly, 87.6 per cent of the managers said that the question was simply not relevant in Hungary, and 10.3 per cent thought that the international cooperation did not cause important problems.)

The problem awareness has somewhat increased since our survey was carried out. Some studies (Siegel and Yancey, 1993; 6 and Kuti, 1993) provoked discussions among the nonprofit leaders. The legal debates on the regulation of the nonprofit sector have also raised the question of adjustment to the European Union standards. This adjustment to any unified EU regulation is on the agenda in the longer run, as a part of a new comprehensive nonprofit regulation. Hungarian decision makers are even trying to guess which of the national nonprofit laws will become the basis for the future EU regulation.

In short, full EU membership is already being considered both as an opportunity and as a challenge in the Hungarian legal debates on the nonprofit sector. It is much less frequently understood in economic terms as presenting competition for the weak and vulnerable Hungarian nonprofits which are not prepared yet to deal with the flow of charitable resources across national borders. The first experiences of the PHARE Democracy Program has been shocking for some Hungarian nonprofit leaders. The process of application and decision making made them feel inferior and worried about the future position of Hungary (and that of the other East European countries) in the European Union. Similarly, the success of fund raising campaigns of some international organizations, and the complete lack of any opportunity to influence the use of the money they collected raised worries among Hungarian nonprofit leaders.

Perhaps as a result of these discussions and experiences, maybe simply because our interviewees were recruited from a different (politically more sensible) group of people, the answers we received this year were more cautious, though still more than half of the interviewees think that the future EU membership does not represent any problem for the Hungarian nonprofit sector.

Current legal issues, trends and debates in legal regulation

As we have shown in Chapter 5, the growth of direct government support for nonprofit organizations is in line with the generally supportive government posture towards nonprofits. By contrast, one must say the opposite about the indirect support of the nonprofit sector. A series of restrictions have been imposed on nonprofit organizations and have been suggested since 1990. The first one was the tax law which limited the tax exemption of nonprofits' business income and set conditions for the tax deductibility of donations in 1992.

The second trial was the first draft of the amendment of theCivil Code which

- suggested the introduction of new legal forms, namely the public law foundation, the public law association and the public benefit nonprofit company;
- wanted to prohibit private foundations and voluntary associations from business activities;
- proposed to impose strict government control on the establishment of service providing nonprofit companies.

This trial failed, the amendment of the Civil Code introduced the new nonprofit forms, but did not significantly increase the government control of private nonprofit organizations.

The third set of restrictions was brought about by the 1994 tax law. The first draft of the law wanted to limit the tax deductibility of donations dramatically. According to the proposal, the limit on tax deductible donations of both private persons and companies would have been 5 per cent of the tax they actually paid in the former year. (Estimates prepared by some experts and the leaders of the nonprofit umbrella organizations show that this 5 per cent of the paid tax equals about 1–2 per cent of the taxable personal income under the present circumstances in Hungary. Both the share and the amount of the tax deductible donations would have been significantly higher for the rich than for low income people. The new tax law would have penalized not only the relatively poor, but also the donors who give regularly and deducted their donations in the former year.) As a result of a united effort of the nonprofit umbrella organizations and the substantive ministries,

the tax bill was passed by the parliament in a significantly modified form: the limit of tax deductibility became 50 per cent of the
tax paid by the donor in the former year.

The fourth set of restrictions is under discussion right now. The
Ministry of Finances has prepared a new scheme of tax deductibility of donations for 1995, which would actually represent a serious
cut of tax advantages. According to the proposal, only 20 per cent
of the donations could be deducted from the tax (and not from the
taxable income) up to a limit of 50 per cent of the paid tax. Tax
incentives would be significantly weakened by this limitation
because the tax rates are higher than 20 per cent in almost all
income categories. (People who earn more than HUF 200,000 i.e.
about US$ 2,000 a year already pay 25 per cent income tax. The tax
rate is 44 per cent above the yearly income of HUF 500,000, i.e. US$
5,000). If the parliament passes this law in the present form, the
restrictions on the tax deductibility of donations will be much
stricter in Hungary than in most countries of the developed
world.

These recent developments raise serious questions about the
future of the Hungarian nonprofit sector. In order to face these
questions we need all the help that can be provided by the international literature on the nonprofit phenomenon.

Chapter 7

CONCLUSION

Theoretical implications

When trying to test the validity of general theories (Hansmann, 1980; James, 1987; Salamon, 1987; Weisbrod, 1986) about the non-profit sector and its development, I must agree with Lyons (1993, p. 306)

> that these common explanations are culturally and temporally bound. They presume the existence of clearly distinguished public and private realms and, within the latter, of private firms. These distinctions, like the firm, are largely the product of nineteenth-century Europe and America. Yet, many important organizations that we recognize as being nonprofit originated in earlier times. Related to the above is that the common theories are concerned only with service-providing organizations, and not those that are formed to facilitate an activity (for example, a sporting club) or to advance a cause (such as Greenpeace).

Since most of the well known nonprofit theories are based on implicit assumptions about the stability and the contours of a given social order, I think none of them is able to explain why and how the nonprofit sector as a whole emerges and develops in any society, not even in their model country, the United States. They catch one or sometimes several important elements of the explanation, they find the rationale for some special kinds of voluntary organizations (especially for service-providing nonprofits) under well-defined circumstances, but most of them do not even try to synthesize the existing theoretical approaches. It would probably be fruitful to use these theories as complementary and not as competitive approaches, fragments of a more exhaustive future theory which will be more helpful in understanding the extremely complex societal process of the development of different nonprofit sectors under different social, political and economic conditions. These fragments cannot provide us with a complex analytical framework, but they suggest important questions and considerations concerning the relationships between the three sectors of the economy, the motivations behind the charitable behaviour, the relations between the political institutions and the civil society, etc. These questions are definitely relevant in the analysis of the Hungarian nonprofit sector, even if its history is much too complicated to produce a black-and-white answer to the question about the relevance of nonprofit theories.

In fact, Salamon's theory which emphasizes the extensive government–nonprofit cooperation applies much better to the development of the Hungarian nonprofit sector than other approaches which argue that an inherent conflict exists between the state and voluntary organizations, but this is only the general picture. If we go into the details, things prove to be much more intricate.

We can easily finish with Weisbrod's median voter theory. There is almost nothing in Hungarian history which would verify this model of the relationship between voting behaviour and government policy. On the one hand, the legitimacy of Hungarian kings, Turkish governors, Habsburg emperors or communist governments did not come from the voters. On the other hand, at least some of them still developed the system of public welfare services and/or supported voluntary service providers, which seems to suggest that governments may have other motivations (e.g. sense of responsibility, ideological commitment, etc.) than just the willingness to win the support of a majority of voters or, more generally, the satisfaction of the majority of citizens.

It is much more difficult to get a subtle picture about the government-nonprofit relationships. If we really want to do more than scratch the surface, we have to differentiate at least

● between national governments and foreign rulers; and
● between service-providing nonprofits and civic associations.

(For the sake of simplicity, I have used the term civic associations to mean all the voluntary organizations that are somehow representing the interests of the civil society, although most of these "civic associations" were actually voluntary organizations involved in some concrete, mostly cultural or social activities in Hungary.)

In general terms, we can state that foreign rulers have obviously more conflicts with and more fear of voluntary organizations than national governments because the latter do not need to worry about movements fighting for independence. Similarly, civic associations representing alternative interests and some alternative power naturally raise much more anxiety and suspicion in government circles than service-providing nonprofits. Consequently, the development of state–nonprofit cooperation and partnership is much more likely in periods when national governments rule the country, and in spheres where service-providing nonprofits play an important role. Most of the restrictions imposed by the government on the nonprofit sector intend to strengthen control over the civic associations. The purpose of encouragement provided to the voluntary sector is generally to promote nonprofit service provision. By and large, the Hungarian history of the nonprofit sector seems to confirm this connection between the state–nonprofit cooperation and the nature of government and nonprofits. The only exception is the state socialist period, when cooperation was almost completely lacking despite the rule of a national government. The explanation can be that only the members of the government were Hungarian, its ideology was fully imported. When it became more "national", i.e. reluctant to servilely follow the Kremlin's instructions, its relationships with the voluntary organizations significantly improved. Nevertheless, with the above reservations, we still can state that cooperation is an essential feature of the history of the state–nonprofit relationship in Hungary.

As far as the "heterogeneity thesis" is concerned, it does not seem to be of much help in explaining the development of the nonprofit sector in Hungary. The present Hungary is ethnically and culturally an extremely homogenous country, only its religious diversity is significant (the shares of Catholics, Calvinists and Lutherans are 66.2 per cent, 20.9 per cent and 4.2 per cent respectively; 2.4 per cent of the population belong to other denominations, 6.3 per cent do not have any relationship with any Church). If the heterogeneity of a country were really crucial in determining the extent to which it develops a nonprofit sector, Hungary should have a significantly smaller nonprofit sector now than it had before the Trianon Treaty, which is obviously not the case.

The "heterogeneity thesis" also fails the test if we use the statistical data which describe the voluntary sector of Hungary in 1878, i.e. before the Trianon Treaty when the heterogeneity of the country was considerable from all (cultural, ethnic and religious) points of view and this heterogeneity was regarded as an important factor of the growth of the voluntary sector. Not only the followers of Weisbrod and James tend to think that heterogeneity has to do with the development of a sizeable nonprofit sector, contemporary activists and analysts were also convinced that many of the voluntary organizations were established under some influence of the ethnic minorities or religious groups. Szádeczky (1913, pp. I/28–9) argues that the idea of establishing the very first voluntary associations and guilds in Hungary came from the German and Flemish settlers, who were invited to the country by King Géza II between 1141 and 1161. Kornis (1925, p. 559) also mentions the German and Lutheran influence on the establishment of secondary modern schools. Gerlóczy quotes several voluntary activists, who admit that competition with the cultural and educational associations of ethnic minorities was among the motivations for creating their organizations, e.g. "The establishment of our voluntary association was a reaction to the Pan–Slavic movement in the northern part of Hungary"; "Our organization was created thanks mainly to the German 'Schulverein' " (Gerlóczy, 1887, pp. 37 and 55).

On the basis of all this anecdotal evidence, one would expect that Hungarian counties with considerable cultural, ethnic and religious diversity developed more sizable nonprofit sectors than those that were more homogenous. The results of the 1878 survey of voluntary associations and the 1880 population census offered an opportunity to check whether the heterogeneity thesis stands up. I used both the number of voluntary associations and members of voluntary associations per 10,000 inhabitants as measures of voluntary sector development in the different counties. The number of ethnic groups representing more than 5 per cent of the county population served as a measure of ethnic heterogeneity. The measure of heterogeneity by religion was the number of denominations representing more than 5 per cent of the population. The correlation coefficients I calculated are displayed in Table 7.1.

Table 7.1

Correlation coefficients

	y = Number of voluntary associations per 10,000 inhabitants	y = Number of members per 10,000 inhabitants
x = Literacy rate	$r = + 0.61$	$r = + 0.37$
x = Ethnic heterogeneity	$r = - 0.08$	$r = + 0.12$
x = Religious heterogeneity	$r = + 0.07$	$r = + 0.15$

These results sharply contradict all expectations: they seem to prove that there is no correlation at all between the development of the voluntary sector and cultural heterogeneity. In contrast, the correlation is quite strong between the level of cultural development (measured by literacy rate) and the number of voluntary organizations. This does not prove, of course, that the heterogeneity thesis cannot be valid in other countries, under different circumstances, in other historical periods or in international comparison, but they clearly show that – in spite of all appearances – heterogeneity was not a crucial factor of the voluntary sector development within Hungary in the nineteenth century. Although contemporary analysts and activists thought religious and ethnic heterogeneity played an important role, this indisputable emotional importance does not appear in the statistical data.

The analysis of the Hungarian nonprofit sector seems to confirm Wunker's (1991, p. 105) statement: "Hungary does not fit neatly within any of the theoretical models proposed in a Western frame of reference." However, some thoughts or allusions of the authors whose theories are not verified by the Hungarian experience still can be useful in understanding the development of the nonprofit sector in Hungary.

For example, Hansmann's (1980) contract failure theory is not directly applicable to Hungary, where consumers cannot really choose between services provided by nonprofit and for-profit entrepreneurs, but his allusion that under certain conditions the nonprofit form can be chosen as the second best institutional form by private entrepreneurs is still worth consideration. Hansmann argues that donatively financed organizations tend to choose the nonprofit form. Many of the founders of the recently created Hungarian nonprofits were probably motivated by this need for donations (including both private and government support) when they decided to establish nonprofit organizations instead of for-profit firms. The trustworthiness of the organizations is not less important if they apply for government grants than if they want to sell their services to private consumers. Consequently, the development of the nonprofit forms is not really surprising in a country on its way from state socialism to a market economy, where government still plays an extremely important redistributive role.

Similarly, the supply side approach of James (1987) can be very fruitful in the historical analysis of the Hungarian nonprofit sector, even if the most elaborated part of it (the one about Churches as benevolent entrepreneurs) does not have much explanatory power in Hungary. I am fairly sure that interests and motivations of the people and organizations (including the government) that establish and support voluntary organizations are not less important factors of development than the demand for the services nonprofits can provide. Hungarian history suggests that besides ideology and religion, political commitment, aims and values of national independence and national identity, moral obligations, altruism, need for legitimacy, problem-solving motivations, status seeking, and many other considerations motivated the behaviour of nonprofit "entrepreneurs" and of members and supporters of voluntary organizations. As some overview articles (e.g. DiMaggio and Anheier, 1990; Douglas, 1987) show, sociologists and political scientists have already made the first steps in order to understand these "mild" factors in nonprofit development, but the appearance of a more or less mature theory which could be tested is not very likely in the near future.

Policy implications

Dynamic as it is, the Hungarian nonprofit sector will most probably reach the inherent limits of its capacity of extensive growth in the near future. After a flying start, it is time to consolidate. Roughly speaking, there are three different scenarios of this consolidation period. In order to build these scenarios, I have to set out first the main assumptions and the key "variables" of the further nonprofit development in Hungary.

The underlying assumption of the whole discussion is that the legal and economic regulation of the nonprofit sector must sooner or later respond to the backlash provoked by a series of disclosure of abuse of the foundation form to shield business ventures from taxation, disguise service fees as tax deductible donations, and exercise political influence through foundation boards. Its change will be, of course, an outcome of government initiatives and those of the voluntary organizations themselves if the latter are able to ally and to develop common strategy. I also assume that this change will not endanger either the freedom of association or any other democratic right. The third assumption is that the government will not completely stop supporting nonprofit organizations and certainly will not try to prevent them from delivering services which were formerly provided by the public sector. Finally, I assume that the private support to nonprofit organizations will remain seriously limited by the low income level of the possible individual donors and the low profitability of corporations in the next couple of years. Within these limits set by the general economic situation, the actual amount of donations will depend greatly on their tax treatment, and the conditions for tax deductibility.

In building the scenarios for the development of the Hungarian nonprofit sector I try to take into account simultaneously options for the following seven key factors:

- *Government–nonprofit relationship.* The state can regard and treat voluntary organizations as opponents representing the society's aims and interests against the political elite; as contractors assisting the government in delivering services in the fields (e.g. education, health, etc.) where the state is clearly responsible for meeting at least basic citizens' needs; or as partners not only in implementing, but also in evolving policies. These different patterns of the government–nonprofit relationship are all viable in a civilized democratic regime, but their consequences for the overall development of the nonprofit sector are obviously very divergent.
- *Direct state support.* The system of direct state support to non-

profit organizations can vary according to the general government attitude towards the voluntary sector, but traditions and
the nonprofits' lobbying capacities also have an important
impact on it. Once government begins supporting voluntary
organizations, it inevitably faces complex and difficult questions of choice. Otherwise, the policy towards the voluntary
sector becomes an indiscriminate and open-ended commitment to support anything and everything that anyone calls
nonprofit, which, of course, cannot be financed even in the rich-
est countries. If the government is not to be indiscriminate in
supporting voluntary organizations, then it has to make
choices. Choices can be made in a haphazard way, public officials may try to balance between the danger of wasting public
money in supporting dilettante initiatives and the danger of
being too conservative, discriminating against the strikingly
innovative organizations. Another opportunity is to develop a
list of well defined services which, once delivered, entitle their
providers to get a certain amount of public support if they meet
all the quality and accountability requirements. Another decision making method again can be the use of "panels of experts"
(consisting of state officials, independent experts and representatives of the sector), a competitive tendering for grants completed by a sophisticated (but still transparent) evaluation
system of both applications and project reports.

- *Tax privileges and "public benefit" test.* In the long run there has to
  be a trade-off between the tax privileges enjoyed by the nonprofit organizations and the state control of their "public benefit character". Unconditional and unlimited tax exemption and
  tax deductibility necessarily produce abuse and scandals,
  which oblige decision makers either to change the taxation of
  nonprofits or to introduce a stricter monitoring of their
  activities. The scale of the possible solutions is large. An
  extreme case is the simple abolishment of all (or almost all) tax
  privileges, which implies that there is not any need for testing
  if nonprofit organizations serve public interest. Another opportunity is that only the nonprofit organizations which have an
  agreement with the government to provide basic public goods
  have the tax exemption and tax deductibility status. Another
  solution can be the development of a sophisticated system
  of tax privileges adjusted to the degree in which nonprofit

organizations serve public benefit. In this case nonprofits have to pass a standardized public benefit test in order to prove their eligibility for the tax exemption and tax deductibility.

- *Private donations.* The tax deductibility of donations obviously has some influence on the charitable behaviour of both individual and corporate donors, although this relationship is not that of "cause and effect". Accordingly, the possible number of donors and amount of donations can be more or less limited if the tax deductibility of donations is abolished or restricted to a small circle of nonprofit organizations.

- *Professionalization.* The institutionalization of the nonprofit sector depends greatly on its organizations' ability to employ well trained staff, which is, in turn, dependent on the financial conditions of the sector. Between the two extremes of the generally low and the generally high professionalization rates characterizing the weak and the well established, strong nonprofit sectors, a polarization can also develop. It may happen that a large, extremely fragile, amateurish voluntary community exists in the shadow of a highly professionalized, government-supported, service-providing minority of nonprofit organizations.

- *Accountability.* As a part of the private sector, and as a representative of the civil society, the nonprofit sector has the right to be free from state scrutiny. On the other hand, nonprofit organizations enjoying either direct or indirect public support are supposed to be accountable to the public; and democratic governments, responsible to the people who elect them, are obliged to enforce the accountability requirements. They can decrease this responsibility by minimizing the support to the nonprofit sector. Another opportunity is to treat accountability as a strict condition of government support. In the case of a harmonious state-nonprofit relationship, the enforcement of the accountability requirements for openness and ethical behaviour can be an outcome of a common effort of the government and the sector itself.

After this short overview of the assumptions and key variables, I can build some scenarios for the further development of the Hungarian nonprofit sector. The three scenarios can be summarized by a simple matrix shown in Table 7.2.

Table 7.2

Key variables in the scenarios for the development of the Hungarian nonprofit sector

Variables	"Laissez-faire" scenario	"State dominated" scenario	"Partnership" scenario
Government/ nonprofit relationship	Government regards nonprofits as opponents	Government regards nonprofits as contractors	Government regards nonprofits as partners
Direct state support	Haphazard	Dependent on services	Planned, transparent
Tax privileges	Negligible	Restricted	Important
Public benefit test	Not applied	Administrative	Standardized
Private donations	Very limited	Limited	Significant
Professionalization	Low	Polarized	High
Accountability	Low	Limited	High

The "laissez-faire" scenario

The worst thing that can happen to the Hungarian nonprofit sector is the disintegration of the new division of labour and government-nonprofit partnership which started to develop after the political changes of 1989. It would be pointless to deny that there is such a danger. Scandals and foundation abuse may prompt the government to stop supporting nonprofit organizations and to cut their tax advantages instead of keeping them accountable; to regard them again as opponents instead of trying to cooperate with them. The consequences of such a *"laissez-faire"* government attitude would be extremely harmful for the sector. The reduction of the government support and tax advantages would probably be accompanied by the decline of earned income and private support, which would prevent the sector from any significant development in the near future.

The "state dominated' scenario

Another, probably more likely, government strategy is the selective support of voluntary organizations. Since some of the services delivered by nonprofit organizations are clearly necessary, the government may decide to support exclusively those nonprofits which provide the citizens with state-approved services on a contract basis. This policy can create a relatively small, but financially very strong, highly professionalized and closely controlled segment within the nonprofit sector, while the majority of nonprofits would be left to their own devices.

The "partnership" scenario

Finally, the ideal scenario is a further development of cooperation between the public and nonprofit sectors. Government bodies and nonprofit organizations would act as partners in identifying and meeting social needs, forming and implementing social policy. A consistent and comprehensive system of nonprofit regulation would be developed in cooperation with the nonprofit umbrella organizations. The legal and tax regulations would try to limit abuse, but at the same time, a large range of tax privileges would be available for genuine charitable organizations. Instead of imposing general restrictions, a correct, carefully thought out, generally known and accepted regulation, clear accounting rules and strict tax inspection would be developed. The government would closely cooperate with the nonprofit umbrella organizations not only in the preparation, but also in the enforcement of the regulation in order to eliminate or at least weaken the "second society mentality" and to help the healthy development of the Hungarian nonprofit sector.

Appendix A

METHODOLOGY

Sample of the empirical survey of nonprofit organizations

Number of foundations and voluntary associations in the sample by ICNPO groups

ICNPO groups	Foundation	Voluntary association	Total
Culture, recreation	82	146	228
Education, research	89	14	103
Health	27	5	32
Social services	45	34	79
Environment	8	5	13
Development and housing	12	10	22
Civil and advocacy associations	6	5	11
Philanthropic intermediaries	5	4	9
International activities	5	7	12
Business and professional associations, unions	5	28	33
Total	284	258	542

Questionnaire of the sample survey

The questionnaire served both the comparative and the Hungarian research project. Consequently, we asked more, and more detailed, questions than would have been necessary for the purposes of the international comparison. I offer here a rough translation of the questionnaire.

1 The legal form of the organization: foundation, voluntary

association, other voluntary organization.

1.1 If other, what kind of voluntary organization?

1.2 If a foundation, does it accept donations?

1.3 If a voluntary association, how many members does it have?

2 Year of establishment.

3 Did the organization have any predecessor?

4 If yes, when did it operate?

5 Who (private individuals and/or organizations) established the organization?

5.1 If individuals, were they Hungarians, foreigners or both?

6 If organizations, what kind of organizations?

7 Regional and local branches (if any) of the organization.

8 International branches of the organization.

9 Membership in national and international umbrella organizations.

10 If yes, which umbrella organizations?

11 Do the answers apply only to the organization itself or to its regional and local branches, as well?

12 What services and activities does the organization carry out?

13 Please tick all specific services and activities from the list (ICNPO) that apply to your organization!

14 Whom does the organization serve: individuals, organizations or both?

15 Can you mention any special social class, layer, group or community which is supported by your organization?

16 Does the organization provide services to its members or to the public?

17 The geographical area served by the organization.

18 Has the organization received any support since its establishment?

19 Who supported the organization in 1991?

19.1 Did the organization receive any loans in 1991?

20 Who was supported by the organization in 1991?

20.1 Did the organization offer any loans in 1991?

21 How do you inform the public about your activities?

22 Do you use the press?

23 Do you use personal information networks?

24 If yes, what kind of networks?

25 How can the clients apply for your support?

26 How do you decide who to support?

27 Criteria used in decision making.

28 Do you publish the list of your supportees?
29 Do you control the use of your grants?
30 Who decides whom to support?
31 How large is your board?
32 Gender, education and social status of the board members.
33 Did the organization play any role during the parliamentary elections?
34 Did the organization play any role during the local elections?
35 Did the government second or lend personnel to the organization?
36 If yes, how many persons for how much time?
37 The number of full-time and part-time employees in 1990 and 1991.
38 How many hours did part-time employees work?
39 Did you have volunteers in 1990?
40 If yes, how many?
41 How much did they work?
42 Did you have volunteers in 1991?
43 If yes, how many?
44 How much did they work?
45 Do you have volunteers at the present time?
46 Are there professionals among your volunteers?
47 Are there professionals among your paid employees?
48 Are there professionals among the persons whom you employ occasionally?
49 Office facilities.
50 What are the major problems confronting your organization?
51 What is your opinion about some of the issues related to non-profit organizations?
52 Revenues of the organization in 1990 and 1991.
53 Expenditures of the organization in 1990 and 1991.
54 The breakdown of operating expenditures by categories of activity.
55 Capital expenditures in 1990 and 1991.
56 The estimated value of in-kind revenues in 1990 and 1991.

Detailed methodological remarks on some data sources and some figures used for international comparison

The total employment and GDP figures come from the Hungarian statistical yearbook. The composition of employees was estimated by an expert of the Central Statistical Office who deals with labour statistics. I had to hire her because the breakdown of the total employment required by ICNPO is not available in the published Hungarian statistics. I needed the help of an expert who was able to estimate the employment figures in accordance with our classification system.

As I have already mentioned, the number of nonprofit organizations was known from the official court registers, but the number of voluntary associations had to be scaled down by the estimated number of dissolved associations. The same correction was not necessary in the case of foundations because they were re-registered in 1990. The classification by ICNPO groups was mostly based on the information published in the foundation and association directories.

The estimate of the third sector expenditures, revenues and employment in 1990 and 1991 come from our sample survey. The calculation of the expenditure and employment figures was fairly easy because we had asked direct questions about the number of employees and the amount of expenditures. The estimation of the cash income was quite sophisticated, I worked out even the minutiae. The figure for in-kind revenue is a rough estimate. The interviewees estimated the value of the in-kind donations their organizations had received and reported on the number of such donors. I have assumed that the breakdown of the number of donors into government/individuals/corporations can be used as a proxy for the distribution of in-kind donations.

The figure for in-kind revenue does not contain the imputed value of volunteer hours (nor does the figure for expenditures). I could estimate the assigned value to volunteer time, but I don't trust the survey results in this field. I have the impression that our interviewees significantly overstated the volunteer involvement in their organizations' work. The reported number of volunteers equals the number of the members in many voluntary associations. The imputed value of volunteer time estimated from our survey is much higher than the estimate we can obtain on the basis of time budget surveys.

The source of the data on third sector expenditures and employment is a survey carried out by the Central Statistical Office in 1993. Unfortunately, this survey has produced only some global figures for the nonprofit sector, it does not provide us with a solid base for any structural analysis.

The 1980 figures used here were estimated from the results of the 1970 and 1982 voluntary association surveys. (There were no foundations at all in Hungary in 1980.) The main assumption in making the estimate was that the voluntary sector developed steadily from 1970 till 1982. I divided the difference between the 1970 and 1982 figures by 12, multiplied by 10, and added the result to the 1970 figure, and in this way I produced an estimate of the 1980 figures.

The 1980 data seriously limited any detailed comparison of the former and present structure of the nonprofit sector. The classification used by the Central Statistical Office when surveying voluntary associations in the 1970s and 1980s was dramatically different from ICNPO. The data they collected on the income structure does not offer any basis for a differentiation between private contributions, government support and private earnings. Employment figures were not collected, at all. Only the data on the number of organizations and amount of expenditures are reliable enough for comparative purposes.

In order to convert the 1990, 1991 and 1992 actual figures into 1980 purchasing power, I used the gross domestic product implicit price deflators.

List of the interviewed politicians and nonprofit leaders

(We give in the first place their position in 1993 when they were interviewed and in brackets their present job if it has changed since then.)

Ágoston, Gabriella[3]
Legal expert
Ministry of Finance
Balázs, Péter[3]
President
Foundation Centre

Bódi, György[3]
President
Foundation for Szeged

Csépe Béla[2]
MP, leader of the Christian Democrat group in parliament
Christian Democratic People's Party

Csepi, Lajos[1]
Director
State Property Agency

Csizmár, Gábor[3]
President
"Fundamentum" Federation of Foundations Serving Children and Young People
(Member of the parliament)

Fodor, Gábor[2]
MP, head of the Parliamentary Committee on National and Ethnic Minorities
Federation of Young Democrats
(Minister, Ministry of Culture and Education)

Gadó, Gábor[1]
Head of department
Ministry of Justice

Gábor, József[3]
Deputy state secretary
Ministry of Culture and Education

Gál Zoltán[2]
MP, leader of the Socialist group in parliament
Hungarian Socialist Party
(President of the Parliament)
Gyergyói, Ildikó[3]
Editor in chief
Kurázsi Foundation News

Harsányi, László[3]
Research director
Research Project on Nonprofit Organizations
(State secretary, Ministry of Welfare)

Hegyesi, Gábor[3]
President
Chamber of Nonprofit Organizations Providing Welfare Services

Jagasics, Béla[1]
Executive director
Federation of Voluntary Associations and Foundations in Zala
County

Kakuszi, István[1]
Deputy state secretary
Ministry of Welfare

Kardos, László[1]
Executive director
Soros Foundation

Kirschner, Péter[3]
Editor of association news
Hungarian Radio

Marschall, Miklós[3]
Deputy mayor
Budapest Municipality
(Executive director, CIVICUS)

Marx, Gyula[2]
MP, head of the Parliamentery Committee for the Support to
Voluntary Organizations
Hungarian Democratic Forum

Minarik, György[1]
President
Internal Revenue Service

Őry Csaba[2]
Secretary-general
"Liga" trade union

Rabi, Béla[3]
Vice-president
Hungarian Association of Educational, Scientific and Cultural
Foundations

Somogyvári, Zsolt[3]
President
Peter Cerny Foundation

Szabon, János[3]
President
Cooperation of Civic Associations and Community Foundations

Szabó, Miklós[1]
President
Chamber of Social Organizations

Szabó, Zoltán[1]
Ministerial counsellor
Ministry of Privatization

Szommer, Ferenc[1]
Cabinet director
Ministry for Environment Protection

Tardos, Márton[1]
Economist, MP
Party of Free Democrats

Judit, Vásárhelyi[3]
Executive director
Independent Ecological Centre

Notes

1 Interviewed by Ildikó Gyergyói.
2 Interviewed by Péter Kirschner.
3 Interviewed by Éva Kuti.

GLOSSARY OF TERMS

capital expenditures are expenditures that are incurred for acquisition of land, construction of buildings, purchase of major equipment and vehicles with a useful life of more than one year.

dues and assessments are income generated through charges which are payed as a condition of membership in voluntary organizations.

fees for service are income generated through service charges which are paid by clients of the nonprofit organizations in exchange for some kind of service, e.g. fees for education, social care, etc.

foundations are organizations governed by a voluntary board (mostly named by the founders). They must have an endowment and cannot have members. They enjoy both tax exemption and tax deductibility. They can be grant-making bodies, grant-seeking, fund-raising organizations, and also service providing, operating foundations.

full-time equivalent employment indicates total number of jobs employment in terms of full-time (forty hours a week) jobs. Part-time employment is converted into full-time jobs, and added to the number of full-time jobs to equal full-time equivalent employment.

GDP (Gross Domestic Product) is the total domestic expenditure, minus imports and plus exports of goods and services. It is measured in Hungary in accordance with recommendations by the United Nations System of National Accounts.

government refers to all branches of the government, including the executive, judicial. It includes administrative and regulatory activities of central, regional and local entities. The terms government, state and public sector are used synonymously.

grants and contracts refer to direct contributions by the central and local governments to nonprofit organizations in support of specific activities and programs.

in-kind revenues refer to non-cash inflows of goods and services that can be used by nonprofit organizations, e.g. material, use of facilities, vehicles, etc.

investment income includes interest on savings and temporary cash investments; dividends and interests on securities, net rental income, and capital gains.

nonprofit sector refers to the whole population of organizations which are formal, private, non-profit-distributing, self-governing, voluntary, nonreligious and nonpolitical, i.e. which are not within the realm of either the government or the market. The terms nonprofit, non-governmental, voluntary and third sector are used synonymously.

operating expenditures refer to the costs of the general operations of nonprofit organizations, including wage and salary disbursements, purchases of goods (other than capital equipment), material and services, fees and charges paid.

private contributions are grants and other contributions to nonprofit organizations by individuals, corporations, foundations, collective fund-raising organizations and other nonprofit organizations.

private earnings are revenues generated by the nonprofit organizations themselves either through their mission-related activities or through business ventures. The terms private earnings and earned income are used synonymously.

revenues are inflows of spendable resources received by nonprofit organizations during the year.

sales refer to the income from the sale of goods and services that are not directly related to the primary mission of the nonprofit organization.

sample survey is an examination carried out by asking questions from people or representatives of organizations chosen in such a way that every member of the examined group is equally likely to be chosen.

sampling population is a particular group of people or organizations that are to be surveyed with the help of a random sample.

Statutory treansfers are contributions by the government which are mandated by law.

third party payments are government payments for reimbursement to nonprofit organizations for services rendered to individuals. These payments are made directly to the organizations in Hungary.

total expenditures are the sum of operating and capital expenditures.

voluntary associations are membership organizations with officers elected by their members. They enjoy tax exemption, but the donations they receive are normally not tax deductible. They can be both member-serving and public-serving organizations; lobbying and advocacy are also among their usual activities.

Appendix C

HUNGARIAN VERSION OF THE INTERNATIONAL CLASSIFICATION OF NONPROFIT ORGANIZATIONS (ICNPO)

Kultúra és pihenés (culture and recreation)

Kultúra és művészetek (culture and arts)

- *Hírközlés, tömegkommunikáció (media and communication).* Production and dissemination of films, radio and television programs, publishing of books, journals, newspapers and supporting these kinds of activities.
- *Vizuális művészetek, építészet, iparművészet (visual arts, architecture, ceramic arts).* Production, dissemination and display of visual arts and architecture, including sculpture, photographic societies, painting, drawing, design centres, architectural associations and foundations supporting visual arts.
- *Előadóművészetek (performing arts).* Performing arts groups, including theatres, dance, ballet, opera, orchestras, chorals, music ensembles; voluntary associations of friends of arts institutions, foundations supporting performing arts organizations.
- *Hagyományőrzés, honismeret, népművészet, irodalom, közművelődés (historical, literary and humanistic societies).* Promotion and appreciation of the humanities, preservation of historical and cultural artifacts, commemoration of historical events; includes historical societies, poetry and literary societies, folk art groups, language associations, reading promotion, war memorials, commemorative funds and associations, foundations supporting the preservation of cultural heritage.
- *Múzeumok (museums).* General and specialized museums; voluntary associations of their friends and supporters; foundations supporting museums and their exhibitions, excavations, education and research projects.
- *Egyéb kulturális és művészeti szervezetek (other culture and arts*

organizations). Multipurpose culture and arts organizations, support and services organizations, auxiliaries, other culture and arts organizations not elsewhere classified.

Sport (sports)

- *Sportklubok (sports clubs).* Provision of amateur sports, training, physical fitness, sport competition services and events.
- *Egyéb sport, a sport támogatása (other sports, promotion of sports).* Voluntary associations of friends and supporters of sports clubs. Foundations for the promotion of sports. Support and services organizations, auxiliaries, other sports organizations not elsewhere classified.

Pihenés, szórakozás (recreation, service clubs)

- *Állatkertek, akváriumok, arborétumok (zoos, aquariums, botanical gardens).* Zoos, aquariums, botanical gardens, voluntary associations of their friends and supporters, foundations raising funds for their projects.
- *Pihenés, szórakozás, szabadidős tevékenység (recreation, leisure time activities).* Provision of recreational facilities and services, playground associations, fitness centres, leisure clubs.
- *Rétegklubok, rétegszervezetek (clubs and associations of special social groups and layers, service clubs).* Country clubs, mens' and women's clubs, voluntary associations of the young and the elderly, clubs of intellectuals, veterans' organizations, alumni's associations, Lions clubs, Zonta International, etc.
- *Hobbykörök (hobby circles).* Voluntary associations of friends of cats, dogs, pigeons; organizations of collectors of stamps, books, antiquities; radio amateurs, model-builders, etc.
- *Vadásztársaságok (hunters' associations).* Provision of hunting facilities, protection and control of the population of wild animals in the territory belonging to the voluntary associations of hunters.
- *Horgászegyesületek (fishermen's associations).* Provision of fishing facilities and services for amateur fishermen.
- *Egyéb rekreációs szervezetek (other recreation).* Multipurpose recreational organizations, support and service organizations, auxiliaries, foundations supporting recreation, other recreational organizations not elsewhere classified.

Oktatás és kutatás (education and research)

Alap – és középfokú oktatás (primary and secondary education)

- *Elemi, alsó – és középfokú oktatás (elementary, primary and secondary education).* Provision of education at elementary, primary and secondary levels. Foundations raising funds for primary, secondary schools and pre-school organizations. Foundations financing fellowships. Voluntary associations of parents and pupils.

Felsőoktatás (higher education)

- *Felsőoktatás: egyetemi szint (higher education: university level).* Higher learning, providing academic degrees. Foundations raising funds for universities. Foundations providing fellowships and financing student exchange. Students' associations.

Egyéb oktatás (other education)

- *Szakmai képzés (vocational, technical schools).* Technical and vocational training. Foundations raising funds for vocational and technical schools. Foundations financing fellowships. Voluntary associations of pupils.
- *Felnőttoktatás, továbbképzés (adult and continuing education).* Institutions engaged in providing education and training in addition to the formal educational system: e.g. folk high schools, language schools, night schools, correspondence schools, etc. Foundations supporting adult education.
- *Egyéb oktatás (other education).* Multipurpose educational organizations, support and service organizations, auxiliaries. Foundations supporting education at regional or national level, not confining their grant-making to a special level of education or to a concrete school. Other educational organizations not elsewhere classified.

Kutatás (research)

- *Orvostudományi kutatás (medical research).* Research in the medical field, e.g. research on specific diseases, disorders, medical disciplines. Foundations supporting medical research. Scientific societies of researchers.

- *Természettudományi és műszaki kutatás (science and technology).* Research in the physical and life sciences, engineering and technology. Foundations supporting this kind of research. Scientific societies of researchers.
- *Társadalomtudományi és politológiai kutatás (social sciences, policy studies).* Research and analysis in the social sciences and policy area. Foundations supporting this kind of research. Scientific societies of researchers.
- *Egyéb kutatás (other research).* Multipurpose, not specialized research organizations, support and service organizations, auxiliaries. Foundations supporting all kinds of research, financing international scientific exchange, giving awards to prominent researchers. Other research organizations not elsewhere classified.

Egészségügy (health)

Kórházak és rehabilitáció (hospitals and rehabilitation)

- *Kórházi ellátás (hospitals).* Inpatient medical care and treatment. Foundations raising funds for hospitals or for special departments of hospitals.
- *Rehabilitációs kórházak (rehabilitation hospitals).* Inpatient rehabilitative therapy to individuals suffering from physical impairments due to injury, genetic defect, or disease and requiring extensive physiotherapy or similar forms of care. Foundations supporting rehabilitation.

Szanatóriumok (nursing homes)

- *Szanatóriumok, idült betegek gyógyintézeti ellátása (nursing homes).* Inpatient convalescent care, residential care as well as primary health care services for the frail elderly, for the severely handicapped, for patients suffering from chronic diseases. Foundations raising funds for nursing homes.

Mentális ellátás, krízisintervenció (mental health and crisis intervention)

- *Ideggyógyintézetek (psychiatric hospitals).* Inpatient care and treatment for the mentally ill. Foundations raising funds for psychiatric hospitals.
- *Mentális betegségek ambuláns kezelése (mental health treatment).* Outpatient treatment for the mentally ill, including community mental health centres and halfway homes. Foundations supporting outpatient mental health treatment.
- *Lelki elsősegélyszolgálat (crisis intervention).* Outpatient services and counsel in acute mental health situations. Suicide prevention. Support to victims of assault and abuse. Foundations supporting crisis intervention.

Egyéb egészségügyi ellátás (other health services)

- *Közegészségügy, egészségnevelés (public health and wellness education).* Promotion of public health and health education. Sanitation screening for potential health hazards, first aid training and services, medical counselling, family planning services. Foundations supporting public health and wellbeing education.
- *Járóbetegellátás (outpatient health treatment).* Nonprofit organizations that provide primarily outpatient health services. Foundations raising funds for outpatient health care.
- *Orvosi rehabilitációs szolgáltatások (rehabilitative medical services).* Outpatient therapeutic care, physical therapy centres. Foundations supporting rehabilitative medical services.
- *Mentőszolgálat (emergency medical services).* Services to persons in need of immediate care. Ambulatory services and paramedical emergency care, shock/trauma programmes and lifeline programmes, ambulance services. Foundations raising funds for ambulance services.
- *Egyéb egészségügyi ellátás (other health care).* Nature cure and acupuncture centres, naturopathic services. Support and service organizations, auxiliaries. Multipurpose, not specialized foundations supporting all kinds of health care. Foundations soliciting donations for the cure of special diseases or the treatment of concrete patients (e.g. children, victims of accidents,

well known artists, sportsmen, etc.). Other health organizations not elsewhere classified.

Szociális szolgáltatások (social services)

Szociális szolgáltatások (social services)

- *Gyermekvédelem, gyermekintézmények (child welfare, child services).* Services to children, child development centres, foster care, adoption services, homes for destitute children. Foundations promoting child welfare and raising funds for the development of child services.
- *Ifjúságvédelem, ifjúságnak nyújtott szolgáltatások (youth welfare, youth services).* Services to youth, e.g. delinquency prevention services, teen pregnancy prevention, drop-out prevention, "drug-stop" services, youth centres and clubs, job programmes for youth. Foundations promoting youth welfare and raising funds for the development of youth services. Youth associations.
- *Családvédelem, családoknak nyújtott szolgáltatások (family services).* Services to families, e.g. family assistance centres, marriage guidance services, single parent agencies, family violence shelters. Voluntary associations of large families, single parents, divorced people, etc. Foundations supporting family services.
- *Egészségkárosultak szociális ellátása (services for the handicapped).* Homes, transport facilities, recreation and other specialized services for the handicapped. Foundations supporting the provision of such services. Voluntary associations and self-help groups of handicapped people. Voluntary associations of parents and relatives of the handicapped.
- *Öregeknek nyújtott szociális szolgáltatások (services for the elderly).* Organizations providing geriatric care, including in-home services, transport facilities, recreation, meal programmes and other services for the elderly. Foundations supporting the provision of these services. Voluntary associations of senior citizens.
- *Önsegítő csoportok, egyéb személyre szóló szolgáltatások (self-help and other personal services).* Programmes and services for self-help and development, including support groups, personal counselling, credit counselling, money management services,

friendly societies.

- *Hajléktalanok menhelyei, hajléktalanok támogatása (temporary shelters, services to the homeless).* Organizations providing temporary shelters to the homeless, including travellers' aid and temporary housing. Foundations supporting services to the homeless.
- *Menekültek támogatása (refugee assistance).* Organizations providing food, clothing, shelter and services to refugees and immigrants. Foundations soliciting donations in order to support service provision. Voluntary associations of refugees and immigrants.
- *Jövedelemkiegészítő támogatás, segélyezés (income support and maintenance).* Organizations (mostly foundations) providing cash assistance and other forms of direct services to persons unable to maintain a livelihood.
- *Természetbeni támogatás (material assistance).* Organizations providing food, clothing, transport and other forms of material assistance to persons unable to maintain a livelihood.
- *Egyéb szociális ellátás (other social services).* Multipurpose charitable organizations. Support and service organizations, auxiliaries. Multipurpose, not specialized foundations supporting all kinds of social services. Other organizations promoting social care not elsewhere classified.

Katasztrófaelhárítás (emergency and relief)

- *Tűzoltóegyesületek (voluntary fire brigades).* Traditionally existing local voluntary associations of citizens serving fire prevention and control.
- *Természeti katasztrófák elhárítása, polgárvédelem (disaster/emergency prevention and control).* Organizations that work to prevent, control and alleviate the effects of disasters, to educate or otherwise prepare individuals to cope with the effects of disasters, or provide relief to disaster victims. Foundations soliciting donations in order to help disaster victims.
- *Egyéb katasztrófaelhárító szervezetek (other emergency and relief).* Multipurpose emergency and assistance organizations. Support and service organizations, auxiliaries. Multipurpose, not specialized foundations supporting emergency and relief. Other emergency organizations not elsewhere classified.

Környezetvédelem (environment)

Környezetvédelem (environment)

- *A környezetszennyezés ellenőrzése, csökkentése (pollution abatement and control)*. Organizations that promote clean air, clean water, reducing and preventing noise pollution, radiation control, hazardous wastes , toxic substances and solid waste management, recycling programs. Foundations supporting these kinds of programs. Voluntary associations of citizens for pollution control. Action groups against environment polluting investments.
- *A természeti környezet védelme (natural resources conservation and protection)*. Conservation and preservation of natural resources, including land, water, energy and plant resources for the general use and enjoyment of the public. Foundations raising funds for the conservation of natural resources. Voluntary associations of citizens protecting their neighbourhood.
- *A környezet szépítése, alakítása (environmental beautification and open spaces)*. Organizations promoting city beautification programs, anti-litter campaigns, programs to preserve the parks, green spaces in urban and rural areas. Foundations raising funds for beautification projects. Voluntary associations of citizens promoting the improvement of living conditions in their neighbourhood.
- *Egyéb környezetvédelmi szervezetek (other environmental organizations)*. Multipurpose environmental organizations. Environmental education and research programs. Support and service organizations, auxiliaries. Foundations supporting several kinds of environmental programs. Other environmental organizations not elsewhere classified.

Állatvédelem (animals)

- *Állatvédelem (animal protection and welfare)*. Animal shelters. Voluntary associations protecting animals. Foundations raising funds for animal protection.
- *A természet élővilágának védelme (wildlife preservation and protection)*. Voluntary associations and foundations promoting wildlife preservation and protection. Sanctuaries and refuges for wild animals. Campaigns for the protection of rare species

threatened with complete extinction.
- *Állatorvosi szolgáltatások (veterinary services)*. Animal hospitals and services providing care to farm and household animals and pets.
- *Egyéb állatvédelem (other animal protection)*. Multipurpose support and service organizations, auxiliaries. Foundations supporting several kinds of animal protection programs. Other animal protecting organizations not elsewhere classified.

Település –, gazdaság – és közösségfejlesztés, lakásügy (development and housing)

Gazdaság –, társadalom – és településfejlesztés (economic and community development)

- *A település és a lakókörzet fejlesztése (community development)*. Organizations working towards improving the quality of life within communities and neighbourhoods. Local development organizations.
- *Gazdaságfejlesztés (economic development)*. Programs and services to improve the economic infrastructure and capacity. Building of infrastructure, e.g. roads, water pipes, sewage pipes, etc. Entrepreneurial programs, technical and management consulting assistance. Rural development organizations. Foundations supporting economic development. Voluntary associations lobbying for local development programs.
- *Szociális fejlesztés, közösségfejlesztés (social development)*. Organizations working towards improving the institutional infrastructure and capacity to alleviate social problems and to improve general public wellbeing.
- *Egyéb gazdaság –, társadalom – és közösségfejlesztő szervezetek (other economic, social and community development organizations)*. Multipurpose organizations promoting programs to help economic and social development. Support and service organizations, auxiliaries. Other developmental organizations not elsewhere classified.

Lakásügy (housing)

- *Lakásegyesületek (housing associations)*. Development, management, leasing, financing and rehabilitation of housing.

- *Lakáshoz jutás támogatása (housing assistance)*. Organizations providing housing search, legal services and related assistance. Voluntary associations, advocacy organizations of home builders, tenants, house owners.
- *Egyéb lakásügyi szervezetek (other housing organizations)*. Multipurpose organizations promoting housing programs. Support and service organizations, auxiliaries. Other housing organizations not elsewhere classified.

A foglalkoztatottság növelése, átképzés (employment and training

- *Átképzési programok (job training programs)*. Organizations providing and supporting apprenticeship programs, internships, on-the-job training and other training programs in order to help their clients to find jobs.
- *Szakmára való felkészítés, pályaválasztási tanácsadás (vocational counselling and guidance)*. Career counselling, aptitude testing and guidance in order to assist people to choose training programs and jobs which suit to their abilities.
- *Foglalkozási rehabilitáció, védett munkahelyek (vocational rehabilitation and sheltered workshops)*. Organizations that promote self-sufficiency and income generation of both handicapped and unemployed people through job training and employment.
- *Egyéb foglalkoztatási és átképző szervezetek (other employment and training)*. Multipurpose organizations promoting employment and vocational training. Support and service organizations, auxiliaries. Voluntary associations of unemployed people. Other employment and training promotion not elsewhere classified.

Polgári jogok, érdekvédelem (civil rights, advocacy)

Állampolgári és érdekvédelmi szervezetek (citizens' rights and advocacy)

- *Az állampolgári aktivitás ösztönzése (civic associations)*. Programs and services to encourage and spread civic mindedness. Citizens advice organizations.

- *Konkrét népcsoportok, rétegek jogainak védelme (advocacy organizations).* Organizations that protect the rights and promote the interests of specific groups of people, e.g. women, children, the elderly, homosexuals, the physically handicapped, etc.
- *Az állampolgári jogok védelme (civil rights associations).* Organizations that work to protect or preserve individual civil liberties and basic human rights such as the freedom of association, the freedom of speech, the freedom of religion, etc.
- *Az etnikai és vallási kisebbségek védelme (protection of ethnic and religious minorities).* Organizations that promote the interests of people belonging to a specific ethnic heritage or religious group. Voluntary associations of members of ethnic and religious minorities.
- *Fogyasztói érdekvédelem (consumer protection associations).* Protection of consumer rights and the improvement of product control and quality.
- *Egyéb állampolgári és érdekvédelmi szervezetek (other civic and advocacy organizations).* Multipurpose organizations protecting civil rights, or advocating the social and political interests of general or special constituencies. Support and service organizations, auxiliaries. Other civic and advocacy organizations not elsewhere classified.

Jogi szolgáltatások (law and legal services)

- *Jogsegélyszolgálat (legal services).* Legal services, advice and assistance in dispute resolutions and court related matters.
- *A bűnözés megelőzése, a közrend védelme (crime prevention and public safety).* Crime prevention to promote safety and precautionary measures among citizens. Foundations supporting the technical development of police services. Voluntary night watch organized by citizens in order to protect their neighbourhood from crime.
- *A bűnözők társadalmi rehabilitációja (rehabilitation of offenders).* Programs and services to reintegrate offenders. Probation and parole programs. Voluntary associations of former criminals.
- *Az áldozatok támogatása (victim support).* Rehabilitation services, counsel, advice and psychological assistance to victims of crime.

- *Egyéb jogi szolgáltatások (other legal services).* Multipurpose organizations providing the citizens with legal services. Support and service organizations, auxiliaries. Other legal service organizations not elsewhere classified.

Jótékonyság, öntevékenység (philanthropic intermediaries and voluntarism promotion)

Jótékonyság és öntevékenység (philanthropic intermediaries and voluntarism promotion)

- *Nem szakosodott adományosztó alapítványok (non-specialized grant-making foundations).* Grantmaking foundations, including foundations established by private individuals, corporations, nonprofit organizations and government bodies, which do not specialize in any concrete field and make grants to a wide range of supportees.
- *Az öntevékenység szervezése, támogatása, nonprofit szervezetek szövetségei (voluntarism promotion and support).* Organizations that promote voluntarism and the development of the voluntary sector. Information services for voluntary organizations. Umbrella groups, consultative bodies and federations of nonprofit organizations.
- *Adománygyűjtés (fund-raising organizations).* Federated, collective fund-raising organizations. United Way.
- *Egyéb jótékonyság, öntevékenység (other philanthropy and voluntarism promotion).* Multipurpose organizations promoting philanthropy and voluntarism. Support and service organizations, auxiliaries. Other philanthropic organizations not elsewhere classified.

Nemzetközi kapcsolatok (international activities)

Nemzetközi kapcsolatok (international activities)

- *Cserekapcsolatok, baráti társaságok, nemzetközi kulturális kapcsolatok (exchange/friendship/cultural programs).* Organizations promoting intercultural understanding between peoples of different countries and historical backgrounds. Programs and services designed to encourage mutual respect and friendship.

- *Fejlesztési segélyszervezetek (development assistance organizations).* Programs and projects that promote social and economic development abroad. Special projects for the promotion social and economic development of the Hungarian minorities living in neighbouring countries.
- *Természeti csapások következményeinek enyhítésére törekvő segélyszervezetek (international disaster and relief organizations).* Organizations that collect, channel and provide aid to other countries during times of disaster, war or emergency.
- *Emberi jogok védelme, békeszervezetek (international human rights and peace organizations).* Organizations which promote and monitor human rights, minority rights and peace internationally.
- *Egyéb nemzetközi szervezetek (other international organizations).* Multipurpose organizations promoting intercultural understanding, monitoring human rights and peace. Support and service organizations, auxiliaries. Other international organizations not elsewhere classified.

Szakmai és üzleti szervezetek, szakszervezetek (business, professional associations and unions)

Szakmai és üzleti szervezetek, szakszervezetek (business, professional associations, unions)

- *Üzletemberek, vállalkozók, munkáltatók szervezetei (business associations).* Organizations promoting, regulating and safeguarding the interests of special branches of business, e.g. manufacturers' association, farmers' association, bankers' association, etc.
- *Szakmai kamarák, érdekképviseletek (professional associations).* Organizations promoting, regulating and protecting professional interests, e.g. bar association, medical association, librarians' association, etc.
- *Szakszervezetek (labour unions).* Organization that promote, protect and regulate the rights and interests of employees.
- *Egyéb szakmai szervezetek (other business and professional associations).* Multipurpose business and professional organizations. Support and service organizations, auxiliaries. Other business and professional organizations not elsewhere classified.

Egyéb, besorolatlan (other, not elsewhere classified)

REFERENCES

A Magyar Korona országaiban 1881-ben végrehajtott népszámlálás fő bb eredményei megyék és községek szerint részletezve (1882), *(Main results of the population census carried out in the countries of the Hungarian Kingdom in 1881 by counties, towns and villages)*, Országos Magyar Királyi Statistikai Hivatal, Budapest.

A Magyar Népköztársaság Polgári Törvénykönyve (1959), *Miniszteri indoklás (Civil Code of the Hungarian People's Republic, Ministerial introduction)*, Budapest.

A Nonprofit Kamara állásfoglalása a Polgári Törvénykönyv egyes rendelkezéseinek módosításáról (1992) (Statement of the Nonprofit Chamber about the bill on the amendment of certain provisions of the Civil Code), Mimeo, Budapest.

Ácsné Molnár, Judit and Fodor, Anikó (1992), *A nonprofit szervezetek adózása, m űködése a számviteli törvény hatálybalépését követően (Taxation and functioning of the nonprofit organizations after the enactment of the law on accountancy)*, Adó – és Pénzügyi Ellenőrzési Hivatal Vizsgálati Módszertani Bizottság, Budapest.

Alhadeff, David A. (1986), Microeconomics and the experimental analysis of behavior, in MacFadyen, Alan J. and MacFadyen, Heather W. (eds.) *Economic psychology intersections in theory and application*, North-Holland, Amsterdam–New York– Oxford– Tokyo.

Alternatív törvénytervezet a Polgári Törvénykönyv egyes rendelkezéseinek módosításáról (Alternative bill on the amendment of certain provisions of the Civil Code) (1992), *Kurázsi*, November.

References

Anheier, Helmut K. and Priller, Eckhard (1991), The nonprofit sector in East Germany, before and after unification, *Voluntas*, 2/1.

Anheier, Helmut K. and Seibel, Wolfgang (1992), The nonprofit sector and the transformation of societies, comparative perspectives from Europe, paper presented at the Annual Meeting of the American Sociological Association, Pittsburgh.

Arató, András (1992), Civil társadalom Lengyelországban és Magyarországon (Civil society in Poland and Hungary), *Politikatudományi Szemle*, 2.

Archambault, Edith (1993), *Defining the nonprofit sector, France*, working papers of the Johns Hopkins Comparative Nonprofit Sector Project No. 7, The Johns Hopkins Institute for Policy Studies, Baltimore.

Aronson, Elliot (1978), *A társas lény* (*The social animal*), Közgazdasági és Jogi Könyvkiadó, Budapest.

Az Országgyűlés bizottságainak együttes jelentése a Polgári Törvénykönyv egyes rendelkezéseinek módosításáról szóló 9434. számú törvényjavaslatról, valamint az ahhoz benyújtott módosító indítványokról (1993), (*Joint report of the Parliament committees on the "Bill No. 9434 on the amendment of certain provisions of the Civil Code" and on the motions to modify it*), Office of the Parliament, Budapest.

Balázs, Magdolna (1991), Az alapítványi élet indulása Magyarországon (The beginnings of the foundation development in Hungary), *Esély*, 1.

Bartal, Annamária (1993), Kié a szegény? (Who owns the poor?), Manuscript, Nonprofit Kutatócsoport, Budapest.

Bauer, Rudolph (1990), Voluntary welfare associations in Germany and the United States, theses on the historical development of intermediary systems, *Voluntas*, 1/1.

Benda, Kálmán (1957), *A magyar jakobinusok* (*The Hungarian Jacobins*), Budapest.

Béry, László (ed.) (1929), *A magyar filantrópia könyve* (*A book on the Hungarian philanthropy*), Légrády Testvérek Nyomdai Műintézete, Budapest.

Bibó, István (1986), *Válogatott tanulmányok*, 1–4. kötet (*Selected papers*, Volumes 1–4), Magvető, Budapest.

Bocz, János, Kuti, Éva, Seresné Gyűrűs, Gabriella, Sebestény, István and Vajda, Ágnes (1994), *Alapítványok és egyesületek. A nonprofit szektor statisztikája* (*Foundations and voluntary associa-*

tions. Statistics on the nonprofit sector), Központi Statisztikai Hivatal, Budapest.

Bocz, János, Gyulavári, Antal, Kuti, Éva, Locherné Kelédi, Ildikó, Sebestény, István and Vajda, Ágnes (1994), *Nonprofit szervezetek Magyarországon, 1992* (*Nonprofit organizations in Hungary, 1992*), Központi Statisztikai Hivatal, Budapest.

Bodolay, Géza (1963), *Irodalmi diáktársaságok 1785–1848* (*Literary societies of students 1785–1848*), MTA KESZ Soksz., Budapest.

Boldisár, Kálmán (1933), *A debreceni casino százéves története 1833–1933* (*Hundred years of the social club of Debrecen 1833–1933*), Debreceni Casino, Debrecen.

Bruszt, László and Simon, János (1992), A nagy átalakulás. Elméleti megközelítések és állampogári vélemények a demokráciáról és a kapitalizmusról (The big transition. Theoretical approaches to and citizens' opinion about democracy and capitalism), *Politikatudományi Szemle*, 1.

Collins, Randall and Hickman, Neal (1991), Altruism and culture as social products, *Voluntas*, 2/2.

Csizmadia, Andor (1977), *A szociális gondoskodás változásai Magyarországon* (*Changes of social care in Hungary*), MTA Állam – és Jogtudományi Intézet, Budapest.

Csorna Kálmán (1931), A szegénygondozás Budapesten (Poverty relief in Budapest), *Statisztikai Közlemények*, 62/1. Budapest.

Czimer, Károly (1929), *A Szeged-Belvárosi Kaszinó százéves története 1829–1929* (*Hundred years of the Social Club of Szeged Inner City*), Szeged–Belvárosi Kaszinó, Szeged.

DiMaggio, Paul J. and Anheier, Helmut K. (1990), The sociology of nonprofit organizations and sectors, *Annual Review of Sociology*.

Dobrovits, Sándor (1936), Budapest egyesületei (Voluntary associations in Budapest), Statisztikai Közlemények, 74/3.

Douglas, James (1987), Political theories of nonprofit organization, in, Powell, Walter, W. (ed.), *The nonprofit sector, a research handbook*, Yale University Press, New Haven.

Egyesületek Magyarországon, 1970 (1972) (*Voluntary associations in Hungary in 1970*), Központi Statisztikai Hivatal, Budapest.

Egyesületek Magyarországon, 1982 (1984) (*Voluntary associations in Hungary in 1982*), Központi Statisztikai Hivatal, Budapest.

Egyesületek Magyarországon, 1989 (1991) (*Voluntary associations in Hungary in 1989*), Központi Statisztikai Hivatal, Budapest.

Előterjesztés a Kormány részére a Polgári Törvénykönyv egyes rendelkezéseinek módosításáról, Tervezet (Bill on the amendment of certain provisions of the Civil Code, Draft) (1992), confidential, but a summary was published in *Kurázsi* (*Változások,* 1992)

Emlékkönyv Dr. Gróf Klebelsberg Kuno negyedszázados kultúrpolitikai működésének emlékére (1925), (*Essays published in honour of Dr. Gróf Klebelsberg Kuno, minister of culture for 25 years*), Rákosi Jenő Budapesti Hírlap Újságvállalata, Budapest.

Erdélyi, László (1925), Bajtársi egyesületek a magyar lovagkorban (Fraternities in the age of chivalry in Hungary), in, *Emlékkönyv Dr. Gróf Klebelsberg Kuno negyedszázados kultúrpolitikai működésének emlékére,* (*Essays published in honour of Dr. Gróf Klebelsberg Kuno, minister of culture for 25 years*), Rákosi Jenő Budapesti Hírlap Újságvállalata, Budapest.

Farkas, János and Vajda, Ágnes (1991), *Két választás Magyarországon 1990-ben* (*Two elections in Hungary in 1990*), Központi Statisztikai Hivatal, Budapest.

Ferge, Zsuzsa (1989), *Van–e negyedik út? A társadalompolitika esélyei* (*Is there a fourth way? Chances of the social policy*), Magvető, Budapest.

Fricz, Tamás (1990), *Állam, közvetítés, civil társadalom* (*State, mediation, civil society*), Akadémiai, Budapest.

Fülöp, Géza (1978), *A magyar olvasóközönség a felvilágosodás idején és a reformkorban* (*The reading public in Hungary in the period of Enlightenment and in the Reform Age*), Akadémiai, Budapest.

Füredi, Enikő (1993), *A negyedik oldal* (*The fourth side*), Kurázsi, June.

Gádoros, Júlia (1992), A "Lelki Sérült Gyermekekért" Alapítvány történetéről (About the history of the Foundation for the Mentally Handicapped Children), in Kuti, Éva (ed.) *A nonprofit szektor Magyarországon* (*The nonprofit sector in Hungary*), Nonprofit Kutatócsoport, Budapest.

Gárdonyi, Albert (1930), *Régi pesti könyvkereskedők* (*Ancient booksellers in Pest*), *Stephaneum Nyomda, Budapest.*

Gayer, Gyuláné, Gondos, Anna, Hegyesi, Gábor, Síklaky István and Szirmai Gábor, (1992) LARES Humán Szolgáltató Kisszövetkezet, majd alapítvány, 10 év az emberek és egy szociálpolitikai paradigmaváltás szolgálatában (LARES Human Service Cooperative, later on Foundation, 10 years in the service of people and a change of paradigm in social policy), in Kuti,

Éva (ed.) *A nonprofit szektor Magyarországon* (*The nonprofit sector in Hungary*), Nonprofit Kutatócsoport, Budapest.

Gerlóczy, Károly (1887), *A Magyarországi közművelődési egyesületek élete* (*Life of the cultural associations in Hungary*), Pesti Könyvnyomda Részvénytársaság, Budapest

Gyergyói, Ildikó (1991), *Alapítvány és spagettigyár* (*Foundation and spaghetti factory*), Sansz, August.

György, István (1992), A közalapítványok vagyona és gazdálkodása a kiegyezéstől megszűnésükig (Endowment and economic conditions of public law foundations from the Compromise till their closure), Manuscript, Nonprofit Kutatócsoport, Budapest.

Hahn, Géza (1960), *A magyar egészségügy története* (*The history of health services in Hungary*), Medicina, Budapest.

Halmai, Gábor (1990), *Az egyesülés szabadsága. Az egyesülési jog története* (*The freedom of association. The history of the law on associations*), Atlantisz Medvetánc, Budapest.

Hankiss, Elemér (1979), *Társadalmi csapdák* (*Social pitfalls*), Magvető, Budapest.

Hankiss, Elemér (1986), *Diagnózisok 2.* (*Diagnoses 2*), Magvető Kiadó, Budapest.

Hankiss, Elemér (1989), *Kelet-európai alternatívák* (*East European alternatives*), Közgazdasági és Jogi Könyvkiadó, Budapest.

Hansmann, Henry B. (1980), The role of nonprofit enterprise, *Yale Law Journal*, 89.

Harangi, László (1986), *Az öntevékeny szervezetek szerepe Magyarországon* (*The role of voluntary organizations in Hungary*), Művelődéskutató Intézet, Budapest.

Harsányi, László (1992), A nonprofit szektor szabályozásának vitás kérdései (Regulation problems in the nonprofit sector), in Kuti, Éva (ed.) *A nonprofit szektor Magyarországon* (*The nonprofit sector in Hungary*), Nonprofit Kutatócsoport, Budapest.

Harsányi, László (1993), Nonprofit szervezetek az átalakuló gazdaságban (Nonprofit organizations in the changing economy), *Napi*, 23 June.

Harsányi, László and Kirschner, Péter (eds) (1992), *Egyesületi címtár* (*Directory of voluntary associations*), Nonprofit Kutatócsoport, Budapest.

Heit, Gábor and Vidra Szabó, Ferenc (1992), A kulturális egyesületek és szabadidős társaságok szerepe a helyi társadalom fejlődésében (The role of the cultural and leisure time associations in the development of the civil society at a local level), in Kuti, Éva (ed.) *A nonprofit szektor Magyarországon (The nonprofit sector in Hungary)*, Nonprofit Kutatócsoport, Budapest.

Heller, Ágnes, Fehér, Ferenc, Bozóki, András and Fricz, Tamás (1992), *Polgárosodás, civil társadalom és demokrácia (Embourgeoisement, civil society and democracy)*, MTA Politikai Tudományok Intézete, Budapest.

Heller, Farkas (1923), *Magyarország socialpolitikája (The social policy in Hungary)*, Németh József Könyvkereskedése, Budapest.

Hodgkinson, Virginia (1990), Mapping the non-profit sector in the United States, implications for research, *Voluntas*, 1/2.

Jagasics, Béla (1992), Félúton, A zalai alapítványok és egyesületek fejlődéséről (Half-way, the development of the foundations and voluntary associations in the Zala county), in Kuti, Éva (ed.) *A nonprofit szektor Magyarországon (The nonprofit sector in Hungary)*, Nonprofit Kutatócsoport, Budapest.

James, Estelle (1987), The nonprofit sector in comparative perspective, in Powell, Walter, W. (ed.) *The nonprofit sector: a research handbook*, Yale University Press, New Haven.

Karácsonyi, János (1985), *Magyarország egyháztörténete főbb vonásaiban 970–től 1900–ig (The main events of the history of Churches in Hungary from 970 till 1900)*, Könyvértékesítő Vállalat, Budapest.

Karner, Károly (1931), *A felekezetek Magyarországon a statisztika megvilágításában (Denominations in Hungary as reflected in statistics)*, Debrecen Szabad Királyi Város és a Tiszántúli Református Egyházkerület Könyvnyomda Vállalata, Debrecen.

Kátai, Gábor (1868), *A Királyi Magyar Természettudományi Társulat története alapíttatásától fogva máig (The history of the Hungarian Royal Society of Natural Sciences since its establishment until today)*, Bucsánszky, Pest.

Katus, József and Tóth, János (eds.) (1986), *On voluntary organizations in Hungary and the Netherlands*, OKK, Budapest.

Kecskés, László (1988), Az alapítványi jog fejlődése (The development of the legal regulation of foundations), *Magyar Jog*, 2.

Kohut, Mária (ed.) (1971), *Források Budapest történetéhez 1873–1919 (Sources of information on the history of Budapest 1873–1919)*, Budapest Főváros Levéltára, Budapest.

Kolosi, Tamás and Róbert, Péter (1992), A rendszerváltás társadalmi hatásai (Social impact of the change in political system),

Valóság, 2.

Konrád, György and Szelényi, Iván (1991), Intellectuals and dominance in post-communist societies, in Pierre Bourdieu and James Coleman (eds.) *Social theory in a changing society*, Westview Press, Boulder.

Kornai, János (1989), *Indulatos röpirat a gazdasági átmenet ügyében* (*Passionate pamphlet about the economic transition*), HVG Kiadó, Budapest.

Kornai, János (1991), A privatizáció elvei Kelet-Európában (The principles of privatization in Eastern Europe), *Közgazdasági Szemle*, 11.

Kornai, János (1992), A posztszocialista átmenet és az állam. Gondolatok fiskális problémákról (The post-socialist transition and the state. Thoughts about fiscal problems), *Közgazdasági Szemle*, 6.

Kornis, Gyula (1925), Realisztikus törekvések a reformkorszak iskolapolitikájában (Efforts to develop technical education in the Reform Age), in Emlékkönyv Dr. Gróf Klebelsberg Kuno negyedszázados kultúrpolitikai működésének emlékére, (*Essays published in honour of Dr. Gróf Klebelsberg Kuno, minister of culture for 25 years*), Rákosi Jenő Budapesti Hírlap Újságvállalata, Budapest.

Kósa, János (1939), *A magyar kölcsönkönyvtárak kezdetei* (*The first public libraries in Hungary*), Magyar Könyvszemle, Budapest.

Kovács, Annamária (1988), Az alapítvány szabályozásának problémái (Problems of the legal regulation of foundations), *Állam és Igazgatás*, September.

Kovács, Annamária (1989), Az alapítványok jogi szabályozásának alakulása (Development of the legal regulation of foundations), manuscript, Művelődéskutató Intézet, Budapest.

Kovalcsik, József (1986), *A kultúra csarnokai I–III. kötet* (*The homes of culture, Volumes 1–3*), Művelődéskutató Intézet, Budapest.

Kozma, György and Petrik, Ferenc (1990), *Társadalmi szervezetek, alapítványok létrehozása és gazdálkodása. Jogszabályok, bírói gyakorlat és ezek magyarázata* (*Establishment and economic activities of social organizations and foundations. Legal regulation, court practice and their explanation*), UNIÓ Lap – és Könyvkiadó, Budapest.

Kulcsár, Adorján (1943), *Olvasóközönségünk 1800 táján* (*Our reading public about 1800*), Egyetemi Nyomda, Budapest.

Kuti Éva (1989a), *A kultúra finanszírozásának és mecénálásának helyzete* (*Financing and sponsoring culture*), Országos Közművelődési Központ, Budapest.

Kuti, Éva (1989b), A kultúra támogatásának új rendszere felé? (Toward a new system of supporting culture?), *Kultúra és Közösség*, 3.

Kuti, Éva (1989c), *The possible role of the nonprofit sector in Hungary. Lessons from nonprofit theories and a comparative study of the Baltimore Museum of Art and the Hungarian National Gallery*, Johns Hopkins University Institute for Policy Studies, Baltimore.

Kuti, Éva (1990), The possible role of the non-profit sector in Hungary, *Voluntas*, 1/1.

Kuti, Éva (1992a), Scylla and Charybdis in the Hungarian non-profit sector, in Stein Kuhnle and Per Selle (eds) *Government and voluntary organizations*, Avebury, Aldershot–Brookfield USA–Hong Kong–Singapore–Sydney.

Kuti, Éva (1992b), Visszaélés prolongálva (Prolonged foundation abuse), *Kurázsi*, November.

Kuti, Éva (1993), *Defining the nonprofit sector, Hungary*, working papers of the Johns Hopkins Comparative Nonprofit Sector Project No. 13, The Johns Hopkins University Institute for Policy Studies, Baltimore.

Kuti, Éva and Somogyvári, Zsolt (1993), The beginning of a contract culture in Hungary, paper given at the conference "Contracting – selling or shrinking? Voluntary and nonprofit organizations and the enabling state in international perspective", London, 20–22 July.

L. Nagy, Zsuzsa (1977), *Szabadkőművesség a XX. században (Freemasonry in the twentieth century)*, Kossuth, Budapest.

Les, Ewa (1994), *The voluntary sector in post-communist East Central Europe. From small circles of freedom to civil society*, CIVICUS, Washington.

Lévai, Katalin and Széman, Zsuzsa (1993), *Társadalmi trigonometria (Social trigonometry)*, Scientia Humana, Budapest.

Lukács, Móric (1847), Néhány eszme az egyesületi jog körül (Some thoughts about the legal regulation of voluntary associations), Reprinted in Tőkéczki László (ed.) (1993), *Magyar liberalizmus (Liberalism in Hungary)*, Századvég Kiadó, Budapest.

Lyons, Mark (1993), The history of nonprofit organizations in Australia as a test of some recent nonprofit theory, *Voluntas*, 4/3.

Magyar, Bálint (1986), *Dunaapáti 1944–1958. Dokumentum-szociográfia I–III (Dunaapáti 1944–1958. Sociography based on official documents I–III*), Művelődéskutató Intézet – Szövetkezeti Kutató Intézet, Budapest.

Magyar Statisztikai Évkönyvek (1886, 1934, 1991) (*Hungarian statistical yearbooks*), Központi Statisztikai Hivatal, Budapest.

Magyarország különböző egyletei (1862) (Various voluntary associations in Hungary), *Statisztikai Közlemények. A hazai állapotok ismeretének előmozdítására IV. kötet*, MTA Statisztikai Bizottsága, Budapest.

Magyary, Zoltán (1988), *A közigazgatás fejlesztése és szervezése* (*Development and organization of the public administration*), MTA Akadémia Államtudományi Kutatások Programirodája, Budapest.

Major, Iván (1992), Privatizációs tervek Kelet-Európában (Privatization plans in Eastern Europe), *Európa Fórum*, 2.

Manchin, Róbert and Nagy, Lajos Géza (1991a), *Ismeretek és vélemények az adóról* (*Knowledge and public opinion about the tax*), Magyar Gallup Intézet, Budapest.

Manchin, Róbert and Nagy, Lajos Géza (1991b), *Vélemények gazdaságról, életszínvonalról, politikai intézményekről* (Public opinion about economy, standard of living and political institutions*), Magyar Gallup Intézet, Budapest*.

Manchin, Róbert and Szelényi, Iván (1986), Gazdasági és jóléti redisztibúció az államszocializmusban (Economic and welfare redistribution under state socialism), *Medvetánc*, 3–4.

Marschall, Miklós (1990), The nonprofit sector in a centrally-planned economy, in Helmut K. Anheier and Wolfgang Seibel (eds) *The third sector: comparative studies of nonprofit organizations*, De Gruyter, New York.

Naplótöredékek a Parlamentből (1993), (Excerpts from a Parliamentary debate), *Kurázsi*, August.

Pach, Zsigmond Pál (1966), The development of feudal rent in Hungary in the fifteenth century, *Economic History Review*, 19/1.

Pajkossy, Gábor (1993), Egyesületek a reformkori Magyarországon (Voluntary associations in Hungary in the reform age), *História*, 15/2.

Pálfalvi, András (1993), A nem kormányzati környezetvédő szervezetek (Non-governmental environmental organizations), Manuscript, Research Project on Nonprofit Organizations, Budapest.

Pálos, Károly (1934), *Szegénység, szegénygondozás* (*Poverty and*

References

poverty relief), Martineum Könyvnyomda, Szombathely.

Pataki, György (1993), Töredékek a magyarországi magán-jótékonyság történetéből a szociálpolitika és az egészségügy terén (Fragments about the history of private philanthropy in Hungary in the field of social care and health care), Manuscript, Research Project on Nonprofit Organizations, Budapest.

Petró, Kálmán (1932), *Az egri norma, 1927–1932 (The model of Eger, 1927–1932)*, Kapisztrán Nyomda, Eger.

R. Kiss, István (1925), Nagy Lajos és az ősiség (King Lajos the Great and the rules of inheritance), in *Emlékkönyv Dr. Gróf Klebelsberg Kuno negyedszázados kultúrpolitikai működésének emlékére (Essays published in honour of Dr. Gróf Klebelsberg Kuno, minister of culture for 25 years)*, Rákosi Jenő Budapesti Hírlap Újságvállalata, Budapest.

Research Project on Hungarian Nonprofit Organizations (1992) Comment on Stephen M. Wunker, 'The promise of nonprofits in Poland and Hungary, an analysis of third sector renaissance', *Voluntas*, 3/1.

Rézler, Gyula (1943), *Egy magyar textilgyár munkástársadalma (The workers' community in a Hungarian textile factory)*, Magyar Ipari Munkatudományi Intézet, Budapest.

Salamon, Ferencz (1885), *Budapest története I–III. kötet (The history of Budapest, Volumes I–III)*, Atheneum, Budapest.

Salamon, Lester M. (1987), Of market failure, voluntary failure, and third-party government, toward a new theory of govern-ment-nonprofit relations in the modern welfare state, *Journal of Voluntary Action Research*, 1–2.

Salamon, Lester M. (1993), *The global associational revolution, the rise of the third sector on the world scene*, Occasional Paper No. 15, The Johns Hopkins University, Institute for Policy Studies, Balti-more.

Salamon, Lester M. and Anheier, Helmut K. (1992a), *Reference Manual of Project Material*, Institute for Policy Studies, The Johns Hopkins University, Baltimore.

Salamon, Lester M. and Anheier, Helmut K. (1992b), *In search of the nonprofit sector I: the question of definitions*, Working Papers of the Johns Hopkins Comparative Nonprofit Sector Project No. 2, The Johns Hopkins University Institute for Policy Studies, Balti-more.

Salamon, Lester M. and Anheier, Helmut K. (1994), *The emerging sector. The nonprofit sector in comparative perspective – an overview*, Institute for Policy Studies, The Johns Hopkins University, Baltimore.

Sárközi, Tamás (1991), Az alapítványok jogi szabályozása Magyarországon (The legal regulation of foundations in Hungary), in Kuti, Éva (ed.), *Alapítványi Almanach*, Magyarországi Alapítványok Szövetsége, Selyemgombolyító Rt, Budapest.

Schindler, Ambros (1991), Az alapítványi világ jellemzői Németországban (The characteristics of the foundation world in Germany), in Kuti, Éva (ed.) *Alapítványi Almanach*, Magyarországi Alapítványok Szövetsége, Selyemgombolyító Rt, Budapest.

Scitovsky, Tibor (1990), *Az örömtelen gazdaság (The joyless economy)*, Közgazdasági és Jogi Könyvkiadó, Budapest.

Sebestyén, László (1993), *Alapítványok nagy szerepe egy kisvárosban (Great role of foundations in a small town)*, Kurázsi, January.

Siegel, Daniel and Yancey, Jenny (1993), *A civil társadalom újjászületése (The rebirth of the civil society)*, The Rockefeller Brothers Fund, Budapest.

Sólyom, László (1985), A társadalom részvétele a környezetvédelemben (The participation of the society in the protection of environment), *Medvetánc*, 4, 1.

Somogyi, Zoltán (1941), *A középkori Magyarország szegényügye (Poverty relief in Hungary in the Middle Ages)*, Stephaneum, Budapest.

Soós, Károly Attila (1993), Hűtlen kezelésről van szó. Alapítványok és hatalomátmentés (It's about misappropriation. Foundations and preservation of power), *Magyar Hírlap*, 17 May.

Stark, David (1991), Privatizáció Magyarországon (Privatization in Hungary), *Közgazdasági Szemle*, 9.

Szabó, Lajos (1989), *A megújuló egyesületek működésének szabályai (Legal rules for the reviving voluntary associations)*, Agrárinformációs Vállalat, Budapest.

Szabó, Máté (1993), *Alternatív mozgalmak Magyarországon (Alternative movements in Hungary)*, Gondolat, Budapest.

Szádeczky Lajos (1913), *Iparfejlődés és a céhek története Magyarországon I–II. (Industrial development and the history of guilds in Hungary I–II)*, Országos Iparegyesület, Budapest.

Szelényi, Iván (1992), *A poszt-kommunista átmenet társadalmi konfliktusai (Social conflicts of the post-communist transition)*, MTA

References

Politikai Tudományok Intézete, Budapest.

Szűcs, István (1870, 1872), *Debreczen város történelme, I–III. Kötet* (*History of the city of Debreczen, Volumes 1–3*), Városi Könyvnyomda, Debreczen.

Szűcs, Jenő (1955), *Városok és kézmívesség a XV. századi Magyarországon* (*Towns and craftsmen in Hungary in the 15th century*), Művelt Nép, Budapest.

Tardos, Márton (1992), A helyzet nem ellentmondásos, hanem rossz (The situation is not contradictory but critical), *Beszélő, 27 June.*

Tóka, Gábor (1992), A szociális védőháló felbomlása és a közvélemény (The disintegration of the social security network and the public opinion), *Európa Fórum, 2.*

Tsyboula, Sylvie (1991), A nonprofit szektor, az alapítványok és a Fondation de France (The nonprofit sector, the foundations and the Fondation de France), in Kuti, Éva (ed.) *Alapítványi Almanach,* Magyarországi Alapítványok Szövetsége, Selyemgombolyító Rt, Budapest.

Változások a nonprofit szervezetek szabályozásában (1992) (Changes in the legal regulation of nonprofit organizations), *Kurázsi,* October.

Vargha, Gyula (1880), *Magyarország egyletei és társulatai 1878 – ban* (*Voluntary associations and societies in Hungary in 1878*), Hivatalos Statisztikai Közlemények, Országos Magyar Királyi Statisztikai Hivatal, Budapest.

Voit, Krisztina (1991), Közintézmények – közalapítványok (Public institutions – public law foundations), Manuscript, Nonprofit Kutatócsoport, Budapest.

Wallerstein, Immanuel (1983), *A modern világgazdasági rendszer kialakulása. A tőkés mezőgazdaság és az európai világgazdaság eredete a XVI. században* (*The modern world-system. Capitalist agriculture and the origins of the European world-economy in the sixteenth century*), Gondolat, Budapest.

Weisbrod, Burton A. (1986), Toward a theory of the voluntary nonprofit sector in a three sector economy in Rose-Ackerman, Susan (ed.), *The economics of nonprofit institutions: studies in structure and policy,* Oxford University Press, New York.

Wunker, Stephen M. (1991), The promise of nonprofits in Poland and Hungary, an analysis of third sector renaissance, *Voluntas, 2/2.*

Zolnay, László (1975), *Ünnep és hétköznap a középkori Budán* (*Work-*

ing days and holidays in Buda in the Middle Ages), Gondolat, Budapest.

6, Perri (1993), Foundations, cross-national policy issues, paper given at the Voluntas symposium 'Foundations', Paris, 22–24 October.

6, Perri and Kuti, Éva (1993), Into the European Community, impacts of future membership on Hungary's nonprofit sector, *Journal of European Social Policy*, 4/3.

ANNOTATED BIBLIOGRAPHY

General works on the nonprofit sector

Theoretical pieces

Arató, András. Civil társadalom Lengyelországban és Magyar-országon (Civil society in Poland and Hungary), *Politikatudományi Szemle*, 1992, 2, 53–80.

Using the concepts of "new evolutionism" and "self–limiting revolution", the author analyses the role of civil society in the late communist and transitional period in Poland and Hungary. The term "civil society" is understood in the study as a sphere of social interaction between state, economy and society. Civil society is distinguished from a political society of parties and political orga-nizations. The author emphasizes the role of independent initia-tives in the democratic political change in both countries. The study ends with an analysis of the relationship of civil society and the new political elite in the post–communist period.

Barbetta, Paolo. A nonprofit szektor gazdasági szerepe (The eco-nomic role of the nonprofit sector), *Esély*, 1991, 1, 11–22.

In his critical analysis, Barbetta describes, compares and evaluates the most important economic theories of the nonprofit sector: Weisbrod's theoretical explanation based on the supply and demand of collective goods (also known as the market failure/government failure theory), Hansmann's, Krashinsky's and Nelson's analysis of the contract failure, and the voluntary failure theory developed by Salamon.

Hegyesi, Gábor. Integrációs modellek és nonprofit szektor (Integration models and the nonprofit sector), *Esély*, 1991, 1, 4–10.

The author develops a typology of nonprofit sectors and nonprofit organizations based on Polányi's system of market, redistribution and reciprocity. He uses both international and Hungarian experiences to test the validity of his hypothesis. He also compares his typology with the models developed by Titmuss and Esping–Andersen.

Heller, Ágnes, Fehér, Ferenc, Bozóki, András and Fricz, Tamás. *Polgárosodás, civil társadalom és demokrácia (Embourgeoisement, civil society and democracy)*. Budapest: MTA Politikai Tudományok Intézete, 1992.

The volume includes two theoretical and two analytical studies on the relationships between embourgeoisement, civil society and democracy. The authors analyse the development of democracy and the role played by citizens and their civic organizations in this process. They also investigate the relationships between the civil society and the political society.

Kuti, Éva and Marschall, Miklós, eds *A harmadik szektor (The third sector)*. Budapest: Nonprofit Kutatócsoport, 1991.

This volume is a synoptic work and includes fourteen essays written by the best known scholars of the nonprofit sector all over the world. It has emerged as a basic reference book in the field. It is a good source of information on economic, political and sociological theories of the nonprofit sector; the public/private relationship; professionalization; the role of nonprofit boards; organizational change; the role of the sector in contributing to health care, personal social services, education, policy advocacy, etc.; sources of support for the sector and their forms; and comparison of nonprofit sectors existing in different political/economic systems.

Analytical attempts to explain the size, scope, structure and role of the Hungarian nonprofit sector

Bocz, János, Kuti, Éva, Seresné Gyúrús, Gabriella, Sebestény,

István and Vajda, Ágnes. *Alapítványok és egyesületek. A nonprofit szektor statisztikája (Foundations and voluntary associations. Statistics on the nonprofit sector).* Budapest: Központi Statisztikai Hivatal, 1994.

This book tries to define the Hungarian nonprofit sector and its different institutions. The authors give an overview of official registers and statistical data sources and compile information from these sources in order to describe the sector. They analyse the changes in the size and structure of the voluntary sector between 1862 and 1992, and the development of private and state support to the nonprofit organizations in the last couple of years. Based on information from a sample survey they also investigate the social and demographic characteristics of the members of voluntary associations.

Bocz, János, Gyulavári, Antal, Kuti, Éva, Locherné Kelédi, Ildikó, Sebestény, István and Vajda, Ágnes. *Nonprofit szervezetek Magyarországon, 1992 (Nonprofit organizations in Hungary, 1992).* Budapest: Központi Statisztikai Hivatal, 1994.

The paper presents the results of the census of nonprofit organizations carried out in 1993 by the Central Statistical Office of Hungary. It evaluates the survey methodology and gives an interpretation of the statistical data on the revenues, expenditures, employees, activities and organizational characteristics of nonprofit organizations. It also sketches out the main points of a plan for further development of nonprofit statistics. In the appendix one can find the questionnaire and the detailed results of the survey.

Kuti, Éva, ed. *A nonprofit szektor Magyarországon (The nonprofit sector in Hungary).* Budapest: Nonprofit Kutatócsoport, 1992.

This volume consists of eleven original essays on the Hungarian nonprofit sector including papers analysing the social and economic roles of the sector; its legal and economic regulation; its relationships with other countries' nonprofit sectors; the contribution of nonprofit organizations to culture, education, health care, personal social services, policy advocacy, community development and the assistance to unemployed and refugees.

Annotated bibliography

Publications dealing with the nonprofit sector in other countries

Knapp, Martin and Susan Saxon–Harrold. Az öntevékeny szektor Nagy–Britanniában (The voluntary sector in Great Britain), *Esély*, 1991, 1, 35–47.

The authors chart the principal dimensions of Britain's voluntary sector – its income, its main areas of service provision, its employment, and changes over the last decade. They also examine the problems of definition, legal regulation and tax policy towards the sector. The professionalization of fund raising and the charity–media relationships are analysed, too. Finally, the authors consider how the efficiency and accountability problems may influence the future development of the British voluntary sector.

O'Connell, Brian and Hodgkinson, Virginia A. A nonprofit szektor felépítése és problémái az Egyesült Államokban (Structure and problems of the nonprofit sector in the United States), *Esély*, 1991, 1, 23–34.

The article describes the essential elements of the national taxonomy of the US nonprofit sector, developed over almost a decade after extensive consultation with agencies in the nonprofit sector and in the government, and reports an initial analysis of the classification of nearly one million nonprofit organizations in the United States. The study also includes a discussion of problems nonprofit organizations face. It analyses the background of attacks on the nonprofit sector and suggests a strategy for repelling these attacks.

Salamon, Lester M. Az állam és a nonprofit szektor kapcsolatai a költségvetési megszorítások időszakában: Az USA tapasztalatai (Government and the voluntary sector in an era of retrenchment: The American experience), *Kultúra és Közösség*, 1989, 3, 24–40.

The author points out that voluntary organizations retained a significant role in the American welfare state, delivering a larger share of government–financed human services than government agencies. By cutting back on government spending, therefore, the

Reagan administration significantly reduced the revenues of the nonprofit sector, while calling on this sector to do more. Although nonprofits survived, they did so chiefly by increasing their income from service charges, rather than their private charitable support. The author raises serious questions about the continued ability of nonprofit organizations to serve those in greatest need, and the opportunity to strengthen the voluntary sector and rationalize government–nonprofit ties.

Schindler, Ambros. Az alapítványi világ jellemzői Németország-ban (The characteristics of the foundation world in Germany). In: Kuti, Éva, ed., *Alapítványi Almanach (Foundation Almanac)*. Budapest: Magyarországi Alapítványok Szövetsége, Selyemgom-bolyító Rt, 1991.

Schindler gives an extensive description of the foundation sector in Germany. He reports on its development, size, structure, legal, economic and tax regulations. He analyses the most important issues of foundation finances and management. He pays special attention to the role of foundations in the process of privatization and to the grant–making policies of German foundations involved in international activities. Finally, he reports on the advocacy, information and service–providing roles played by the Federation of Foundations in Germany.

Seibel, Wolfgang. A kormány és a nonprofit szektor közötti kap-csolat. Nemzetközi összehasonlításban: Franciaország és az NSZK (Government/third sector relationship in a comparative perspec-tive: the cases of France and West Germany), *Esély*, 1991, 1, 48–60.

Cross–national differences of the division of labour between the government and nonprofit sectors are illustrated in this paper with respect to France and West Germany. The autonomy of the state, the nature of the dominant actors and their style of interac-tion are identified as crucial variables shaping the linkage patterns of government/third sector relationship. The cross–national com-parison allows for the hypothesis that different patterns of this relationship also shape different degrees of institutional adaptive-ness in a changing political and economic environment.

Tsyboula, Sylvie. A nonprofit szektor, az alapítványok és a Fondation de France (The nonprofit sector, the foundations and the Fondation de France). In Kuti, Éva, ed., *Alapítványi Almanach* (*Foundation Almanac*). Budapest: Magyarországi Alapítványok Szövetsége, Selyemgombolyító Rt, 1991.

The author gives a short overview of the history of state/third sector relationship in France and analyses its consequences for the French nonprofit sector. She differentiates between voluntary associations, nonprofit organizations of public benefit and foundations, then describes their economic and tax regulations. In the second part of her paper, she reports on the revenues, expenditures, activities and grant–making priorities of the Fondation de France which is the largest French community foundation.

Historical background

Balázs, Magdolna. Az alapítványi élet indulása Magyarországon (The beginnings of the foundation development in Hungary), *Esély*, 1991, 1, 82–91.

Using historical evidence, Balázs tries to prove that urbanization and the development of the foundation sector are closely correlated. She gives several examples of the creation of foundations and makes an attempt to estimate the size of the foundation sector in the nineteenth and early twentieth centuries. She pays special attention to the foundations involved in education and hospital care. She also ventures to identify the founders and donors of the epoch, and examines their aims and motivations.

Burucs, Kornélia. Nők az egyesületekben (Women in voluntary associations), *História*, 1993, 15, 2, 15–18.

The author gives an overview of the women's voluntary organizations in the nineteenth and in the first half of the twentieth century. She points out that these mostly religious and charitable organizations played an important role in the emancipation movement, as well. Lots of innovative services and institutions were started on their initiative, especially in the field of education, culture, social care, women's employment and in the protection of children. Women's associations were crucially important in the fight for the political rights of women.

Halmai, Gábor. *Az egyesülés szabadsága. Az egyesülési jog története (The freedom of association. The history of the law on associations).* Budapest: Atlantisz Medvetánc, 1990.

The freedom of association as a basic human right. The treatment of the freedom of association in legal theories. Models of the regulation of voluntary associations. Changes of the regulation of voluntary associations in Hungary between 1949 and 1989. The sociological and legal classification of voluntary associations. Regulation of their internal rules and external relationships. The history of the legal regulation of political parties.

Pajkossy, Gábor. Egyesületek a reformkori Magyarországon (Voluntary associations in Hungary in the reform age), *História*, 1993, 15, 2, 6–9.

The author examines the development of the voluntary associations in Hungary in the nineteenth century. He emphasizes the importance of the German influence and the impact of the emergence of a new bourgeoisie. He describes the legal regulation and estimates the size and structure of the voluntary sector. Analysing the voluntary associations' prominent role in the everyday life of the cities, he suggests that there was close interrelation between the urbanization and the development of the voluntary sector. The last part of the article offers a rough comparison of voluntary sectors in the countries of the Austro–Hungarian monarchy.

Reisz, László. Egyletek a dualizmuskori Magyarországon (Voluntary associations in Hungary in the period of dualism), *Statisztikai Szemle*, 1988, 10, 930–946.

The author investigates the characteristics of voluntary associations established in Hungary at the end of the nineteenth century (in the era of the Austro–Hungarian monarchy), relying on the secondary processing of the data from a national survey of voluntary associations carried out in 1878. The types, activities and regional distribution of associations and the social layer, nationality and religion of their members are analysed. Besides the analysis of the nonprofit phenomenon, the author also tries to identify some typical features of the Hungarian society of the epoch.

Legal position

Egriné Rónai, Márta and Pettendi, Zsuzsa. *Alapítványok létesítése és m űködtetése (Establishment and management of foundations)*. Budapest: Közgazdasági és Jogi Könyvkiadó, Pallas Közlöny – és Kiadványszerkesztő Igazgatóság, 1990.

The book includes all the laws and government decrees which regulate the foundation sector as a whole, or some aspect of the establishment and management of foundations. It summarizes the rules of accounting, as well. Besides publishing the actual text of laws and decrees, the authors also give detailed explanations and several examples helping founders and foundation managers to better understand and follow the regulations.

Kecskés, László. Az alapítványi jog fejlődése (The development of the legal regulation of foundations), *Magyar Jog*, 1988, 2, 104–16.

Kecskés undertakes a broad international comparison of the legal treatment of foundations. He distinguishes five different legal models, namely: (1) the foundation which is a legal person as an endowment; (2) the foundation which is a legal person as an organization; (3) the foundation which is not a legal person, just a financial commitment, "donatio sub modo"; (4) special properties, "vakf" in the Islamic law; (5) "trust" in the English law. He also analyses how the foreign examples have influenced the concept and legal regulation of foundations in Hungary through their history and in more recent times.

Kovács, Annamária. Az alapítvány szabályozásának problémái (Problems of the legal regulation of foundations), *Állam és Igazgatás*, 1988, September, 788–97.

The author gives a short overview of the development of the legal regulation of foundations under state socialism. She claims that the new regulation was designed to further the general interests of political democracy, but legislators did not consider practical problems which may emerge in the case of a too loose regulation. The paper specifies and explains all these problems together with their likely consequences and suggests several changes in the regulation of foundations.

Sárközi, Tamás. Az alapítványok jogi szabályozása Magyarországon (The legal regulation of foundations in Hungary). In: Kuti, Éva, ed., *Alapítványi Almanach (Foundation Almanac)*. Budapest: Magyarországi Alapítványok Szövetsége, Selyemgombolyító Rt, 1991.

In his critical analysis, Sárközi summarizes the main characteristics of the legal regulation of foundations in Hungary. He claims that the rather liberal regulation, which emerged at the end of the state socialist period as a reaction to the former prohibition, leaves too much room for foundation abuse. He argues that the legal form of "public law foundation" should be introduced into the Civil Code in order to strengthen government control over the state–supported part of the foundation sector.

Szabó, Lajos. *A megújuló egyesületek működésének szabályai (Legal rules for the reviving voluntary associations)*. Budapest: Agrárinformációs Vállalat, 1989.

After a short overview of the history of regulation, the book explains how the "Association Law" passed in 1989 has changed the rules of establishment and management of voluntary associations. It summarizes the rules of accounting, as well. Besides publishing the actual text of laws and decrees, the author also gives detailed explanations and several examples helping founders and managers of voluntary associations to better understand and follow the regulations.

Policy

Anheier, Helmut K. and Seibel, Wolfgang. A nonprofit szektor és a társadalmi átalakulás (The nonprofit sector and the transformation of societies), *Európa Fórum*, 1993, 3, 22–37.

The study explores the emergence and development of the nonprofit sector in the process of societal transformation from state socialism in three Central Eastern European countries: the former German Democratic Republic, Hungary and Poland. The authors introduce a conceptual scheme which contrasts and compares the third sector in the context of changing state/society relationships. They point out that the role of the nonprofit sector in the transformation process varies significantly, had different starting points, is passing through different phases and will lead to different outcomes.

Kuti, Éva. A nonprofit elméletek és a nonprofit gyakorlat lehetőségei Magyarországon (Nonprofit theories and the possible role of the nonprofit sector in Hungary), *Közgazdasági Szemle*, 1991, 1. 18–30.

The author undertakes a short overview of the nonprofit theories and points out their neglect of the role played by nonprofit organizations in the redistribution process. She develops two different models of the possible public policy responses to social inequalities: the welfare state model and the nonprofit–based model. Then she considers what will be the role of the new Hungarian voluntary sector; what are the possibilities of following the Western European route – a version of the welfare state model – or the American way – a nonprofit–based model bolstered by "third party government".

Kuti, Éva and Marschall, Miklós. A nonprofit szektor fogalma. Egy definíciós vita és ami mögötte van (The concept of the nonprofit sector. A definitional debate and its background), *Esély*, 1991, 1, 61–9.

The paper compares the nonprofit definitions valid in different countries and examines the main elements of the definition of nonprofit organizations in Hungary. The authors suggest that the hot issues (the non–distribution constraint, the public benefit character of NPOs, the accountability requirements, etc.) of the definition debate are closely correlated with the most important ethical and policy issues of the sector. They also suggest that the outcome of the debate on the nonprofit definition will have serious consequences for the Hungarian nonprofit sector.

Siegel, Daniel and Yancey, Jenny *A civil társadalom újjászületése: A nonprofit szektor fejlődése Kelet–Közép–Európában és a nyugati segítségnyújtás szerepe (The rebirth of civil society: The development of the nonprofit sector in East Central Europe and the role of Western assistance)*, Budapest: The Rockefeller Brothers Fund, 1993.

The report gives an overview of the development of nonprofit sectors in three East Central European countries: the Czech and Slovak Federal Republic, Hungary and Poland. The analysis is based on approximately 450 interviews with foundation officials, leaders of non–governmental organizations and representatives of government. The report contains the authors' sober assessment of the challenges and opportunities facing the nonprofit sectors in the emerging democracies and suggests areas where Western assistance has been constructive as well as those in which it has been less helpful or even counter–productive. The authors make twelve specific recommendations for concrete action by foundations and others who want to be usefully involved in the democratization effort.

6, Perri and Kuti, Éva *A közös piac veszélyei és kihívásai a magyar nonprofit szektor számára (Future EU membership: impacts on and challenges for Hungary's nonprofit sector)*, *Közgazdasági Szemle*, 1993, 2, 110–24.

Hungary, like many other countries, hopes to join the European Union within the not too distant future. This would expose its burgeoning nonprofit sector to an encounter with the Western European sectors. This paper considers what that encounter might mean for the Hungarian nonprofit sector and policy makers in both the European Union and in Hungary. Using recent theoretical models and a range of plausible predictive assumptions, scenarios are developed as descriptions of possible impacts, which are then appraised and compared.

Annotated bibliography

Major ICNPO groups

Kuti, Éva. A kultúra támogatásának új rendszere felé? (Towards a new system of financing culture?), *Kultúra és Közösség*, 1989, 3, 3–12.

The paper examines the possible role of the nonprofit organizations in the process of decentralization and denationalization of financing culture. The author suggests that the emerging foundations can be of crucial importance both in fund raising for cultural institutions and in the development of a new system of distribution of government support to culture. She argues that before any strategic decision on the reform of financing culture, all the benefits and drawbacks of a mixed system should be taken into consideration.

Lévai, Katalin and Széman, Zsuzsa. *Társadalmi trigonometria (Social trigonometry)*. Budapest: Scientia Humana, 1993.

The book compares the welfare models of the developed countries, Eastern Europe and Hungary, and examines the roles played by the state, market, voluntary and informal sectors in the provision of welfare services in these different models. Then it gives a detailed description of four extremely important organizations of the provision and financing social services in Hungary, namely the Hungarian Red Cross, the largest Catholic charity, the Soros Foundation and the local governments of some districts of Budapest.

Sólyom, László. A társadalom részvétele a környezetvédelemben (The participation of the society in the protection of environment), *Medvetánc*, 1985, 4, 217–42.

The article starts with the description of three different environmental movements, two of them initiated by voluntary associations. The author analyses the nature of political conflicts between the government and the environmental movements. He claims that these conflicts reflect all problems of the democratization process. He also deals with the infrastructural and organizational problems of the environmental movements, and suggests that a radical change of the legal regulation of voluntary associations would be necessary in order to strengthen the citizens' participation in the protection of environment.

Szabó, Máté. *Alternatív mozgalmak Magyarországon (Alternative movements in Hungary)*. Budapest: Gondolat, 1993.

The book compares the alternative movements in Hungary with those in Western Europe (especially in West Germany), East Germany and Poland. It analyses the history of the Hungarian social movements, the role played by the alternative movements under state socialism, and then their role in the process of democratization. It focuses mostly on the peace movements and the activities of the environmental organizations.

Várhegyi, György, ed. *Az alapítványi és magániskolák. Tudományos tanácskozás. (Foundation schools and private schools. Papers of a symposium)*. Budapest: Oktatáskutató Intézet, 1992.

This volume is a selection of papers given at a symposium on the problems faced by foundation schools and private schools in the early 1990s. It includes papers on the nonprofit sector as a whole; the history of private and nonprofit schools; the legal regulation of private education, the relationships between public, private and foundation schools; the problems of financing nonprofit education. Reports on the discussion in several sessions present the special problems of different levels of education and different types of private and nonprofit schools.

Bibliographies, data bases, and other resource material

Bocz, János. Egyesületi statisztika Magyarországon (Statistics on voluntary associations in Hungary), *Statisztikai Szemle*, 1992, 10, 840–52.

The author makes an attempt to characterize the role of voluntary associations, its changes and the state/civil society relationship through presenting the changes in the statistical concept of associations and in their legal regulation. He gives an overview of the difficulties of statistical surveys of voluntary associations, then he lists and compares all the association surveys carried out in Hungary in the course of the last two centuries. He pays special attention to the methods and classification used by statisticians and to the comparability of the data from different surveys.

Dobrovits, Sándor. Budapest egyesületei (Voluntary associations in Budapest), *Statisztikai Közlemények*, 74, 3, Budapest: Központi Statisztikai Hivatal, 1936.

The author gives a detailed overview of the problems and difficulties of statistical surveys on voluntary associations. He describes the methods used in the 1932 survey and presents the most important data gathered about the voluntary associations in Budapest.

Egyesületek Magyarországon, 1970 (Voluntary associations in Hungary in 1970). Budapest: Központi Statisztikai Hivatal, 1972.

This volume presents the results of the statistical survey of voluntary associations carried out by the Statistical Office of Hungary in 1970. It includes detailed data about the number, regional distribution, activities, members, publications, revenues and expenditures of voluntary associations.

Egyesületek Magyarországon, 1982 (Voluntary associations in Hungary in 1982). Budapest: Központi Statisztikai Hivatal, 1984.

This volume presents the results of the statistical survey of voluntary associations carried out by the Statistical Office of Hungary in 1982. It includes detailed data about the number, regional distribution, activities, members, publications, revenues and expenditures of voluntary associations.

Egyesületek Magyarországon, 1989 (Voluntary associations in Hungary in 1989). Budapest: Központi Statisztikai Hivatal, 1991.

This volume presents the results of the statistical survey of voluntary associations carried out by the Statistical Office of Hungary in 1989. It includes detailed data about the number, regional distribution, activities, members, publications, revenues and expenditures of voluntary associations.

Magyarország különböző egyletei, 1862 (Various voluntary associations in Hungary in 1862). Statisztikai Közlemények. A hazai állapotok ismeretének előmozdítására IV. kötet. Budapest: MTA Statisztikai Bizottsága, 1862.

This volume presents the results of the statistical survey of voluntary associations carried out by the Statistical Committee of the Academy of Sciences of Hungary in 1862. It includes detailed data about the number, regional distribution, activities, members, publications, revenues and expenditures of voluntary associations.

Vargha, Gyula. *Magyarország egyletei és társulatai 1878–ban (Voluntary associations and societies in Hungary in 1878).* Hivatalos Statisztikai Közlemények. Budapest: Országos Magyar Királyi Statisztikai Hivatal, 1880.

This volume presents the results of the statistical survey of voluntary associations carried out by the Statistical Office of Hungary in 1878. It includes detailed data about the number, regional distribution, activities, members, publications, revenues and expenditures of voluntary associations.

INDEX